THE STRONGEST
MEN ON EARTH

THE STRONGEST MEN ON EARTH

When the Muscle Men Ruled Show Business

GRAEME KENT

The Robson Press

First published in Great Britain in 2012 by
The Robson Press (an imprint of Biteback Publishing Ltd)
Westminster Tower
3 Albert Embankment
London SE1 7SP
Copyright © Graeme Kent 2012

ISBN 978-184954-371-2

10 9 8 7 6 5 4 3 2 1

A CIP catalogue record for this book is available from the British Library.

Set in Garamond

Printed and bound in Great Britain by
CPI Group (UK) Ltd, Croydon CR0 4YY

CONTENTS

ACKNOWLEDGEMENTS

I would like to thank my agent Isabel White for her enthusiastic support and considerable input into the writing of this book from beginning to end. I am also indebted to my editor at the Robson Press, Hollie Teague, for her guidance, encouragement and meticulous editing skills.

INTRODUCTION

They were nothing if not adaptable. Achieving real fame and fortune in the brief golden age of strength athletics, some of the professional strongmen and women were prepared to take almost any risks and put their bodies through the most reckless forms of endeavour to attain their coveted top-of-the-bill status.

One of the first of them was Jack Holtum, a former Danish sailor. He earned a steady living by flexing his mighty muscles and lifting heavy weights onstage, but these displays were not enough to mark him out from his competitors. Instead he added a new finale to his act in which, twice nightly, he caught a cannonball fired at him from point-blank range. This was enough to transport him to the ranks of superstars, even if it did cause a group of his female fans in Paris to circulate a petition begging him to return to his previous posing display and not risk marring his beautiful physique by offering it up for such dangerous target practice.

Rosa Richter went one better in the high-risk stakes. As a child she toured as a boy in a strongman act with a Japanese circus. Realising that this was never going to bring in the wealth she dreamt of, at the age of fourteen she became the first female human cannonball, being fired a distance of seventy-five feet onto a trapeze before dropping into a net. It was an incredibly perilous way of earning a living, but, while still in her teens, she commanded a fee of £200 a week during the 1870s and became one of the first circus strongwomen to take her act into the music halls and vaudeville.

An Italian called Luigi Brinn had an impressive enough strongman act. Supporting on his back a rowing boat containing fourteen sailors who pretended to row, he would stagger around the stage supporting his burden. But even this proved insufficient to the braying crowds and, in order to compete with his fellows, he enlarged his repertoire by supporting a heavy artillery piece and a uniformed attendant on a platform on a pole balanced upon his chin, and assimilated the recoil with barely a stagger when the weapon was fired.

The emphasis among these would-be Hercules was always on determination. Australian Don Athaldo was three times discharged from his country's armed forces for being medically unfit yet developed his strength to such an extent that he trained thousands of his fellow countrymen with his postal strongman courses. He was capable of towing a touring car and six passengers for eight hundred metres up the steep incline of a Sydney thoroughfare.

A few of them had to remain alert to avoid the attention of law-enforcement agencies, especially some of the strongmen who branched out into the lucrative area of postal bodybuilding courses. Alois P. Swoboda, who emigrated from Austria to the USA, numbered President Herbert Hoover among his clients and was a millionaire before he was thirty. But when he launched his 'Conscious Evolution' course and claimed to be able to regrow lost limbs by the use of willpower, he incurred the wrath of the American Medical Association.

Ostensibly these strength athletes were competing to see which of them could claim the title of world's strongest man or woman. In reality, the exhibitionists of both sexes strutting and preening onstage represented the embodiment of the whole modern ideal of physical culture, even if most of this self-absorbed fraternity did not know it.

By the closing decade of the nineteenth century, a number of events and forces had combined to focus public attention on the subject of health and physical development and make the advent of professional strength athletes an enthusiastically received form of popular entertainment for the next twenty-five years.

A revival of interest in the Greek physical ideal, brought about by research into Greek statuary, and the importation of the Elgin Marbles to Great Britain as the result of judicious bribery; the development of photography; the sudden establishment of sporting and athletic clubs among the middle classes, allied to a new national fascination with professional sport; the springing up of the Young Men's Christian Association with its emphasis on physical fitness; the concept of muscular Christianity conceived by Charles Kingsley and taken up by Thomas Arnold of Rugby and other public school headmasters; the concern of the government about the lack of fitness generally exemplified by the poor physical condition of the new city-dwelling recruits for the armed forces: all played a part in the national consciousness. Everywhere the strongmen were taking over as bill-toppers in music halls and vaudeville theatres as they became, for several decades, the new public heroes.

Among Victorian women, too, there was a sudden interest in such sports as tennis and bicycling and an increasing tendency among some of them to compete on equal terms with men. This found expression in the wider world of the Suffragette movement, with its principle of equal rights for women. A handful of its members, specially trained in ju-jitsu, became known as the Bodyguard, deputed to look after the safety of the leaders of the movement. This led in turn to an interest in public exhibitions of self-defence for and by women, which for a time became a small but well-patronised branch of show business.

These new idols of both sexes came from many different backgrounds and nations. Many of them were sufficiently charismatic and interesting to sustain the interest of the crowds flocking to the halls to witness their performances. Eugen Sandow had become an itinerant circus performer to avoid being conscripted into the Prussian army. Almost by chance he became the figurehead of a worldwide physical culture movement and one of the first 'dumb acts' to make a considerable fortune on the halls, as well as improving the health and physiques of thousands of the students of his revolutionary postal bodybuilding courses. His great rival, Charles Aloysius Sampson from Alsace-Lorraine, was the last of the old-time chest-beating, moustache-twirling strongmen. In order to enter the new world of vaudeville he turned cheating into an art form and continued to call himself the world's leading strongman, despite all evidence to the contrary.

Some of the strongest of the strength athletes had fatal flaws to prevent them from scaling the heights of their adopted profession. The Frenchman Louis Uni performed under the heading of Apollon and might have been the strongest man of them all. Alas, he was too lazy to try hard and was constantly reviled by his discontented wife after he failed in his attempt to enter the upper echelon of the performers' hierarchy as a lion tamer. The hirsute Canadian Louis Cyr had enormous physical strength but had the misfortune to look like a cross between Ghengis Khan and a yeti, and could never draw the crowds. The Saxon Trio (with an ever-changing line-up) had a most impressive strength and balancing act but tended to turn up onstage in a state of extreme intoxication and hurl weights willy-nilly into the stalls. Olympic champion Launceston Elliot was a crowd-puller with his onstage simulated gladiatorial combat. Unfortunately, his main opponent in his company had delusions of grandeur and tended to fight back too hard, causing the bruised and battered Elliot to call it quits and replace the fight scene with a gentler act featuring a bevy of underclad young ladies.

Among the women, Kate Sandwina struck a blow, literally, for her sex, by defeating her adoring future husband in a wrestling contest, and then carrying him off to her tent to revive him. Little Annie Abbott, the Georgia Magnet, weighed around 100lbs but resisted the efforts of the strongest of men to lift her from the ground.

Little has been written about this brief but fascinating heyday and this book intends to change that: witness the golden age of professional strongmen and women.

'SEE, HE DOES NOT COME!'

On the evening of 2 November 1889, the strongest man in the world was performing his act on the stage of the Imperial Theatre at the Westminster Aquarium in London. The 30-year-old Charles Aloysius Sampson, born in the disputed border territory of Alsace-Lorraine between France and Germany, was wearing tights and gladiator boots. A strap over one shoulder glittered with medals he had won in physique contests and exhibitions of strength. With his bulging muscles, dark, greased hair parted in the middle and large curling moustaches he presented an imposing figure, heaving aloft a dumbbell from the selection of weights and other apparatus littering the stage. A contemporary newspaper reporter described the strongman as looking considerably younger in the flesh than he did in the posters advertising his performances. Sampson was a naturalised American citizen, 5ft 8in. tall, measuring 44in. around the chest and weighing 212lbs. He claimed to have 18in.-flexed biceps, although contemporary photographs do not bear this out. The skin on his hands and arms had been coarsened by a decade of work with weights and cables.

Reporters liked Charles A. Sampson, even if his fellow music hall performers, tired of his constant boasting, did not. He was always good for a story and, if some of them tended to strain credibility, they still filled the column inches. His latest piece of self-aggrandisement had consisted of a rambling account of how he had been attacked with a sword by a drunken American officer on his recent tour of the USA. The officer had smashed the flat of the blade down on the strongman's head, shouting, 'If you are so strong, you can try to break this!' According to Sampson, he had retaliated with a single punch, breaking his assailant's shoulder blade in three places, subsequently earning himself a fine of $25 in a local courthouse.

He also claimed that in the previous year, 1888, he had brought production at a small factory to a halt by the simple process of wrenching an engine from its moorings, thus putting it out of action until the engineers could repair it. The strongman gave no reason for this burst of Luddite vandalism.

Sampson was always adept at publicising himself and his performances. In his newspaper interviews he gave many embellished accounts of a sickly, undernourished childhood, of how he had been written off by the medical profession yet transformed overnight into superhuman strength after a bolt of lightning struck him at fourteen years old. He also alleged that he had nursed himself back to health and strength after being wounded in the Franco-Prussian War.

Actually, like most strength athletes of the time, Sampson seems to have been a well-developed youth who had increased his natural power by a system of lifting heavy weights. Apprenticed to a circus strongman, he had begun to pick up both barbells and the tricks of his chosen trade. Willing to travel the world, he had ended up in the USA just as the new dime museums were flourishing. Displaying all sorts of freak shows and novelty acts they remained open from ten in the morning until ten-thirty at night for an all-inclusive fee of ten cents, with new performances starting every hour.

Sampson had done so well in his new milieu that he had been emboldened to try his luck in Great Britain and had secured his first booking in London. He had done reasonably well on his initial engagements but had antagonised indigenous strongmen with his arrogance and refusal to fraternise with his contemporaries. His rivals were also quick to spot that many of the newcomer's performance feats, like their own, were obviously faked. One English strongman, Tom Pevier, was particularly disgusted with Sampson's clumsy effrontery when it came to breaking in half what were plainly previously weakened coins. 'His tricks were so apparent to us all that he was challenged and offered genuine coins to break,' wrote the indignant rival Hercules.

In fact, Pevier's intervention was rather more dramatic than he claimed. Rounding up a group of other music hall artistes, the raucous group had attended one of Sampson's exhibitions and offered him the coins to break. When the strongman refused, Pevier and his friends started throwing the money at him, with other members of the audience following suit with enthusiasm. Theirs was something of a pyrrhic victory. After the curtain had fallen, Sampson and his partner Cyclops scurried eagerly about the stage picking up the coins and bearing them off in several canvas bags to the bank.

One aspect of his billing matter which particularly marked Sampson out from his competitors was his self-imposed title of the world's strongest man. He was genuinely a strong athlete but he was not above embellishing his performances when he thought that he could get away with it. His famous challenge barbell occupied a prominent place on the stage throughout his act and was sometimes placed in an open-topped box. The strongman would lift the weight above his head and then carefully replace it in the container. Sampson would then challenge any man in the audience to lift the weight. Many tried but none was successful. This was not surprising: the barbell was now screwed to the stage, kept in place by catches at the bottom of the box, which Sampson had removed surreptitiously just before lifting the weight. He would then replace the catches when he lowered the barbell back into the box, or his colleague Cyclops would do so when he pretended to clean the weight before an attempt was made to lift it. As a variation on this theme, the strongman's assistants would wheel a flimsy-looking cart bearing the barbell on to the stage. In reality the vehicle was made of heavily disguised lead and weighed more than 400lbs. When the weight was clipped to its surface no man could hope to shift it.

Another ploy was to have a barbell placed across the tops of two barrels. As a preamble, spectators would be invited onstage before Sampson attempted his lift. They were defied to manhandle the weight off the top of the barrels. Again, none would succeed. Then, with mighty roars and much stalking up and down the stage while he beat his chest with his fists, the strongman would swoop upon the barbell and thrust it painfully overhead, to great acclaim.

On these occasions the secret of the strongman's success lay in the fact that the barbell had been deprived of much of its weight before the unsuspecting eyes of the audience, after the challengers had failed to budge it and before Sampson made his own effort. This was achieved by two concealed holes in the orbs on the ends of the supporting bar. They were opened by Sampson's innocently hovering manager as the strongman distracted the spectators with his florid warm-up antics at the front of the stage. This allowed the heavy sand with which the weights were packed to run down unnoticed into the barrels, rendering the weight much lighter by the time Sampson attempted his own lift.

Tonight, the audience watched Sampson's demonstration of power lifting with pleased anticipation, waiting for the contest that was supposed to follow. The newspapers had been full of it for days. In his book *Sandow on Physical Training*, G. Mercer Adam, a friend and occasional collaborator on the strongman's books, summed up the public's interest: 'If the fate of the Empire had hung in the balance, more keenness in the coming match could not have been shown.'

Every seat in the house was taken and hundreds of would-be spectators had been turned away. Many of the disappointed were still milling about outside the theatre, disrupting the horse-drawn traffic in London's Tothill Street.

The reason for the excitement was indicated on the posters in the foyer. '£500 Challenge!' they proclaimed. Any man able to duplicate Sampson's feats of strength would receive this worthy sum.

With his cynical blend of genuine strength and barefaced chicanery, so far Sampson had defeated all comers, but tonight he was genuinely worried. The challenge had been accepted. Only a few days before, a young Prussian strongman, appearing under the stage name of Eugen Sandow, had defeated a strapping ex-blacksmith billed as Cyclops, the stage name of Franz Bienkowski, a protégé of Sampson's. Now the newcomer was about to meet Cyclops's master.

At least that had been the intention. As Sampson's performance was drawing towards its close, Sandow still had not arrived. From the wings Sampson's manager maintained a wary scrutiny. If the challenger did not appear within the next ten minutes, Sandow would lose the match by default.

The audience began to get restless. The promised competition had caught the fancy of sporting London. Some of the spectators had paid as much as a shilling for a balcony seat. A place in the gallery cost threepence, while twice this amount would secure a seat in a so-called private box holding fifty occupants. These were not inconsiderable prices at a time when a glass of beer sold for twopence and cigarettes cost a penny for five.

At that moment, Eugen Sandow was held up in the crowd outside the theatre. As he struggled through the mob he was followed by his agent Albert Fleming, a tough gymnasium owner, gambler and general fixer; his trainer and mentor Louis Atilla; and Captain Molesworth, the manager of the Westminster Aquarium, who was there almost by accident having ventured forth innocently into the night in search of the missing athlete and was now locked out of his own theatre with him.

Sandow was a blond, handsome bisexual native of Konigsberg, a port on the Baltic, and weighed in the region of 196lbs. He was a stocky, broad-shouldered, generally unassuming man offstage. A few days earlier the *Daily Telegraph* had described him as 'a short, but perfectly built young man of twenty-two years of age, with the face of a somewhat ancient Greek type, but with the clear blue eyes and curling, fair hair of the Teuton'. So far, in his young and not notably successful life, he had been an acrobat, artist's model, weightlifter and wrestler. He had toured the Continent with small fairs and circuses, often hungry and frequently unemployed. Originally he had changed his name from Friedrich Wilhelm Müller to avoid being drafted into the army in his home country, before embarking upon his present itinerant lifestyle. Now, ever hopeful, he was trying to embark upon a career as a music hall strongman. At the moment, his command of English was limited.

In the packed street, people soon began to recognise Sandow and made way for him, but progress was still excruciatingly slow.

The press was thickest outside the front entrance of the theatre, so the four men, led by Captain Molesworth, asserting the leadership qualities that must have led to the granting of his commission, plunged down a side alley and headed for the stage door.

Inside the theatre, Sampson was still lifting weights with hoarse bellows of self-approbation. His act was polished, if lacking in drama, and he had a good following. In his way, Sampson could be compared with his near contemporary, John L. Sullivan, the heavyweight boxing champion. Just as Sullivan had a claim to being the last of the great bareknuckle champions and also one of the first of the gloved fighters, so Sampson's strongman career spanned circuses and travelling shows that had their origin in medieval times, and he was about to gain a foothold in the emerging music hall and vaudeville spectacles about to be sparked off by the publicity engendered by this evening's much-hyped contest with Sandow.

Outside, the crowds continued to jostle around the theatre, demanding to be let in. The Westminster Aquarium, sometimes known as the Royal Aquarium, was a large complex several storeys high, not far from the Houses of Parliament. It was a flourishing establishment with a permanent staff of around three hundred men and women. It catered to the growing Victorian demand for sensationalism in public performances as music hall acts grew ever more spectacular.

The building derived its name from a huge but ill-fated aquarium in its basement. After several diminutive whales had died in the water and a talking walrus had been dismissed for its lack of persuasive coherence, the tank was now used mainly for swimming and diving displays. There were also a number of cafes and restaurants in the building, together with a row of cheapjack stalls and booths, a long promenade frequented every evening by dozens of prostitutes, and the Imperial Theatre itself. Arthur Roberts, a music hall comedian and inventor of the popular card game Spoof, had celebrated in song the slightly more mature charms of some of these avaricious ladies of the night:

> I strolled one day to Westminster,
> The Royal Aquarium to see,
> But I had to stand a bottle
> Just to lubricate the throttle
> Of a lady who was forty-three.

This hall specialised in eccentric acts, better known as freak shows, and as a result fought a series of running battles against suspicious and censorious local and national licensing authorities. One of its most popular performers was the celebrated Human Cannonball, an acrobat called Zazel. An iron tube on wheels, roughly resembling a cannon, contained in its barrel an assemblage of highly tuned rubber springs designed to propel Zazel into a net on the far side of the stage. The contraption's resemblance to an artillery piece in action was heightened at the moment of projection by an accompanying spectacular explosion and puff of smoke, which had no connection at all with the workings of the weapon.

Forerunners of Sampson on the Aquarium's role of honour included the Maravian Wild Women, the Two-Headed Nightingale, Pongo the Gorilla, the Missing Link, the Man with the Elastic Skin and Captain Costentenus, proclaimed as the most heavily tattooed man in the world.

Since its inception, the Royal Aquarium had been a thorn in the flesh of the former Home Secretary R. A. Cross. Throughout the decade the minister seemed to have been embroiled in a series of running battles with Captain Molesworth and his enterprising staff. Upon the completion of the Anglo-Zulu War in 1879, Cross forbade the Aquarium's intention to import three Zulu princesses, a royal baby, a chief called Incomo and twenty-three assorted warriors from the recently defeated nation to present a series of indigenous dances upon the stage of the Imperial Theatre.

However, Molesworth conducted such a skilful series of public protests that, bowing to public pressure, the Home Secretary reluctantly gave way and allowed the importation of the Farini's Friendly Zulus, headed by the amazing Princess Amazulu and her entourage. The show was such a success that the Zulu warriors remained *in situ* for two years, performing three times a day, with displays of singing, dancing and much enthusiastic hurling of *assegais* (a type of spear) in all directions. Disgruntled rival showmen, however, were heard to mutter that a considerable proportion of the fighting *impi* had been recruited from the ranks of black seamen discharged for deserting from their vessels at the Port of London.

Mr Cross had also objected, on the grounds of public safety, to Zazel being propelled so violently from the mouth of the cannon onstage. Captain Molesworth had come late to show business from his former maritime duties but was catching on fast when it came to matters of hype. Apparently the management of the theatre had replied by inviting the minister to take the acrobat's place for one performance. The offer was ignored, but Captain Molesworth contrived to insert copies of the relevant correspondence in the act's advertising matter. Zazel was allowed to continue, although the performance suffered a brief setback when it was discovered that she had once toured with a strongman troupe as a boy. The pretty teenager's increasingly curvaceous body, however, left no doubts about her true sex.

Also indisputably a member of the female sex was the well-endowed aerial artiste billed as Zaeo, another cause of friction between Captain Molesworth and his ever-present hovering watchdogs. Only recently the beleaguered manager had emerged successfully from a prolonged dispute with the scandalised members of the Central Vigilance Society for the Repression of Immorality. These ladies had objected to posters revealing the charms of the scantily clad trapeze artist. Molesworth had fought such a masterly delaying campaign against the reform group that most of London's male population who were interested in such matters had become pleasantly acquainted with the plump Zaeo's generous displays of flesh, causing her performances to be sold out before the manager had been forced to take down the offending posters.

This evening, with only minutes remaining, Sandow, Fleming, Atilla and Molesworth had reached the stage door, but there was a further complication. A frightened doorkeeper refused them admittance, even when his employer Captain Molesworth joined in the urgent demands from the alley to be let in. Sandow was not about to give up at this late juncture. While his companions made way for him among the cheering crowd the Prussian backed off and then ran at the locked door, hurling his shoulder against it. It was said later that the sound of the shattered hinges could be heard even above the noise of the throng in the street. The door crashed open, bowling over the unfortunate doorman cowering inside the theatre. As Sandow and the others galloped over the prostrate custodian, Fleming dropped a mollifying £10 note on his motionless body.

The panting newcomers entered the auditorium of the music hall so dramatically that the event could have been stage-managed. By this time Sampson had come to the end of his act and his manager was issuing his usual challenge to the audience from the footlights. The strongman, who spoke little English, glowered menacingly in the background. The content of the manager's speech has not been recorded, but the man must have made play with the fact that so far Sandow had not put in an appearance, because at one point Sampson lumbered forward and shouted, pointing contemptuously, 'See, he does not come!'

He had spoken too soon. Eugen Sandow and his breathless backers came running down the aisle. The *Daily News*, perhaps exaggerating, gave an even more hectic version of events: 'Soon a commotion (was) created by a number of gentlemen reaching the stage by flying leaps from box to box, panting and tousled after fighting their way through the frenzied crowd outside.'

Panic-stricken in case he was too late, Sandow began bellowing in German at his fellow strongman, and Fleming demanded that his charge be allowed up on to the stage. Sampson's manager refused angrily, declaring that Sandow had arrived too late. Anyway, he went on, his man's challenge was intended only for amateurs. Sandow was a professional strength athlete. Instead, suggested the manager hopefully, why not let Sandow and Cyclops have a return match for a stake of £1,000 a side? They had already met once only a few days before, when Sandow had won easily.

Fleming refused to be sidetracked. He declared that Sandow had come for the express purpose of competing with Charles Sampson. The spectators, he went on, had turned up in large numbers tonight to witness such a contest. At this the fascinated onlookers broke into cheers, demanding that the bout be got underway.

Captain Molesworth took charge. He hurried up onto the stage and ordered Sampson to meet Sandow's challenge. The captain was no fool. He had seen irate crowds get out of hand before.

He was not going to let this happen at the Imperial if he could help it.

Taking advantage of the distraction provided by the theatre manager's appearance, Sandow now attempted to run up onto the stage. Sampson saw him coming and stamped over to push his challenger down. The gallant Molesworth broke off his argument with Sampson's manager to race over to the two strongmen. Courageously, if foolishly, he interspersed himself between Sampson and Sandow. The younger of the two strongmen seemed to be wearing full evening dress and incongruous Roman sandals (a few days earlier, when he had defeated Cyclops, the Prussian had also sported a monocle). Retaining his evening dress trousers he took off his upper garments to reveal the pink singlet of an athletic costume. By this point the enthralled crowd had entered into the spirit of the occasion, cheering every fresh development on the crowded platform.

Finally, Captain Molesworth managed to restore some semblance of order, although the two strongmen were still glaring threateningly at one another. Molesworth walked down to the footlights and addressed the crowd. The contest would take place without further ado, he announced sternly. Would the judges please come up and take their places?

Gravely the Marquess of Queensberry and Lord de Clifford, appointed to oversee the forthcoming trial of strength, took their seats in the centre of the stage. They were said afterwards to have conducted themselves with typical British aplomb. Such a fracas would not have been a novel experience for either peer – both men had been nurtured on a nineteenth-century diet of illegal prize-fights and fixed horse races – and beneath their aristocratic veneers they were as tough as old boots.

John Sholto Douglas, eighth Marquess of Queensberry, was smoking a large cigar and wore a customary gardenia in his buttonhole. He had given his name to the first set of regulations to govern gloved fighting and was something of a joiner, having spent much of his life as an inactive member of the army, navy, House of Lords and a variety of gentlemen's clubs. Six years later he was to achieve notoriety when he instigated the trial and imprisonment of the homosexual playwright Oscar Wilde, after the latter had conducted an affair with Queensberry's son, the minor poet Lord Alfred Douglas.

De Clifford, 'Ned' to his highly placed friends and to absolutely no one else, was a fixture at most major sporting events, often officiating as a judge, stakeholder or timekeeper. Seven years earlier, after a celebrated racing scandal, he had been one of the stewards at the Four Oaks Park meeting who had reported the reprobate 'Squire' Abingdon Baird to the National Hunt Committee for foul riding, subsequently securing the warning-off of the inappropriately named gentleman rider.

At last, matters in the hall settled down and the contest got underway. Desperately Sampson picked up several bottles and juggled with them, then he challenged Sandow to emulate this feat. Peremptorily the judges ruled that this had only been an example of dexterity, not strength. As such it could not be entered into the competition.

After some muttering, Sampson grudgingly kicked the bottles away. He picked up an iron bar. In quick succession he struck the rod viciously against his wrists, biceps, calves and neck, bending the bar in a number of directions before throwing it away with a contemptuous glance at his adversary.

Sandow picked up a similar piece of metal and repeated each of the blows just performed by Sampson. His efforts were clumsier than the other man's had been, but just as effective. While each competitor recovered his breath after these exertions, the ubiquitous Fleming nipped forward cheekily to announce that this had been the first time his charge had attempted the routine.

The crowd applauded appreciatively. Irritably Sampson picked up a leather belt and set himself to tear it in half. Again the judges conferred and then intervened. They declared that only feats of strength involving weights, chains and cables could be attempted.

For a moment it looked as if the enraged Sampson was going to stride over and strike Lord de Clifford, the spokesman for the judges. Effortlessly the peer faced him down. He was no stranger to confrontation and knew how to deal with tough customers like the furious strongman. Indeed, only nine days later de Clifford was to be involved in another sporting controversy. Just as he was about to act as timekeeper for an ill-tempered bareknuckle bout on a muddy field in Flanders, between the black Australian Peter Jackson and the British heavyweight champion Jem Smith (which ended with the Englishman's disqualification), 'Parson' Davies, Jackson's manager, had objected long and loudly to 'a bloody lord' being given such a responsible position. The manager's objection was to fall upon deaf ears.

The mocking crowd in the Imperial Theatre shouted to the defending champion to get on with it. Sullenly Sampson seized a length of thick wire cable. His manager twisted it into position around the strongman's chest, securing the cable at the back before stepping back. Sampson took a deep breath, inflated his chest and shattered the wire.

Sandow picked up a similar length of cable. It took Albert Fleming some time to secure it in position behind the young Prussian's back, but eventually he managed it. Sandow dealt with this latest challenge as summarily as his opponent had done, breaking it in half with one mighty heave of his barrel chest.

Suddenly, Sampson grabbed a bottle from the stage. It was not clear whether he was introducing another exhibition of juggling or was contemplating striking Sandow with the improvised weapon. A cool word of warning from the Marquess of Queensberry was sufficient to cause the strongman to drop the bottle.

It was plain that Sampson was losing his temper. His self-control was not assisted by the taunts of the audience, now solidly behind the young challenger. But the champion was not finished yet. It was time to introduce his speciality. From his manager he took a hinged steel bracelet and attached it around one of his mighty upper arms. Slowly the strongman flexed his biceps. The steel ring shattered and flew apart.

Such an impressive feat of strength temporarily silenced the audience. Somewhat mollified, Sampson tossed a similar bracelet to Eugen Sandow and strode imperiously to the back of the stage.

In vain Sandow struggled to wrap the band around his biceps. It was much too small to go round the Prussian's arm. Sampson's manager shouted jubilantly, claiming the victory for his man. With a smirk Albert Fleming reached into his pocket and produced two steel bracelets of his own, which he handed to Sandow. At this, both Sampson and his manager rushed at Fleming. These new bracelets, they complained, were plainly of inferior make. They clamoured for Sandow's disqualification.

Sandow was mortified. Throughout his professional career he was dismissive of such displays as chain breaking, bottle juggling and coin tearing, referring to them as 'knacks' owing more to showmanship and sleight of hand than real strength.

Their lordships hesitated. Fleming saved the day and proved

worthy of his percentage by announcing calmly that the concealed bracelets were from the same firm that had manufactured Sampson's steel rings.

The champion strongman and his manager scoffed at the suggestion. Disdainfully Fleming waved them into silence and motioned to someone sitting in the stalls. This gentleman rose and announced to the cheering audience that he was a representative of the manufacturer in question. Producing an invoice from his wallet he handed the scrap of paper to the judges. Lord de Clifford scanned it and confirmed that the bill did indeed state that Sandow's bracelets were of the same strength and texture as Sampson's.

Fleming bowed with smug satisfaction. An astute and streetwise man, he had noticed in Sandow's previous contest with Cyclops that the Prussian's arms were indeed enormous. The agent had guessed correctly that the bracelets employed in his act by Sampson would not fit the challenger and had accordingly ordered the duplicates to be prepared.

Sandow fixed the bracelets around his arms. In stentorian tones, Fleming reminded the audience that Sampson had used but one steel ring. As silence descended, Sandow slowly flexed both arms. At the climax of his grimacing, sweating efforts, the two bracelets splintered and split like children's toys.

There was a momentary lull in the activity on the stage. Years afterwards, Sandow's critics claimed that on this occasion, so early in his music hall career, Sandow had proved to be every bit as devious as Sampson when it came to breaking the bracelets on his arms. It was later claimed that the Prussian had planted an accomplice in the audience that evening. Her name was Sarah E. White an attractive American music hall artiste touring Europe as an underwater aquatic act, which she claimed was the first to be undertaken in public by a woman. Her stage name was Lurline, the Water Queen.

According to her story, later given under oath in a court of law, secreted on her lap among the voluminous bags and muffs that evening were two more chain bracelets, almost identical to the ones just produced onstage by Fleming. Sarah claimed that one of the links on each bracelet had already been loosened in order to facilitate their breaking when Sandow flexed his upper arms. Earlier, when Fleming had passed the bracelets among the stalls to be examined, Sarah had surreptitiously substituted the genuine chains for a more brittle pair specially made and doctored for a fee of £20 by a specialist in such matters called Mr Schlag. For good measure, Sarah insisted, Sandow had also asked Mr Schlag to make a number of coins so brittle that they would break easily, in case Sampson included this feat among his challenges.

If it was a scam, on this occasion it worked. Jeering spectators shouted at Sampson to concede the match. The stubborn Frenchman ignored them. He hurried into the wings and returned with a length of chain. He threw it to the younger man, challenging him to break it. Sandow was willing enough to make the effort but Fleming ordered him to drop the steel shackles. Strength feats of this nature had not been included in the original challenge. Even when Sampson broke the cable himself, Fleming would not allow his man to attempt the deed.

By now the crowd was with Sandow all the way. Its members began chanting 'The weights! The weights!' Sensing the threatening atmosphere behind the apparent light-heartedness, the judges ordered that the contest should conclude at once with a weight-lifting competition to decide which man on the stage was the stronger of the pair.

Beginning an incredible few minutes, Sandow picked up a dumbbell weighing 280lbs and lifted it over his head with one hand. Still holding the weight aloft, he lowered himself to the floor and then scrambled to his feet again. He deposited the weight on the stage. While Sampson looked on glumly, Fleming affixed a steel chain around Sandow's other arm. Lifting a 220lb dumbbell overhead with his free arm, at the same time he inflated the other bicep and, with a roar, broke the chain.

It was the end of the contest and everyone present knew it. Sampson could not hope to follow that. The strongest man in the world had been thoroughly beaten.

The ex-champion did not take defeat gracefully. George Mozart, a music hall comedian in the audience that night, said that for a moment it looked as if a fight was going to break out between the two strongmen. Fortunately the cheers of the crowd engulfed the victor, who was embraced by Fleming and Atilla.

After a few minutes, an excited Sandow came forward to claim his prize money. He was to be disappointed. Charles Sampson and his manager had slipped off the stage during the celebrations and now were nowhere to be seen. Later, the Frenchman claimed 'I left the stage when I saw that I could not obtain fair play.' Albert Fleming complained bitterly to the sympathetic audience. The Marquess of Queensberry and Lord de Clifford agreed that the young Prussian should be recompensed in full, although both judges added hastily that they were in no way responsible for finding the missing cash.

That left only Captain Molesworth. The manager of the Westminster Aquarium was no stranger to controversy at his establishment, having been in a similar position when the Prussian had defeated Sampson's partner, Cyclops. With a £100 prize for the winner, neither Sampson nor Cyclops could produce that sort of money when Sandow had triumphed. Molesworth, who had been in the audience, had guaranteed the cash, thus averting trouble. Again, ever the pragmatist, Molesworth realised it would be cheaper to pay Sandow off than incur a bill for a wrecked theatre.

Reluctantly agreeing to do what he could on this occasion, the manager left the stage and started scouring the building for ready cash. There was nothing like the advertised sum on the premises. After much scurrying around the various tills and box offices in the building, Captain Molesworth could only return with £350 in his hand. Sheepishly he presented this sum to Albert Fleming.

Sandow's agent would have preferred the full amount but realised that his strongman had secured much more than a thousand pounds' worth of publicity upon the stage of the Imperial Theatre that evening. It remained only for him to start exploiting Eugen Sandow's newfound fame.

There was to be one inconvenient coda to what so far had been an evening of almost unmitigated triumph for the Prussian. Jerome K. Jerome, the celebrated comic author of *Three Men in a Boat*, was, at the time, a poorly paid junior clerk living in a cheap London boarding house. In an account in his autobiography, Jerome recalled how his landlord had evicted a fellow lodger, a burly young fair-haired German with curling moustaches, for celebrating too noisily in his room upon his return from a night out. The over-enthusiastic reveller was Sandow, returning from his triumph at the Westminster Aquarium.

But even as the dispossessed strongman tramped the inhospitable streets of London with his luggage in the small hours of that morning, the Prussian could not have been too disheartened. He suspected that great things lay in store for him.

So far, 1889 had proved to be an eventful year. The exploits of the serial killer Jack the Ripper were still terrifying the inhabitants of the East End of London. Dockworkers at the Port of London had successfully gone on strike for a rate of sixpence an hour, the so-called 'dockers' tanner'. At Mayerling in Austria, Crown Prince Rudolf, heir to the Hapsburg Empire, and his 17-year-old mistress had been found dead in a remote hunting lodge. No one seemed certain whether it had been a suicide pact or if the prince, trapped in a loveless marriage, had killed his mistress and then himself. The Eiffel Tower opened in Paris. A dam collapsed at Johnstown, Pennsylvania, drowning more than two thousand in the ensuing flood. Thomas Edison had displayed the first moving pictures and President Benjamin Harrison had opened Oklahoma to white settlers.

And the golden age of the professional strongman was about to begin.

2

A NEW CRAZE

For days after the showdown between Sandow and Sampson newspapers were full of the event. *The Sportsman* reported:

> Athletics had an exciting, not to say uproarious field night on Saturday at the Westminster Aquarium. The rival athletes, Samson [sic] the Alsatian and Sandow the German gave a public trial of strength, with the object of proving which was 'the strongest man on earth'.

Several newspapers poked fun at Sampson's ungracious acceptance of defeat. The *Glasgow Herald* wrote satirically:

> It is painful to hear that Samson [sic], the strongest man on earth has been subjected to destructive criticism, as if he were an historical myth like William Tell's apple.

As far away as New York, the *Brooklyn Eagle* had its own take on the contest, referring to Sandow as a Pomeranian:

> As the Pomeranian snapped length after length of the steel chain bracelets with his biceps and burst the wire ropes with his pectoral

muscles, men rose in the audience and waved banknotes of big denominations as an invitation to Sampson to beat Sandow if he could, but the former sulked and declined.

Almost at once a popular song about the contest was being sung on the halls. With lyrics by Edward Roden and music by F. F. Venton, it was called 'The Strongest Man on Earth'. The song began 'In days of old a Sampson bold', while the chorus went:

> Up jumped Sandow like a Hercules,
> Lifting up the iron bars
> And breaking them with ease.
> Sampson looked astonished and said it wasn't fair.
> But everyone knows that Sandow was the winner there.

The song became the signature tune of an 18-year-old singer, dock labourer and former prizefighter, Alec Hurley, who a few years later was to marry the reigning Queen of the Music Halls Marie Lloyd.

By now the music halls were flourishing. There were forty in central London alone and many more in the suburbs. Some of them were rough and ready establishments, but new ornate halls were being built all the time. Contemporary music hall artistes like Vesta Tilley trilled such favourites as 'Burlington Bertie' and 'Jolly Good Luck to the Girl Who Loves a Sailor'. Marie Lloyd warbled 'Don't Dilly Dally on the Way' and 'Oh, Mr Porter'. Eugene Stratton crooned 'Lily of Laguna' in blackface; Charles Coburn was renowned for his rendition of 'The Man Who Broke the Bank at Monte Carlo', once being called upon to sing the chorus ten times in succession before an appreciative audience would let him go, while the substantial Talbott O'Farrell, known to the irreverent as 'that bloody great barrel' gave his all to 'That Old Fashioned Mother of Mine'.

Within weeks of the Sandow–Sampson contest, and driven by the newspaper publicity, the two major strongmen were basking in the ultimate accolade of being parodied on other stages. At the Empire, Leicester Square, the comedians known as the Brothers Griffith were soon putting on a burlesque sketch of the Sandow–Sampson competition. Dressed as the famous strongmen, the scrawny siblings exchanged dialogue in heavy cod foreign accents. Part of their exchange went:

'What is your name?'
'Gorgonzola.'
'Mein Gott! You must be strong!'

The comic Tom Wootwell devised another parody inspired by the Prussian's success against Sampson. He would wander on to the stage in a tatty costume, emulating the tights and vest of a strongman. Beneath this costume his calves and upper arms were absurdly inflated to resemble muscles. At the end of the act, after a great build-up, Wootwell would fix a chain around his biceps and attempt to burst it by flexing his arm. When he did so, the sawdust taking the place of his arm muscles would leak, deflating the biceps rapidly.

As the winner of the contest, Eugen Sandow profited straight away from his triumph. He accepted a six-week run at the Alhambra music hall at an impressive £150 a week. This was a considerable sum for the time. It was not in the class of the actress and mistress of the Prince of Wales, Lillie Langtry, the 'Jersey Lily', who had embarked upon a series of tours of North America for a fee of £250 a week, expenses and a percentage of the profits, nor did it compare with the income of Annie Oakley, 'Little Miss Sureshot', who was currently touring Great Britain with Buffalo Bill Cody's Wild West Show. Her feats of marksmanship were drawing her an income of $700 a week.

Two artistes about to break through to the big time were earning music hall salaries more typical of 1889: Dan Leno, the clog-dancing comedian, and the young singer Marie Lloyd. In 1889, Leno was earning £28 a week in pantomime while the weekly appearance fee of Marie Lloyd, preparing for her first tour of the USA, was £30.

Sandow's new income was immeasurably more than the young strongman had ever earned before and it was a colossal sum compared to that paid to other strongmen at the time. Even the established Sampson had only commanded £10 a week at the Imperial Theatre, plus a small share of the profits.

The young Prussian enjoyed being feted and revelled in meeting the great and the good. In a period in which the proliferating music halls were eager to broaden their repertoires and encourage more spectators into their theatres, famous legitimate actors were offered such good money to perform that they were happy to appear in twice-nightly sketches. This led to a sometimes incongruous meeting of different backgrounds and cultures. Music hall executive George Alltree reported on the reaction of the imperturbable and ultra-refined classical actor, Herbert Beerbohm Tree, waiting in the wings with his wife at a London hall, just as two perspiring acrobats scurried off the stage at the conclusion of their performance. Always keen to observe the niceties, the great actor had drawled, 'I don't believe you've met my wife. Maud – the two Whacks. The two Whacks – Maud.'

Taking advantage of his sudden good fortune, Eugen Sandow spent most of the next twelve months on a triumphal tour of the provincial music halls, although whenever possible he took time out to further his contacts within his new profession on the halls. He took great pains in teaching the actor George Alexander how to throw a mutineer over the side of a ship for a West End production. For the time being he continued to employ Louis Atilla as an assistant onstage and a trainer and consultant behind the scenes. Showing the ruthless business streak that was to become his hallmark, the young Prussian pruned his payroll by dismissing his agent Albert Fleming immediately and began his canny lifelong practice of handling all his own financial affairs. Fleming accepted his dismissal phlegmatically and soon left for South Africa, where he operated a gymnasium and promoted boxing matches. It was not long before the Prussian had also dropped Atilla and embarked upon a successful solo career. Atilla was to prove less sanguine about the summary severance and launched a vindictive campaign to find another strongman to challenge and defeat Sandow.

Sandow was a single-minded man who always seemed to know what he was doing and why he was doing it. The journalist and politician (and new friend to Sandow) T. P. O'Connor described the strongman as a curious mixture of great shrewdness and a simplicity that amounted sometimes to childish naivety. Sandow was also inclined to be quick tempered and his language could be rough and ready.

For a while Sandow toured with a magician called Bertram in a show entitled 'Music, Muscle and Mystery'. Already Eugen Sandow was devoting a great deal of care to the planning of his act and doing his best to avoid the routine of lifting inanimate weights deployed by most other strongmen. He was determined to make his act stand out and to sustain the top-of-the-bill status into which his recent Imperial Theatre success had catapulted him. In the 1880s, almost all the music hall bill-toppers were singers or comedians. So-called 'speciality acts' like Sandow's appeared emphatically at the bottom of the bill, largely disregarded by the audience as it arrived or prepared to take its leave. Many of the strongmen only secured work as 'disappointment acts', recruited at the last minute when other performers dropped out. Nevertheless, after the furore caused by his Westminster Aquarium victory, Eugen Sandow wondered if he could dare to hope to raise the status of these 'dumb acts' in general and his own planned muscle routine in particular. He knew that this was his big chance and one not likely to be repeated. A natural businessman and fiercely ambitious, he was convinced that he had the courage and determination to make the most of the opportunity so suddenly presented to him. All he needed was a gambit to establish his style, and already the Prussian had a pretty good idea of the form this was going to take.

As befitted his new title of the strongest man in the world, at first Sandow included much powerlifting and many displays of force in his performances, but these soon were smoothly assimilated into dramatic and humorous sketches to appeal to a wider audience. This approach involved the manipulation of unusual objects, not just the dull, repetitious routine lifting of barbells and dumbbells and tearing packs of cards in half.

For one of these brief sketches, the curtain would rise on a pianist playing rather badly. The strongman would appear, mime his displeasure at the standard of performance and then tiptoe up behind the musician. Suddenly Sandow would dive, seize both the piano and its player, lift them both off the ground and carry his load apparently effortlessly into the wings. As he did so, the pianist, who was also Sandow's offstage boyfriend, would start playing 'You Should See Me Dance the Polka', while the strongman, still encumbered, would break into an appropriate skittish dance as the stage lights dimmed.

Striking a more patriotic note, Sandow would march onto the stage in the tunic of a British sergeant and would stop at a set depicting a fissure in a tropical terrain. More soldiers wheeling a cannon would follow him and stop in dumb confusion, indicating their concern at being unable to go any farther to fire upon their unseen foes. At this the resourceful Sandow would drop into an arched wrestler's bridge, supporting himself upon his hands and heels as he stared up at the roof. A long board was balanced across his heaving raised chest, and the troops and their artillery piece would proceed over the improvised human bridge in a line to the other side of the gap.

These were genuine innovations in a strongman's repertoire, far removed from the usual huffing and puffing and heaving overhead of standard weights of dubious provenance, accompanied by much over-dramatic slapping of chests and biceps.

The great difference, however, between the young Prussian's stage performance and those of most of the behemoths who had preceded him lay in his superb physique and the onstage uses to which he was to put it. Unlike most of his contemporaries, Eugen Sandow was a beautifully built man, with a chiselled musculature and the ability to display it to its best advantage. His mentor Atilla had noticed this years before when the itinerant Sandow had first wandered into his Brussels gymnasium. He had taken the young man under his wing and devised a special weight-training programme for him involving many repetitions of the lifting of comparatively light weights in order to isolate the different muscle groups and enable them to stand out in high definition when flexed.

The contrast with the shapeless, amorphous body of the average professional strongman, who trained only to develop his power, was marked. For years it had enabled the young Sandow to secure a steady living as a professional artists' model as well as a strongman and wrestler.

Atilla encouraged Sandow to concentrate in his stage act on his natural advantages of grace and athleticism. Unlike most other strongmen the Prussian would devote a whole section of his performance to a display of posing, depicting famous statues and paintings, embellished by spectacular lighting effects. The results were so impressive that before long Sandow numbered many women among his fans, as well as men. In her memoirs, *Recollections of Vesta Tilley*, published in 1934, music hall artiste and male impersonator Vesta Tilley remembers the strongman showing her a box filled to the lid with items of jewellery pressed upon him by adoring female followers.

From the beginning, Eugen Sandow concentrated on promoting himself and his music hall act. He was always available for interviews with newspapers and took part willingly in any exploits required of him. An assistant who toured with the strongman in his early days on the road recounted how even then Sandow would take every opportunity for self-advertisement. When he and his company were waiting for a train connection at one of the junctions on a Sunday, when artistes were travelling all over the country from one music hall to another, Sandow would make a great show of pulling one of his performer's heavy trunks away from the others, wait until a crowd had gathered, then lift the hamper by one corner and push it above his head before dropping it with a clatter. The assistant added that the prudent Prussian always made sure that it was never the trunk bearing his labels and possessions that was dented in the final crashing descent.

Although he had lost his crucial challenge match with Sandow, the defeated and irrepressible man from Alsace-Lorraine, Charles A. Sampson, also cashed in on the sudden public interest in strong-man acts. After all, he and the Prussian were suddenly by default the best-known strength athletes in Great Britain, perhaps in the world, and although it was already apparent that there was a muscle-man fad in the making, Sampson and Sandow for the moment occupied the inside track. For a start he refused to admit that Sandow had defeated him. Days after the competition at the Westminster Aquarium, he was still complaining to newspapers that the judges had not allowed him to go through his normal repertoire in the stage contest. In the *Birmingham Gazette* of 5 November 1889, he grumbled 'how any referee can tell me in the face of my challenge what feats I may and may not do is beyond all comprehension; it is his business to see that the feats are fairly done'.

Nevertheless, in the wake of the newspaper coverage of the events at the Imperial Theatre, the astute Sampson completed his run there and then hired the Royal Albert Hall, advertising the occasion with his usual hyperbole, still billing himself as the world's leading strength athlete.

Royal Albert Hall

Unprecedented attraction and positively for two nights only. Friday and Saturday evenings, Nov 22 & 23. By special arrangement and at the request and express desire of a very large number of influential patrons and friends, C. A. Sampson, the strongest man on earth! After sixteen weeks engagement at the Royal Aquarium, and the most successful on record, will give two of his marvellous exhibitions at the above hall, on which occasion he will be assisted by the elite of the profession. Forming for the evening's programme one of the most scientific, elegant and recherché entertainments ever witnessed. (Evanion Catalogue, British Library)

Unfortunately, one of his vaunted supporting acts was soon to get the much put-upon strongman into more trouble. A comic in his show performed a song that offended the susceptibilities of the capital's licensing committee, somehow reaching the ears of no less a person than Queen Victoria herself. The thought that a lewd ballad could have been sung at the establishment named after her late and much missed husband, Prince Albert, caused her to order enquiries to be made. Her Secretary, Sir Henry Ponsonby, a member of the licensing committee, wrote back abjectly:

Sir Henry Ponsonby presents his humble duty to Your Majesty and is afraid that he cannot entirely free himself from the affair of the Albert Hall. When asked some time ago if he saw any objection to Sampson performing his feats of strength there he said he did not. He knew nothing about the Comic Songs, etc. with which it is stated the performance was accompanied, but he thought that exhibitions of strength were such as could legitimately be performed there. He now sees to his regret that the entertainments which accompanied it were by no means such as should have taken place at the Albert Hall, and these certainly should not have been allowed.

Ejected from the Albert Hall, Sampson decided to emulate Sandow and embarked upon a lucrative provincial tour. Throughout he continued to assert that he had been robbed of his title at the

Imperial Theatre and took every opportunity to fan the embers of his feud with the Prussian. He told a reporter from the *Birmingham Gazette* that he was far from satisfied with the result of the recent competition. The interviewer said of the strongman: 'He is too good a sportsman not to acknowledge that he has met a formidable antagonist, but he declares that he has not been allowed to put him to the test for which he, Samson [sic] stipulated.'

Charles Sampson's troubles were not yet over. One afternoon, in a Birmingham theatre, he left his trick barbell screwed to the stage in readiness for that evening's performance. Politely, an acrobat on the bill, the muscular Frank Boisette, asked Sampson to move the weight, so that he and his troupe could practise. Brusquely Sampson told the acrobat to move it himself. Obligingly the acrobat gripped the bar and tore it from the stage, bringing up several planks with it.

Poor Sampson seemed to experience more than his fair share of failed tricks. Perhaps he was particularly ham-handed, or it might have been that his overbearing manner so antagonised most of his peers that any mishaps accruing to his name were eagerly repeated and soon became common currency among members of the profession on the circuit. After a time, appreciating that all publicity is good publicity, the strongman stopped trying to cover up his mishaps and actually started enumerating them to reporters in search of stories.

Among the accidents that had befallen him in the course of his stage performances, he declared that he had burst a blood vessel in his stomach while lifting a heavy weight, and dislocated his thumb and damaged a kneecap while performing his celebrated Roman Column trick. This involved the strongman perform-ing feats of strength while being suspended in an upside-down position against a substantial pillar. Once, he claimed, he had been in a kneeling position supporting on his back a revolving platform containing a dozen elegantly dressed beauties. The platform had collapsed on top of the strongman, breaking three of his ribs and severing a muscle in his right arm. He had then replaced the young ladies with seven polar bears. At the climax of his act, so he claimed wildly, he would wrestle the largest of these animals – twice a night. On one occasion, a keeper inadvertently had left a door of a cage open and the other six bears had rushed out and joined in the fight wholeheartedly, mauling the strongman and smashing a bone in his right forearm, necessitating thirty-seven stitches in the limb.

A more thoroughly documented catalogue of misadventures during the theatrical tours of Charles A. Sampson occurred when the ever-ambitious strongman decided to include the lifting of an elephant (hired from a local zoo) from the ground as a part of his act. It was a spectacular addition to his repertoire and a sign that, until the arrival of Sandow, Sampson had always been much more of a showman than most of the other strongmen around. But there were a number of built-in risks to such an ambitious policy. In fact, the consequences became known in the trade as Sampson's Follies.

In the first place, it was a very difficult trick to pull off. Besides the elephant, it involved the use of an elaborate piece of apparatus and the collaboration of a number of assistants and stagehands. An elephant was positioned on a platform at stage level. Charles Sampson climbed a ladder to a second platform located above the animal's head. He then shrugged into an impressively powerful set of harness consisting of a labyrinth of chains and leather straps extending down through a hole in the top platform and wrapped around the body of the specially trained elephant below. Jealous rivals were quick to contend that it was only quite a small and exceedingly docile elephant.

After a great deal of appropriate music and much use of flashing lights and drum rolls, Sampson would place his hands upon his knees, grimace grotesquely and slowly straighten up. As he did so, the harness around his shoulders would tighten and gradually seem to lift the elephant underneath him some 6in. above the stage. At this Sampson would give a great shriek of triumph, lower the elephant back to the stage and then collapse dramatically in a crumpled heap on his platform. Somehow, supported by acolytes, he would always recover in time to take the requisite number of curtain calls.

It was an open secret, as well as a matter of sheer common sense, in the strongman fraternity, that the elephant was being lifted by a system of concealed mechanically operated pulleys, hoists and other machinery. However, when it succeeded it was an impressive and dramatic presentation, especially viewed from the front.

The elephant was renowned for behaving impeccably through-out the performance. It was the human element that sometimes went woefully wrong, especially on tour. On one occasion it was the fault of the locally recruited stagehand, who had been trained to stand offstage, poised to operate the lever to start the process of winding the beast off the ground. After Sampson had gone through his opening preamble and the music had reached a climax, absolutely nothing happened. The elephant remained immobile. When Sampson's assistants rushed backstage to ascertain the cause of the catastrophe, the stagehand, upon whom so much depended, was discovered lying comatose in a beatific drunken coma next to the lever.

An even more embarrassing moment befell the strongman. Having performed the routine perfectly, Sampson crashed to the floor of the platform as assistants rushed to his side to revive their boss with brandy. To his amazement, the fraught moment was greeted with roars of laughter instead of the usual applause. The machinery had failed and the elephant seemed to be suspended with no means of support in mid-air.

Nevertheless, such occasional hiccoughs excluded, Sandow and Sampson had arrived in the public eye at just the right time for the sakes of their respective careers, and were ideally situated to spark off the professional strongman vogue.

Carefully supervised and embellished by Sandow, controlled details of the new star's early life began to emerge. He had never had it easy. He claimed to have been the son of an ex-army officer who had become a jeweller, although there is no proof of this. Similarly, his repeated claims to have been a weakly, underdeveloped child were probably all part of his later efforts to sell his popular body-building courses.

The young Sandow was good at games and took an interest in weightlifting. When he was eighteen he left Konisberg to dodge the draft and became an acrobat in a travelling circus. After several years the circus went bankrupt, leaving the young Sandow adrift and penniless in Brussels. Here he was fortunate enough to meet up with the diminutive but broad-shouldered gymnasium owner, Louis Atilla, who became his mentor. Atilla's real name was Louis Durlacher. He had been an unsuccessful song-and-dance performer who had graduated to the role of partner to a professional strong-man. Like Sandow he was a great believer in self-promotion. To this end, he was seldom seen without an apparently ordinary walk-ing stick, which he would toss casually to a new acquaintance. The stick, reinforced with metal, weighed 25lbs, resulting sometimes in embarrassing results for anyone attempting to catch it.

Their act had been crude and dull but Atilla learned enough from it to set himself up as a physical training instructor. In those days most strongmen gave exhibitions with barbells, consisting of two enormous hollow iron globes joined together by a long steel bar. In most cases they did not weigh nearly as much as was proclaimed from the stage. At his gymnasium, Atilla came up with the idea of filling the hollow globes with pieces of metal. These made the weights more adjustable for training purposes. As a lifter became stronger and more experienced, he could add more weight to the globes, thus progressively developing his physique and strength. It was a sensible idea and revolutionary for its time.

At first Atilla's physical culture classes flourished, but gradually, for one reason and another, the trainer's pupils tired of the strenuous weightlifting exercises involved in developing their bodies and began to abandon him. Soon even the resourceful Atilla was finding it difficult to scrape a living.

It was then that, fortuitously, the muscular, eager Sandow came along to work out at the Brussels gymnasium. Atilla could spot a good thing when he saw one. Sandow was intelligent and hard working and, just as important, he was a 'fast-gainer', able to pack on extra muscle quickly when he needed to. Atilla urged the young Prussian to become a professional strongman under his tutelage. Sandow was not exactly being overwhelmed with career opportunities at the time, so he accepted

The year was 1887. Strongman acts may not often have topped the bills but successful practitioners could earn a decent living if they were prepared to travel to secure bookings. Eugen Sandow was handsome, well built and charismatic. There was a fair chance that he might be able to provide Louis Atilla with a reasonable living until something better turned up.

First there were preparations to be made. Atilla put the eager German through an intensive course of physical development. Although he was only 5ft 8in. tall and his wrist measurement was an unexceptional 7in., Sandow showed that he was indeed capable of sculpting his body to even more impressive proportions. The young ex-acrobat soon put on bulk without losing the definition that made his physique such an attractive one. Atilla also concentrated on developing a stage presence for his pupil, grooming him in readiness for the big breakthrough, which eventually took the form of his contests with Cyclops and then Sampson.

It was during this period of physical regeneration that the young strength athlete changed his name to Sandow, a corruption of his mother's maiden name of Sandov. Later it was claimed that the name Eugen had been adapted by the two men from the race-improving science of eugenics. After he had become famous, Sandow adopted the spelling of Eugene for his first name (though he was known as Eugen and Eugene throughout his career).

At first the new team was a flop. Sandow and Atilla secured bookings for their double act in Antwerp and Rotterdam but miniscule audiences greeted their routines with apathy. The two disheartened men returned to Brussels and almost starved. Staggering on to Amsterdam they found that no one wanted to know them. Sandow even offered in vain to appear at a music hall for the equivalent of fifteen shillings a week. It looked as if the Prussian's strongman career was over almost before it had started.

Then, as was to happen frequently in Sandow's career, the power of publicity came to the strongman's rescue. Later both Atilla and Sandow claimed to have devised the ploy. It certainly got them off the hook.

Scattered around the streets of the city were dozens of coin-operated 'Try Your Strength' machines. The punter paid and then squeezed a handle with both hands, watching an indicator purporting to display the amount of pressure exerted. One night, after dark, Sandow swooped on three of these instruments in different areas of Amsterdam. Obediently he squeezed the handles as hard as he could. Each device went into convulsions and then erupted, spewing out broken springs and other vital parts. The next night Sandow sallied forth again. This time he destroyed three more machines.

In a quiet week for news the epidemic was reported with relish in the local newspapers. The local police force was affronted by the suspicion that a nocturnal gang of hooligans armed with hammers had apparently invaded their city. It was decided to place guards on the surviving strength machines.

On the third night, with Atilla lurking discretely in the background, Sandow approached one of the machines which had escaped his earlier ministrations. He nodded sedately to the suspicious policeman on duty, placed his hands on the grip and squeezed until the tortured appliance collapsed. While the police officer marched a compliant strongman off to the nearest lockup, Atilla was racing away to the offices of the largest newspaper in Amsterdam.

Their actions sustained enough publicity to secure the double act an engagement at the prestigious Paleis voor Volksvlijt. Here they prospered for a few weeks until the engagement was over. Atilla then secured them a booking at the Crystal Palace in Sydenham. Spending almost every penny they had on fares, they sailed for London. The trip, embarked upon with such high hopes, was to prove a catastrophe. Soon after their arrival Atilla injured himself and they were unable to perform as a pair, as contracted, with the theatre's management refusing to employ Sandow as a solo performer.

Dispiritedly the two men returned to the Continent. They split up for a while: Atilla returned to Brussels to allow his injury time in which to heal, while Sandow secured temporary employment as an artists' model, including posing for Aubrey Hunt, a celebrated artist and member of the Royal Academy, as a Roman gladiator. He supplemented his income by giving weightlifting exhibitions and conducting lessons in physical culture.

Once again times were hard for the young wandering Prussian. One night, as he was passing a café in Paris, a friend from his Konisberg days, a small, out-of-work music hall acrobat named Françoise, hailed him. On the spur of the moment, and acting mainly out of desperation, the two of them teamed up.

For a few months they toured Europe as the Rijos Brothers, with an ingenious mime act they called 'L'Afficheure' (the Billsticker). Sandow played the part of the billsticker, apparently juggling with a doll, portrayed by the tiny Françoise. In the course of their performance Sandow would hurl his partner against the wall, to which the latter would cling and make patterns with his multi-coloured costume, imitating well-known posters. The strongman remembered later with pride, 'It was only after a time that the audience realised that Françoise was not really a rag doll of huge proportions.'

The Rijos Brothers were definitely small-time, for the most part touring with third-rate circuses and sideshows. Once again Sandow was forced to perform feats of strength on the side. He also wrestled, taking on all comers. The latter sideline broke up the act when Sandow incurred a damaged arm in a bout in Venice.

In the meantime, the restless Atilla had moved to London and opened a gym in Bloomsbury. He was soon rejoined by a down-and-out Sandow who, while working as a model for Aubrey Hunt and perhaps enjoying a homosexual liaison with the artist, had been given, claimed the young trainer and writer W. A. Pullum, a letter of introduction from Hunt to John Fleming, a wheeler and dealer in London's sporting world.

There is some confusion as to the events that followed in London. Accounts, some of them given in forensic detail, state that Sandow reported to the august National Sporting Club in London. He attracted a great deal of attention with his displays of strength and muscle flexing, which culminated in him lifting a surprised portly member of the club above his head.

In fact, the sporting club was not to open its doors for another couple of years, in 1891. It is possible that Sandow arrived at an ad-hoc meeting of bored aristocrats who later founded the NSC, but there is also a chance that the young strongman turned up instead at the raffish Pelican Club, a gambling establishment for young bloods and old roués, and where John Fleming had served in an administrative capacity.

Fleming was under a cloud at the time, being suspected of fixing a fight between the British heavyweight champion Jem Smith and the visiting Australian Frank Slavin, so it is more likely that the man about town would have been lying low at this particular time. What is certain is that John Fleming's son Albert became Sandow's British agent. In conjunction with Louis Atilla, he masterminded Sandow's challenges to Cyclops and Sampson and unwittingly laid the foundations for the rapidly approaching great strongman cult.

3

THE STRONGMEN ARRIVE

For years the embryonic halls of entertainment had been content to feature mainly singers and comics. Now, with audiences increasing, there was a demand for more varied forms of entertainment, and managers were doing their best to provide these. As early as the 1860s, showmen had experimented with presenting celebrities on their bills. The acrobat Leotard and the high-wire walker Blondin had made personal appearances at London halls, while the Native American professional runner Deerfoot had presented himself and his trophies at theatres all over the country. Deerfoot's stage appearances had been limited to a few embarrassed words to the audience and, in order to boost his marquee value, he had even taken part in a shame-faced publicity stunt in Worcester, when he had pretended to scalp an associate.

By the 1890s, the halls were experimenting with all sorts of speciality acts, including acrobats, trick cyclists, animal shows, mind readers and escape artists. Now only the new fashion for strength athletes seemed to have potential for top-of-the-bill status and it was not long before word began to spread among the scattered international strength fraternity of the comparative riches to be secured in the English music halls for anyone who could replicate the successes of the pioneering Sandow and Sampson. Impresarios and agents began to hunt for suitable strongmen and soon muscle-bound titans were arriving in London from all over the world. There was an increasing probability that the existing champions sooner or later would be upstaged.

Sampson, with his rigged feats and penchant for concealed mechanical forms of assistance, was particularly vulnerable to challenges from his peers. He lived in a state of permanent suspicion and was constantly afraid of being shown up during his public displays. Once, when he was appearing in London, a far superior strongman, a Frenchman called Louis Uni, who performed under the name of Apollon, came up on to the stage, ostensibly to accept Sampson's invitation to check the validity of the weights being lifted. Afraid that the rival strongman would challenge him to a contest, Sampson had blanched. Speaking rapidly in French in low tones he had begged Uni not to interfere in the livelihood of a fellow strongman.

By 1891, the *New York Herald* was able to give a list of the thirty most prominent strength athletes already criss-crossing the Atlantic to fulfil top prestigious theatrical engagements in Europe and the USA. They included the names of Sampson and Sandow, as well as Cyr, Cyclops, Kennedy, Ajax, Hermann, Sebastian Miller, Milo, Marks, Hercules, Dodnetti, Andrew Hall, Wilson, Ayres and Montgomery.

Newspapers were not slow to recognise that the major strongmen were already forming themselves into mutually supportive cabals. The *Brooklyn Eagle*, examining the burgeoning strongman craze, pointed out: 'They have entered into a combination by which they play in different cities [and] give each other points on the best ways of increasing the financial profits of the union.'

Some of the newly emerging strongmen had in fact been around for some time but had been forced to find employment in the lowly regarded fairs and circuses. Typical of these veteran British strongmen now blinking in the glare of hype were the McCann brothers, Louis and Henry, from Birmingham, who performed professionally as the 'Marvellous Muscular Men, Hercules and Samson' (the latter being an unimaginative but common sobriquet for stage strongmen). As early as 1883, they were on record as writing to the proprietor of the Brighton Aquarium asking for work and outlining their act: 'Our great and unrivalled feats of strength, with the heaviest weights and dumb-bells in the world, including lifting at every performance.'

Soon there were hundreds of strongmen touring the halls, many of them as headliners during the great initial popular fascination with strength athletes. They came from many different countries and backgrounds, although most of them were artisans impelled to take up their new careers by the prospect of making a steady and even glamorous living, and get away from dull or dangerous jobs or escape boring domestic routines. They were mostly naturally big and strong men who suddenly realised that their muscles could be used for something more lucrative than swinging hammers in forges or dragging loads across factory floors.

First, however, a would-be professional strongman had to attract the favourable attention of a manager or agent to guide him through the hazards and pitfalls of a show business livelihood. Some like Edward Aston and Donald Dinnie first attracted attention by winning strength events at such professional athletics tournaments as the Grasmere Games and the Highland Games. Staff Sergeant Moss developed his physique as a physical training instructor in the British army but resigned to tour the halls and sell his physical culture correspondence course. His military background, however, soon told against him when he was marked down for being too heavily tattooed when he entered an international physique contest. Monte Saldo entered the profession by being officially apprenticed to Eugen Sandow when he was eighteen years old. Albert Treloar, one of the first American strongmen, also gained his knowledge of the trade from Sandow by working on tour as one of the Prussian's stage assistants. Gunner Moir won and held briefly the title of British heavyweight boxing champion, which secured him a week's engagement at £40 at a London music hall, performing feats of strength.

William Bankier, Alexander Zass and Louis Uni were all well-built, restless lads who ran away from home and ended up as odd-job men in circuses, later graduating to helping the resident strongmen and learning the ropes. Don Athaldo was a blacksmith's apprentice, living in a remote area of Australia. He was so determined to become a professional strongman that he enrolled on a correspondence course and developed his physique even further.

John Marx was noticed unloading a brewer's dray with obvious ease. Joe Bonomo, as a boy was entranced by the strongmen's sideshows on Coney Island and learned everything he could from them before turning professional when he grew older. Both Bobby Pandour and Otto Arco started as gymnasts. In the process they developed such magnificent muscles that later in their careers they could easily make the transformation to weightlifting. Several broke into the profession by emulating Sandow and leaping on to the stage and challenging touring strongmen and doing so well that the strength athletes they defeated either paid them to go away or recommended them to agents or managers.

Once they had made the initial breakthroughs, the young wannabes then had to find agents to guide them, for a percentage, through the complexities of their budding music hall careers. There was plenty of work available for suitable acts with syndicates increasingly putting together groups of theatres. Artistes could be booked to tour all the theatres in a single chain. Businessmen like Oswald Stoll, Edward Moss, William Broadhead, the Livermore Brothers and Walter de Freece exerted enormous influence over the halls and the performers who appeared on their stages. There were also hundreds of independent halls, all eager to book the best entertainers. In New York, in 1881, Tony Pastor had opened his family-orientated Fourteenth Street Theatre, the first of many that were to follow and provide employment for artistes.

By the closing decade of the nineteenth century, the billings of the major strongmen, usually based on heroes of mythology, screamed down from fly posters on the walls of theatres and city streets all over the UK and USA: the French Hercules, the Scarborough Hercules, Hercules and Samson, the Iron Samson, the Cowboy Samson, the Iron Master, the Muscular Marvel, the Man with the Grip of Steel, Champion Athlete of the World, Champion Club Swinger of the World, the Beast of the Jungle, the Tipperary Wonder – the bombastic and congratulatory list seemed to have no end.

The managers and committees running the halls liked strongmen because their flamboyant acts lent themselves to publicity stunts outside the music halls, which the proprietors hoped would lead to an influx of spectators in the evenings. The strength athletes needed no second bidding to strut their stuff in public, hauling huge laden carts through city streets or defying the efforts of two horses to pull them apart. Most of these stunts had been performed since medieval times and were not as difficult as they looked. A favourite was towing a cart by a harness held between the strongman's teeth and draped over his shoulders as he lumbered backwards. The attention of the gawping onlookers was directed to the strongman's mouth, but throughout the journey most of the weight of the cart was being taken on the puller's legs and body. It also helped if the route taken was down an almost imperceptible slope.

The problem, which persisted, was that most of these would-be music hall strongmen still had no acts to speak of. The veterans among them brought along their circus performances of lifting weights, breaking chains and dragging heavy loads. These were usually horrendously dull to watch. The complete novices among them, no matter how powerful their muscles, did not even have a shop window in which to display their basic strength skills. It became obvious to the strongmen and their employers that they would have to develop acts of their own, and this simply could not be accomplished overnight. It could take years for a variety performer, by a laborious process of continuous trial and error, to put together a polished routine. On the plus side, once assembled and slotted into place a single performance could be trotted around the country by its owner virtually unchanged for years.

Newspaper reports of the displays of these enthusiastic novices popping up everywhere became almost blasé:

Another Strong Man

Yesterday afternoon at the Royal Music Hall, an exhibition was given by a 'strongman' calling himself Milo. Milo is a young Italian, of short stature, but of powerful and well-proportioned frame. His initial feats, like those of the former strong men, consisted in balancing a dumbbell of 150lb, tossing a[n] 80lb weight around in the manner of a juggler, holding 150lb in his teeth while he stood on his hands, and so forth. Then he played with a hollowed dumbbell containing a clown in each extremity, and next raised a 250lb bell above his head. Then came the final feat, in which two full-sized chargers and two men habited as Life Guards, standing on a platform, were raised simultaneously from above by Milo. This feat evoked much cheering. The weights were tested by a committee.

Still smarting after his summary dismissal by Eugen Sandow, Louis Atilla had spotted the Italian Milo, whose real name was Luigi Borra, wrestling at the Folies Bergère. The embittered trainer was determined to produce a young strongman capable of defeating the Prussian in a contest of strength in London. He persuaded Borra that it would be easier and much more lucrative to lift weights for a living than grapple against all comers in the ring.

As may be seen from the newspaper report of his debut, Milo's stage performance was stilted and hackneyed, owing much to the existing acts of Sandow and Sampson. Atilla, who had a talent for such choreography, set to work to polish the Italian's routine and make him stand out from the crowd. The Italian proved a ready pupil. Before long, Atilla had sent his latest protégé zooming up the billing order, performing stunts including balancing a pole on his chin on top of which would be a platform bearing a man and a field gun and carriage, which were discharged at the climax of his performance. Atilla also taught Milo how to hang by his teeth from a trapeze with both arms extended fully to the sides while holding a 50lb dumbbell in each hand, in what was known in the profession as a crucifix.

What with the firing of the cannon and the dropping of heavy weights, Milo's act became known as one of the noisiest on the music hall circuit. This gave rise to the story that after one particularly poorly attended first house performance, Milo trudged off the stage in dispirited silence to be quizzed in the wings by a hopeful waiting chorus girl:

'Did you manage to wake them up, Mr Milo?'
'Two of them.'
'What happened?'
'They got up and walked out!'

Sandow and Sampson apart, the stage performances of the first wave of strongmen were nothing to get excited over. Managers and bookers began to wonder if the strength bubble might be about to burst. A typical stage performance of the time was that of Cyclops, the former pupil of Charles Sampson, and another strongman calling himself Vulcan, who had become the new partner of Cyclops. They managed to secure a booking at the Royal Aquarium but their performance did not come over well. The two young men, who were both under thirty, juggled with weights to open the show. Then they stood back to back. Cyclops lifted a 112lb barbell over his head and threw it backwards to Vulcan, who caught the weight and returned it in the same manner.

They played catch in this fashion for some time, before Cyclops lifted what he claimed to be a barbell weighing 350lbs from the floor to an overhead position. The performance ended with both men breaking chains by inflating their chests and tensing their biceps.

Other veteran strongmen were responding in droves to the call of the unprecedented salaries suddenly on offer in London and the provinces, like elderly warhorses hearing the first rumblings of gunfire for a long time. They brought with them years of experience of the circuses, fairs and dime museums of the world. Most of them were genuinely strong but had passed the stage where they could be persuaded to add an element of Sandow's much-needed showmanship to their acts. One of the most powerful physically of the first arrivals was John Marx, a native of Luxembourg. His real name was Gruen or Gruenn – his billing varied considerably. Marx was so confident in his ability that he never bothered to learn more than a smattering of English nor furnish much of a spectacle in his performances. He lifted heavy weights but, according to George Alltree who booked him often, the strongman restricted his utterances to a terse, memorised 'Me John Marx, the greatest strongman in the world. My weights so heavy, no man can move. I do move – so! Overhead – so!'

Actually, Marx's specially constructed barbells and dumbbells were not only genuinely heavy but their bars were also enormously thick. The 6ft 4in. tall giant had very large hands, over 8in. long and 4in. wide. He utilised this asset in the design of his weights, so that challengers from the audience could seldom even grasp the bars properly, let alone lift them overhead.

As a young man he had visited the USA, where he had worked as a labourer in a brewery or a saloon, sources differ. A travelling professional strongman who performed under the name of Aloysius saw the young man loading beer barrels with ease on to a delivery cart and persuaded him to turn professional and tour with him under the heading of the Brothers Marx. Their theatrical bills announced: 'We Challenge the Universe: Feats of Herculean Strength!' Later Marx toured with circuses on the Continent before visiting Great Britain when he heard of the wealth and fame suddenly on offer there.

Houdini, the great escapologist, sometimes appeared on the same bills as Marx and had a soft spot for the big man, saying that he reminded him of a two-footed baby elephant. The escapologist admitted in his published study of contemporary strongmen, *Miracle Mongers and their Methods*, that the weightlifter had one major weakness. 'In spite of his sovereign strength, Marx was no match for a pair of bright eyes. All a pretty woman had to do was smile and John would wilt.'

Marx also had a quick temper. While Charles A. Sampson was appearing at the Royal Aquarium, he and John Marx had an altercation. One of Sampson's assistants, a man called Dewell, came to the assistance of his boss, only to be struck by the man from Luxembourg. Subsequently Marx was charged with assault and fined at Westminster police court.

On another occasion the lumbering strongman met his match at the hands of a famous performer – this time offstage. Marx was sharing a dressing room at the St James's Hall in Plymouth with the comedians George Mozart and Alec Pleon. Pleon was a highly strung, reckless man and only 5ft tall.

The two comics arrived at the dressing room, which had an extremely low ceiling, some time before the strongman from Luxembourg. Carelessly they took up more than their fair share of space. When Marx arrived, stooping and complaining because of the low ceiling, he was enraged to discover that his fellow artistes had left no room for his make-up on the dressing table. With an angry grunt he swept Pleon's make-up box off the table with his ham-like fist. When the comic protested, Marx threatened him physically. Pleon seized an empty water jug and jabbed it forcefully into the pit of Marx's stomach. Marx straightened up in agony and struck his head against the ceiling, stunning himself. There was no John Gruen Marx at the first house performance that night.

It could not be said that Marx learned from experience. On

several other occasions he put himself out of action by persisting with a trick that simply did not want to be performed. A chain was stretched tautly between two uprights. Marx then hovered over it and brought his fist down hard, with a tremendous yell, breaking the chain in half. It was a spectacular effect but had its repercussions for its protagonist. On at least two occasions Marx broke the little finger of his right hand in the execution of the blow. Very reluctantly he discarded chain breaking from his repertoire; however, he persevered with his trick of straightening horseshoes. This aroused the suspicion of his peers: it was commonly held among the strongman fraternity that these implements could not be manipulated unless they had been specially treated in advance. But, as Marx always carried a substantial wad of banknotes in his pocket to bet on himself against other strength athletes, he was seldom challenged.

Another early strongman on the halls, who was to become a major force in the physical culture cult, was William Bankier who billed himself as Apollo, the Scottish Hercules. Although he was to have a long and distinguished career in different aspects of show business, Bankier was unlucky. He had everything that Sampson and Sandow had, and was probably brighter and more enterprising than either of his rivals. One of the few strongmen to have lived a genuinely interesting and adventurous life, he could have been a major player in the strongman game. But he was not the first on the scene, and that always told against him. A sense of wanderlust and an impulse to try his hand at every opportunity that presented itself had taken the Scot halfway round the world at a very young age. By the time that he returned to Great Britain, Sandow had already established himself. For years Bankier did his best to compete on equal terms with the Prussian but never quite accomplished this, and it rankled.

He was born in Banff in 1870, the son of two schoolteachers. Naturally big and strong from an early age, Bankier started running away from home when he was twelve, and eventually embarked for Canada on a ship called *Cynthia*, which was shipwrecked off the coast of Montreal. Bankier, not yet fourteen, swam ashore, crossed great swathes of prairie on a train on his own and found work on a Manitoba farm, where he was overworked and underpaid.

Once again he took to the road. This time he ended up as a labourer in a travelling circus. He studied the repertoire of the tent show's professional strongman and found that even at his tender age he could emulate most of the weightlifter's stunts. When the strongman did not recover from a drunken bender in time, Bankier took his place at that evening's performance. His routine proved so satisfactory that after the strongman recovered Bankier joined his act as an assistant and general gofer. It was during his time with this and other circuses that Bankier became a considerable acrobat. He was particularly adept at climbing a 30ft rope, using his arms only, with his legs extended horizontally below him. As a result of this exercise he developed particularly massive biceps.

He spent a year at this work and then joined a tent show run by the great William Muldoon, a wrestling champion and a pioneer of physical education in the USA. Muldoon renamed Bankier Clyde Clyndon and billed him as the Canadian Strong Boy. He also taught the youth how to wrestle.

Always restless and eager to better his condition, Bankier, now a strapping and immensely strong young man, joined a troupe of touring prizefighters, headed by Jake Kilrain, who had unsuccessfully fought John L. Sullivan in the last recorded contest for the world bareknuckle heavyweight title. Under Kilrain's tuition, Bankier was able to add boxing to his physical skills. At the age of seventeen not only was the handsome young Scot as strong as a gorilla he could offer a variety of honed strongman and combat skills to any potential employer.

No less a person than Colonel W. F. 'Buffalo Bill' Cody, the great Indian fighter and cavalry scout, took advantage of this and Bankier toured with the former scout's Wild West and Congress of Rough Riders show before returning to Great Britain, after a short stop in Ireland, to do more circus work as a strongman. By now Bankier was working under the name of Apollo. He developed the stunt of lifting one of the circus elephants using a harness lift. Bankier always claimed that, unlike C. A. Sampson and many other strength athletes, all his lifts were genuine, the results of strength and technique.

On arrival in Britain, Bankier found that Eugen Sandow had established himself as the supreme strongman of the music halls. This always irked the Scot. He considered, perhaps with reason, that he was every bit as strong as the other man and that his physique was certainly a match for that of the world's strongest man. He developed his own strongman act and soon attained top-of-the-bill status, but in the eyes of the public he always stood in Eugen Sandow's shadow. This incensed the Scottish Hercules. He took to issuing vitriolic public challenges, always ignored by his rival. A typical example was published in the *Glasgow Evening Times*:

Sir – I hereby challenge Sandow to a contest of strength for £100 a side, for which I send £5 now to show I mean business: the contest to consist of weightlifting from the ground, six feats each… This is no bombastic challenge, but simply a desire to prove to the public that there are better athletes in Britain than ever came from Germany… Yours strongly, Apollo, the Scottish Hercules.

The jingoistic William Bankier always shared the commonly held public belief that one Briton was worth half a dozen foreigners. Later, when he was promoting ju-jitsu and wrestling matches, he caused something of an international furore when he publicly decried the sneaky fighting methods of other nations compared with those of his fellow countrymen.

With his background and experience Bankier had no difficulty in putting together a music hall act. Like Sandow, he was short and very well formed; being 5ft 6in. tall, weighing 180lbs and with a chest measurement of 49in., he was able to open his act with an effective posing display from a pedestal. For these performances he wore a very skimpy loincloth. Although he was a heterosexual, Bankier, like Sandow, had a considerable gay following which would follow him from theatre to theatre. Changing into a more regulation leotard, Bankier would then go into a display of strength activities. He would support a piano with a number of musicians and a dancer on a plank across his shoulders, lift weights and perform his celebrated lifting-the-elephant display. He was also extremely agile and could jump over the back of a chair holding a 56lb weight in either hand. He would follow this, still holding the dumbbells, by performing a standing somersault. He kept the use of orthodox weights to a minimum, preferring to use everyday objects with which his audience could relate, like anvils and even bicycles.

Bankier was scornful of the more blatant trickery performed by some of his fellow strongmen and incurred their dislike by expressing his reservations in public, insisting that many of the more spectacular tricks were not nearly as difficult as they appeared. He also claimed, with justification, that many strongmen exaggerated the weight of the pounds they claimed to lift and also their own physical measurements. 'There are strong men on the stage who claim to lift 300lbs,' he scoffed in his autobiography, *Ideal Physical Culture and the Truth About the Strong Man*, 'but that's all balder-dash!' He poured scorn on such staples of the strongman's art like chain breaking and horseshoe straightening, claiming that these pieces of apparatus invariably would had been doctored in advance by compliant blacksmiths in their foundries.

Apart from Sandow, Sampson and Bankier, few of the pioneering strongmen of the last decade of the nineteenth century were famous enough or possessed enough showmanship and charisma to demand top billing from the start. One other who could, however, was Launceston Elliot. He was a weightlifter and all-round athlete and was the first British winner at the initial Olympic Games of the modern era, held in Athens in 1896. He was a huge, handsome man and his Olympiad victory made him a drawing card on the halls from the start. He owed his unusual Christian name to the fact that he had been conceived in the capital of Tasmania. Not long after his birth in India, his mother died in a fall from a hotel window, where the family was staying. Elliot's father, a colonial magistrate and a distant relative of the Earl of Minto, then married the receptionist at the hotel and, with some haste, took her (already pregnant) and Elliot back to India. Elliot did not arrive in England with his father and stepmother until he was thirteen. He grew into a strong if temperamental athlete with a pronounced adventurous streak, ready to try his luck at most things. He won several national amateur weightlifting tournaments while still a teenager and was placed prominently in a couple of physique contests. At one stage he became a pupil of Eugen Sandow.

He took part in the ad-hoc Greek Olympiad, like all the other entrants, by simply turning up in Athens in time for the opening ceremony. The overall competition was not noted for its smooth running. The three yachts which finally arrived for the sailing ceremony were promptly placed in quarantine, forcing the races to be cancelled. The two English representatives who entered for the cycling were working in humble capacities at the British Embassy at the time and there was much debate as to whether these athletes could be considered 'gentlemen' because of their inferior positions. In the end, they were allowed to take part.

Launceston Elliot entered whichever competitions appealed to him. He was eliminated in the first heat of the one-hundred metres sprint, when he finished fourth. However, as the sprints took place on the first day of the Olympiad, Monday 5 April, it has been claimed that Elliot was the first British athlete to compete in the modern Olympics. As he was born in India, did not see the United Kingdom until he entered his teens and was fiercely proud of his Scottish heritage, however, Elliot never made any such assertion.

Competing in weightlifting, Elliot tied with the Danish entrant Viggo Jensen in the two-handed barbell contest, but the judging panel, headed by the Prince of Denmark, awarded first place to Jensen for displaying superior style. A few minutes later the same two men contested the one-hand dumbbell lift. This time Elliot won easily, sweeping the weight from the ground to an overhead position without pausing at the shoulder. He was awarded the victor's silver medal, no golds being issued at this Olympiad.

The other competitions proved something of an anti-climax for the strongman. In the Greco-Roman wrestling heats he was matched against a much smaller German called Carl Schuman, a gymnast who had already picked up three first places in the gymnastics and a third in the weightlifting. He proved much too good for Elliot, who was disqualified and escorted from the arena for fighting on after the bell. The big man also stormed out of the climbing event when he could not get to the top of the rope.

Elliot's subsequent stage act was also out of the ordinary. Falling out with his father, he left the family farm in Essex and started by touring with his wife and pretty daughters in an act choreographed by strongman and trainer Bill Klein. As the distaff side became more and more popular with male audiences he gradually increased his female supporting staff to a nubile dozen. In addition to lifting the usual weights and juggling with wooden clubs, he devised an act called the Spinning Cyclists. Elliot would settle a long bar across his huge shoulders. A cyclist and his mount would be attached by wires to each end of the yoke. Elliot would start by revolving slowly in time with the riders as they pedalled round the stage. As the two men increased speed their cycles left the ground and the strongman started spinning more quickly. A drummer in the pit would increase his tempo and as the curtain fell both cyclists would be spinning through the air level with the strongman's shoulders.

It was difficult to top such a display but Launceston Elliot did his best. He concluded each performance with a simulated gladiatorial display, based on those of the arena of ancient Rome. Elliot used a permanent company of eight strongmen for this event, four black and four white. Whenever possible he would enlist another eight gladiators at whichever city in which he happened to be appearing. The display included a bout with *cestus*, heavy leather riding gloves designed to resemble the deadly steel strips used as fist coverings in the ancient arenas. Such an exciting climax always brought the audience to its feet.

Unfortunately one night the contest became a little too realistic. Spurred on by the screaming crowd, Elliot bundled into his opponent particularly vigorously. The strongman's partner, a second-rate professional boxer, fought back with a will. At the end, the two contestants were so severely battered that neither was able to appear at the second house performance that evening. Wisely, Elliot subsequently abandoned the gladiatorial display as a part of his performance.

Throughout the decade, strongman acts showed no sign of declining in popularity. However, the public was eclectic and the shows had to be increasingly colourful and fast moving. This meant that some would-be professional strongmen fell at almost the first hurdle. Some just were not strong enough. Others were lacking in stage presence. A number possessed a great deal of muscular strength and skill but their chosen stage specialities were mind-numbingly dull.

One of these unfortunates was an Australian from Ballarat, Tom Burrows, who billed himself as the King of Clubs. Originally arriving in Britain in 1892, alongside a couple of Australian boxers who soon faded from the public's sight, he secured a post teaching boxing at the Royal Military Gymnasium at Aldershot. There he found that his rather pointless hobby of swinging wooden Indian Clubs amazed his pupils, so he added it to his teaching curriculum.

The enthusiastic and persuasive Burrows actually managed to get club swinging introduced into the British army's physical education programme. He then went one step further and became a professional strongman on the halls. In 1895, he set a supervised world record of swinging a pair of 3lb clubs, 24in. long, for twenty-four hours, swinging at least fifty complete circles per minute, with no rests, pauses or artificial aids. Later, on a tour of the world, he set a record of twenty-six consecutive hours of club swinging in Cairo.

Burrow's arrival in London with his two lightweight boxers

coincided with the launching of the strongman craze on the music halls. He managed to secure a few engagements and even once appeared before Kaiser Wilhelm of Germany when the latter attended an army gymnasium display at Aldershot, but he never managed to become famous. There were two main reasons for this. In the first case his act was definitely unexciting. This was compounded by the fact that his monotonous routine was visibly doing him a great deal of physical and mental harm.

When music hall audiences realised that the so-called highlight of the Australian's act, indeed the whole *oeuvre*, consisted of his standing rooted to the spot for days at a time twirling his clubs busily around his head, at a time when the acts of the best of the top-of-the-bill entertainers seldom lasted for more than twenty minutes, his efforts were met increasingly with boos and catcalls. He was forced to transfer his efforts to private clubs and arcades, where the everyday life of the organisations would carry on around him as Burrows stood almost unnoticed in a corner, going through his act, muttering to himself. His wife or assistants would feed him solicitously throughout on soups and jellies.

Eventually, so many dreary repetitions of his meaningless but arduous physical movements with clubs weighing over 3lbs each had their effect upon the strongman's constitution. He began to collapse towards the end of his longer performances and display signs of mental instability. He set a new world record of continuous club swinging for one hundred hours but as soon as he had finished he started tottering about the stage in a delirious state. When people went to his assistance, he struck a close friend and knocked him to the floor. He had to be overpowered by members of the audience until he collapsed into a coma and was carried home on a stretcher.

In an effort to remain fully awake during his competitions on home territory at Aldershot, Burrows would sometimes be accompanied by the band of the Royal Hampshire Regiment. Should this not be considered sufficient, an elaborate mechanism for the administration of oxygen would be displayed at the rear of the stage.

In an attempt to break his record of one hundred hours, he collapsed after ninety-seven hours and thirty-five minutes. At the climax he was reduced to crawling piteously about the platform in a stupor, blindly groping for his discarded clubs. The *New York Times* reported, 'His wife gave him hot tea and placed ice on his head'. In Edinburgh he collapsed again and had to be brought around with stimulants.

Later, Burrows undertook a poorly attended tour of the world, taking in the Far East, South America and South Africa. Desperately Burrows sought for competitors against whom he could defend his spurious title of world champion. For a time, he thought he had found one in the American club swinger Henry Lawson. However, a much-feted contest between the two men ended in disaster when the unexpectedly fragile American collapsed after a paltry sixty hours and sank weeping into a chair. Unperturbed, Burrows went on swinging for another six hours and thirty-five minutes. He claimed that during each of these long-distance competitions he lost on average 7lbs in weight.

Towards the end of his career, at the beginning of the twentieth century, Tom Burrows was thrown an unexpected lifeline by the public's growing fondness for silent moving pictures. He became a fixture at the primitive cinemas springing up in towns and cities, standing beneath and a little to one side of the screen, swinging his clubs, while the flickering images were projected on the wall above him. His advertising material emphasised that patrons would get full value for their money – 'one shilling, evening; sixpence, afternoon: Doors will be open to the public all day and all night. First class programmes of pictures will be presented each evening, with Burrows swinging in full view.' At the same time the management assured the paying customers that their view of the novel electric pictures would not be curtailed for a moment by the club swinger.

For a brief time Burrows went into partnership with a showman and opened his own cinema in London where he could twirl his clubs to his heart's content, while his associate selected the programmes and attended to the business side. Eventually the venture failed and Burrows returned to any halls that would still pick him. This time he took with him a partner, a dedicated 'long-distance' pianist called Charles Parnell. Burrows would start swinging his clubs first and Parnell would join in at the piano some time later. They endeavoured to finish their act together in a crescendo of synchronicity. The effect was marred a little because at most halls they were instructed to conclude by eleven in the evening at the latest. The records they claimed for these joint marathons were sixty-two hours and two minutes for Burrows, and thirty-eight hours and two minutes for his accompanist.

Eventually, Tom Burrows retired to join the great pantheon of other failed strongmen who had misjudged the public's taste, sharing company with Maciste, the Italian Hercules, whose *pièce de résistance* lay in opening a tin of sardines with his fingers, and the Birmingham strongman billed as Polias whose offering of lifting a sofa on to his head while his wife reclined languorously upon it may have presented a picture of domestic bliss but emphatically did not pull in the crowds. Harry Houdini, who was touring the halls of the world at this time, was especially scathing of the efforts of one rather puny unnamed Italian strongman whose routine consisted of lying on his back on a platform, raising a heavy barbell to the full extent of his arms, and then releasing the weight and allowing it to crash down on to his chest. Houdini remarked pessimistically that he did not know what became of this particular strength athlete, but he could guess.

To these failed attempts to develop a crowd-pleasing physical routine could be added the efforts of Charles Matthews, a celebrated English long jumper. Realising that he did not possess the musculature to present a strongman act, instead Matthews based his routine on leaping over a piano onstage. This might have been a good trick so far as it went but, as the leaper discovered, it was difficult to build an entertaining fifteen-minute routine around it.

Young Miles's act consisted of calling up a volunteer timekeeper and endeavouring to walk a mile, round and round the stage, inside eight minutes. The stages were invariably small, and bored onlookers were usually throwing things at the puffing and trundling champion pedestrian long before the allotted time was up.

Perhaps the most off-putting of all the peripheral strongman acts was that presented by the American wrestling champion Martin 'Farmer' Burns. Burns had such a strongly muscled neck, developed over hundreds of bouts in which he performed his celebrated wrestler's bridge, resting most of his weight on his neck and shoulders, that he had the notion of presenting a stage show in which he allowed himself to take a drop from a genuine executioner's hanging platform, with a rope around his neck, and dangle there for three minutes while he whistled the popular minstrel melody 'Dixie'. Curiously, Burns may not have died in the process but on most nights his act assuredly did.

Most strongmen, however, made genuine efforts to improve

their music hall acts and make them more wide ranging and attractive to the eye. Established strongmen like John Gruen Marx were famous enough not to have to pander to their audiences and could continue with the straightforward weightlifting performances they had been presenting for years. Lesser, more prudent and acquiescent strongmen and their agents who took advantage of the new demand for their services on the halls realised that they would have to spend much time and ingenuity in appearing more powerful to their audiences than perhaps they really were.

Fortunately, through the ages there had been a strong tradition of obfuscation, not to say downright chicanery, in the lengthy folklore of feats of strength. The new arrivals and their advisers and managers could study, emulate and profit from them. It was true that, before Sandow, strongmen had not featured highly on the roll of honour of entertainment for the masses. For centuries, however, in different civilisations there had been legends about such mythical and semi-mythical strongmen as Gilgamesh, Hercules, Samson, Goliath and Milo.

After that, ancient kings and leaders accumulated their own legends of feats of strength, but these were almost certainly the results of court sycophancy and a general reflex eagerness to please the mighty. The Emperor Maximus of Rome was reputed to have drawn a loaded chariot over the ground. William the Conqueror was said to have been capable of vaulting from the ground into the saddle of his warhorse – while he was wearing heavy armour. King Erius of Denmark was recorded as single-handedly overcoming four strongmen in a tug-of-war competition, without even getting to his feet. Robert the Bruce, it was claimed, had slain a giant in single combat while leading the Scots against the English.

Peter the Great of Russia acquired the reputation of being able to break coins between his fingers.

From the Middle Ages onwards, the main ways for strength athletes to earn livings from their prowess lay in travelling fairs and circuses or by attracting the patronage of a nobleman or prince. Among the genuine strongmen of history a few emerged from obscurity because of their exceptional feats of strength or colourful private lives, or simply because they were so big that people noticed and remembered them.

One of the first of these giants was Thomas Topham, a carpenter from Islington, London, and later proprietor of a public house. Among his feats in travelling fairs was resisting the efforts of a horse to move him. After his death it was realised from contemporary drawings of the strongman in action that he had employed basic laws of physics and physiology in his tug of war with the horse: Thomas Topham always sat on the ground and pulled on a rope against the horse. By anchoring his feet against two tree stumps or a low wall, the strongman was able to combine his knowledge of carpentry with a basic knowledge of physics. Keeping his arms and thighs straight meant that Topham assumed the role of the longer arm of a lever and so was able to keep the animal in check. On one occasion the tree trunk shattered and Topham was injured.

He also rolled up pewter plates in his hands, lifted two heavy hogsheads of water using the harness system later to become so popular, lifted a 27-stone clergyman into the air, supported five standing men on his body as he lay between two chairs, and bent pokers by striking them against his forearm, a trick gratefully adapted by Charles Sampson over a century later.

Topham was a skilled self-promoter and drew large crowds in his professional capacity but was less successful in his marital endeavours. He was nagged constantly by a shrewish wife, whom he suspected of being unfaithful, and stabbed her in a quarrel in 1749, before committing suicide with the same knife. He had not yet reached his fortieth birthday. His wife recovered.

A considerable amount is known about Thomas Topham because he attracted the attention of a contemporary French scientist and philosopher, and later member of the Royal Society, John Theophilus Desaguliers, who had settled in England when a child in 1694. He wrote copiously about Topham in his book, *A Course of Experimental Philosophy*. Desaguliers noted that, like some of the strongmen of the following century, Topham scorned any attempt at showmanship: 'He has shewed [sic] feats of strength; but he is entirely ignorant of any art to make his strength seem more surprising.'

Nevertheless, Thomas Topham established such a reputation during his lifetime that he was not even allowed to rest easily in his grave after his death. The *Daily Advertiser* of 16 August 1749, reported:

> For these few days past there has been a great commotion in Shoreditch parish, an apprehension that a resurrection had begun it, and several witnesses have been examined by the magistrates in relation thereto. Yesterday it was said that Topham, the Strong Man, had, the night before, with the assistance of some surgeons, got the better of his grave, though some eight feet of earth had been laid on him.

Another noted strongman was William Joyce or Joy. A guide book entitled *A Journey Round the Coast of Kent*, published in 1818, declared that he 'broke a rope which could sustain thirty-five hundred weights, lifted up 2,240 pounds and was drowned at 67'.

During a brief sojourn as a sailor he was allocated a daily double helping of rum because he always did the work of two seamen.

The Strong Man of Kent, as he was called, sometimes displayed his feats of strength before Queen Anne. Unfortunately for his career prospects at court, Joy also moonlighted as a smuggler. He is believed to have drowned while wading ashore carrying some kegs of brandy. Taking advantage of the fact that the giant could no longer be offended and retaliate, the carver of his headstone smugly pointed out how transient was human strength and fitness:

> At last lies here, his breadth and length.
> See how the mighty man is fallen.
> To death the strong and weak are all one
> And the same judgement doth befall
> Goliath great as David small.

A touring German strength athlete named John Charles van Eckenburg visited many countries with his act, which laid the foundation for his successors for several centuries. He could break ropes and climaxed his act by lying in a wrestler's bridge with an anvil on his chest while a brawny partner placed rocks on top of the anvil and shattered them with blows from a hammer. This was a trick to be replicated by generations of succeeding strongmen. The anvil was heavy but Eckenburg knew what he was doing. The weightier the anvil was, the more it absorbed the blows from the hammer.

In another stunt, van Eckenburg would break a thick rope. He managed to do this because the rope moved round a cylinder through a metal eye. To the spectators the rope seemed to move smoothly but in fact it was constantly snagging and fraying on the metal. Van Eckenberg concentrated on breaking the rope where it was most shredded and at its weakest.

Both Topham and van Eckenburg secured good livings from their natural strength but both were outshone by the French strength athlete Barsabas, who was reputed to have rescued the coach of King Louis XIV from the mud by lifting its wheels from the ground, thus earning himself a pension for life from the grateful monarch. Louis Uni, who later achieved fame as Apollon, would also do well from an encounter with the aristocracy.

For most strongmen their physical endeavours were a full-time job but one Italian performer could truly claim to be a polymath. His name was Giovanni Battista Belzoni, known profession-ally as the Great Belzoni. He was born in Padua in 1778 and, at age sixteen, he entered a monastery in Rome, where he studied hydraulic engineering. He became engaged in political agitation when Napoleon's army entered Rome, forcing him to flee from Italy and make his way to Great Britain, although his detractors claimed that he was merely fleeing to avoid conscription. Having read a translation of Daniel Defoe's *Robinson Crusoe*, Belzoni had succumbed to an urge to see the world. A big strong man and newly married, he joined a circus and toured with it for twelve years as the Patagonian Samson.

His act went over well almost everywhere. On 28 September 1811, he appeared at the Old Theatre on the Isle of Man. The follow-ing day, the *Manx Advertiser* said that, among other feats, Belzoni 'balanced a heavy coach wheel on his chin and a boy on a pole 12 feet high'. For his finale, under a flowing cloak he wore an iron cage, while a wide leather belt went round his waist. A number of men clung to him, securing footholds on the belt or cage, while he supported others on his back and shoulders and carried one under each arm. He would then shuffle across the stage with his human pyramid, waving a flag. Sometimes, just for the sake of variety, Signora Belzoni would attach herself to the top of the mobile pyramid, waving a flag like her husband.

Like later strongmen, Belzoni sometimes had difficulties with elaborate stage tricks. Throughout his circus years, Belzoni continued to experiment with his study of waterpower, though not always with complete success. At the Crow Theatre in Dublin he was hired to design and construct for the last scene a hydraulic temple. It went badly wrong, flooding the set and causing the musicians in the pit to flee. The actor playing the part of Harlequin commented philosophically that the accident had the effect of 'leaving Columbine and myself, with the rest, to finish the scene in the midst of a splendid shower of fire and water'.

Belzoni toured Europe and the Middle East with his act. Finding his way to Egypt he tried unsuccessfully to persuade the Pasha to adopt the strongman's invention to increase the supply of water to the former's palace. Nothing if not versatile, Belzoni then followed the suggestion of the British Consul General Henry Salt that he excavate for archaeological treasures and send them back to the British Museum in London – for a price. Belzoni was no intellectual, but he was strong, determined and fearless, with a gift for languages, well able to put down mutinies among his crew with his fists. He took to his new vocation and became equally well known for finding a number of tombs in the celebrated Valley of the Kings and for his ruthless and destructive methods of excavation.

Though he claimed to be engaged in research, Belzoni spent much time robbing tombs in Timbuktu and later died of dysentery in 1823.

Belzoni wrote a number of books but he never mentioned

his sideshow years as the Patagonian Giant, perhaps because his circus days did not gel with his newfound wealth and fame as an archaeologist. Most of his new professional colleagues regarded Giovanni Belzoni as an opportunistic rogue. It was claimed that he had taken more loot out of Egypt than Napoleon's entire invading French army.

However, it was apparent from the Italian's book *Narrative of the Operations and Recent Discoveries within the Pyramids, Temples, Tombs and Excavations in Egypt and Nubia*, that his earlier training as a strongman had sometimes stood him in good stead:

> Of some of these tombs many persons could not withstand the suffocating air, which often causes fainting. A vast quantity of dust rises, so fine that it enters into the throat and nostrils, and chokes the nose and mouth to such a degree that it requires great power of lungs to resist it... In some places there is not more than a vacancy of a foot left, which you must contrive to pass through in a creeping posture.

By the nineteenth century, strongman acts were being featured in many circuses. One of the best known of these weightlifters was a Frenchman called Hippolyte Triat, who made a significant advancement to weight training by inventing the prototype of the dumbbell, first built in 1838. This consisted of a short bar joining two globes, which could be lifted with one hand. The first one weighed 185lbs but due to an accident in the foundry one orb came out slightly heavier than the other, making the apparatus unwieldy and difficult to use.

With such an encouragingly vague history of the feats of ancient strongmen behind them, the new breed of strength athletes could be eclectic when they claimed to be carrying on the great traditions of the past. Drawing on the story of Samson slaying an army of Philistines with the jawbone of an axe and the emperor Commodus – 'conqueror of a thousand warriors' – they began to introduce mock gladiatorial displays into their performances. Emulating the precedent of Milo travelling a great distance with an ox on his shoulders, they experimented with carefully rigged, in both senses of the word, displays which seemed to involve the effortless lifting of horses and other animals from the ground. Both Polydance of Thessalonia and Hercules were reputed to have grappled with lions, leading to a subsequent ill-fated attempt by Eugen Sandow to do the same. Salvius of Rome was renowned for walking up a ladder carrying 200lbs on his shoulders, 200lbs in his hands and another 200lbs attached to his legs, a feat attempted by nineteenth-century strongmen. In 1905, a German strongman called William Pagel toured with his own circus and climbed a ladder carrying a horse in a harness on his shoulders.

And when there were no more classical examples upon which to draw in order to embellish their acts, the new breed of professional strongmen could always resort to cheating.

4

THE IRON DUKE

Most strongmen embellished the tricks they performed upon
the stage but a few went even farther, living their lives
under a veil of deception. One such strongman was an American
called William Muldoon, who accepted the sobriquet of the Solid
Man of Sport, based on a vaudeville comic song. Muldoon, almost
single-handedly, transformed professional wrestling in the USA
from a squalid, hole-in-the-corner affair to a razzle-dazzle peak of
fixed showmanship. He was one of the first to tour the hinterland
of his country with polished strongman shows, trained the reprobate boxer John L. Sullivan to a level of fitness beyond the fighter's
wildest dreams or desires, established a physical fitness empire,
and ended up as the autocratic Chairman of the New York State
Athletic Commission. He also rewrote his *curriculum vitae* with
such care and attention as to make Baron Munchhausen seem a
pillar of reliability. Most important of all, he established the strongman business in the USA. He and Eugen Sandow never met but
conducted their physical culture interests virtually in tandem on
different sides of the Atlantic.

There had been a few strongmen displaying their wares before
the arrival of Muldoon. Most of them attained only local fame, but
in the nineteenth century the English bareknuckle champion Jem

Mace and his half-Romany cousin Pooley Mace toured the USA in a series of tent shows, giving boxing exhibitions, muscle flexing and weightlifting displays, and posing in the style of the statues of Roman gladiators. Pooley also gave a renowned strongman exhibition, which included hammering an anvil lying upon his chest. He also used a version of beating an iron bar out of shape by striking it against different parts of his anatomy.

Inspired by the idea, P. T. Barnum, the great circus proprietor, and other showmen started scouring the countryside for outsized men. At first they employed them as sideshow freaks in their dime museums and travelling circuses, but there they did not attract much more than a fleeting interest. Perhaps that was because the impresarios all adhered to the same programme of finding someone tall, exaggerating his height and then declaring that the paragon was capable of extremely far-fetched and completely unsubstantiated feats of strength. Barnum, in particular, had always liked to have strength athletes on his books as adjuncts to his more spectacular acts like the midget General Tom Thumb and the bearded lady Madame Clofillia, and was never afraid to publicise them.

Among the early successes among the big men displayed in his sideshows throughout the second half of the nineteenth century was one especially imported from Fuzhou in China, via a tour of England. Called Chang the Giant, this Chinese strongman was billed as having 'the strength of Hercules and the beauty of Apollo'. He was about 6ft 5in. tall but was always displayed in flowing robes on built-up shoes. His publicity matter claimed that he was 8ft in height.

Colonel Routh Goshen of Kentucky was billed as the Palestine Giant. In reality about 7ft tall, he was naturally billed as being 8ft 6in. Unlike many giants he was genuinely strong and could pull a heavy cannon across a circus ring. Goshen was married three times, with one of his wives eloping with their lodger. He complained to a local newspaper that she had taken with her a large sum of money, a horse and an educated goat. He missed the goat but Mrs Goshen could go straight to Hades and tell them that he had sent her.

From Cape Breton in Nova Scotia came Angus MacAskill, a genuine giant, over 7ft 9in. tall and weighing more than 400lbs. He was perfectly proportioned and very strong. He emigrated from Scotland with his parents when he was six years old and, until he was a teenager, he was of normal size, until he hit puberty and grew to his later enormous stature. He developed a local reputation for his ability to lift anchors, masts and barrels and was soon recruited by Barnum, the master showman, for a tour of North America and the West Indies. The affable giant looked after his money and returned home contentedly with what was referred to with some awe locally as 'a snug fortune'. With his savings MacAskill purchased several farms, a mill and a general store, but died early at the age of thirty-eight.

The best known of all P. T. Barnum's circus strongmen, however, were Hiram and Barney Davis, known professionally as Waino and Plutanor, the Wild Men of Borneo. Born in 1825 and 1827 respectively, they were a pair of very strong dwarf brothers who each grew to a full height of 40in. and a weight of about 45lbs. Despite this they were both enormously strong and could lift heavy weights, and wrestle and defeat grown men. Barnum claimed that they had been discovered on Borneo by a group of sailors, who only captured them after a titanic struggle in the jungle. In fact, both brothers had been purchased from their destitute mother and sold on to Barnum at a profit. At first the brothers conformed to their billing by running around muttering gibberish, but their strength acts were so impressive and popular that for much of the time they could concentrate on these. They stayed with the circus for more than twenty-five years.

But despite Barnum's skill as a showman, it was William Muldoon who lay best claim to having brought strongmen out of such freak shows and into the mainstream sporting arenas. He was born in Caneadea in upstate New York in 1852, although later he claimed that 1845 had been the year of his birth. A big youth, he grew even stronger from constant outdoor work on the land. Towards the end of the 1860s he arrived in New York City and secured employment driving a horse and cart for $12 for a sixty-hour week. Always keen to accumulate cash he also worked in a warehouse and had regular shifts as a saloon bouncer. In his spare time and given his obvious strength, he started wrestling in small clubs and arenas.

Muldoon was introduced to professional wrestling, he claimed, when, as a part of his professional duties ejecting recalcitrant customers from dives and bars, he encountered one youth sporting a spectacular black eye. As he was being propelled into the street the young man told Muldoon proudly that he had received the bruise while earning $2 wrestling in a club on Houston Street. Sensing a chance to accumulate even more loot, the young bouncer dropped his informant on to the cobbles and wasted no time in hurrying to the club and offering his services there.

He was engaged and soon attained a reputation in the city as a ferocious young grappler. He worked his way up to fighting in main events at Harry Hill's notorious club, which offered its patrons, food, drink, boxing, wrestling and young women, and was a popular haunt of bucks and swells of all ages 'hunting the elephant', the current euphemism for voyeurism, or having a risky night out in unsavoury areas. The saloon had a rudimentary code of conduct and was indeed a cut above most of its dangerous contemporaries. The *Police Gazette* gave the establishment its ultimate recommendation: 'It is 'Arry's boast that no one has ever been robbed or killed in his place.' Entry cost twenty-five cents for men and nothing for ladies. One of the patrons, the inventor Thomas A. Edison, personally supervised the installation of his patented electric light system in the saloon.

At this time, grappling was just catching on as an attraction in urban areas. There had been a number of different regional styles, like the collar and elbow, practised in different parts of the country since the days of the early settlers. By the 1870s, the more spectacular catch-as-catch-can form was replacing the rather static traditional Greco-Roman in the favour of fans. The catch-as-catch-can form allowed holds below the waist and was the forerunner of the modern all-in and freestyle modes of the sport. The introduction in 1870 of padded mats meant that the more spectacular throws and falls of the catch-as-catch-can version could be practised with less physical damage to the participants, providing a cushion against the more violent throws.

In the absence of an official governing body, championships could be claimed by anyone. Despite grandiose claims of large side stakes for bouts, purses were pitifully low and results were often pre-arranged to accommodate betting coups. From quite early in his career it was rumoured that Muldoon, often wrestling as the Iron Duke, could be bought, either to win or lose, if the price was right and his cut of the wagers acceptable.

A fillip to professional wrestling was provided when overseas scufflers started arriving to challenge the local champions. Muldoon was quick to see the commercial value of international matches and encouraged these new arrivals. He even became the undercover manager of some of them, taking a slice of their winnings. One of the first of his protégés was a former Japanese sumo wrestler called Matsuda Sorakichi. Too small to hope for much success among the behemoths of the Japanese style, Sorakichi decided to try his luck in the US and managed to secure a job wrestling in a circus, where he was spotted by Muldoon.

In order to build up his pupil's reputation, Muldoon matched himself against Sorakichi in New York, taking care to lose so that a lucrative rematch could then be promoted. At least one sports writer commented on the surprise upset in their first encounter:

> Matsada Sorakichi, the Jap, is rapidly forging to the front as one of the best all-round wrestlers in the world, and the comparative ease with which he defeated William Muldoon, best three in five, while it surprised me greatly, at the same time forced this conclusion more firmly into my mind.

In this instance Muldoon's plotting came to nothing; Sorakichi was not really big enough for the burgeoning professional wrestling circuit. Instead he tried to establish himself economically with an advantageous marriage. This turned sour by 1885 when Ella, the wife of the Japanese wrestler, claimed that her husband and his friends had frittered away her inheritance, moved a girlfriend into the marital home and threatened her with violence.

Sorakichi was only one of many arrivals from overseas who found the American strongman scene too hard and vicious. Another visitor was the towering Scottish strength athlete, Donald Dinnie. Dinnie flourished at such hitherto parochial events as tossing the caber and throwing heavy stones and hammers. He was at the same time a taciturn and avaricious man who once spurned the glory of performing before Prince Albert, the consort of Queen Victoria, unless his usual match fee of £2 sterling was paid up front. He was 6ft 2in. tall, weighed 203lbs and at the time of his arrival in the USA was in his late twenties. He claimed to have won over 1,500 prizes at Caledonian Games events held in his native country.

By the early 1870s, Scottish exiles to the New World were forming their own Caledonian societies all over the Continent and putting on annual versions of the Scottish Games, which drew large crowds. In 1872, Dinnie led the surge of homegrown talent across the Atlantic to compete for prizes at these events. When he appeared in Detroit his advertising handouts described him as the champion all-round athlete of Great Britain. His speciality events and personal bests were given as:

Throwing the 56-pound stone: 22 feet 8 inches
Throwing the 32-pound stone: 35 feet
Throwing the 18-pound stone: 39 feet 7 inches

Dinnie also challenged anyone at throwing the caber, a pole 18ft long and 6in. in circumference at one end, and 8in. at the other. He was also prepared to engage in sprint races and Highland wrestling bouts against all comers.

While he was visiting New York, Muldoon persuaded the big man to take up catch-as-catch-can wrestling, dubbed him the Scottish champion and, again, arranged a number of lucrative matches for himself against the visitor. The cautious Dinnie insisted that at least some of these contests should take part in the Scottish grappling style, at which he was unparalleled, even if he did lose regularly in the catch-as-catch-can and Greco-Roman events against Muldoon and other Americans. Dinnie was never a good loser, causing one newspaper writer to comment after a bout: 'Dinnie behaved himself with regard to one or two matters more like a spoiled child than a grown man.' The big Scot never had the skill in the Greco-Roman and catch-as-catch-can styles to match his prowess in Highland Games wrestling.

The growing wrestling and strongman industries were given constant publicity by the raunchy *National Police Gazette*. This was a lurid scandal sheet concentrating on reporting sport, crime, show business and sex. It was purchased in 1877 by Richard K. Fox, who became its publisher and a sponsor of all sorts of different sports. Its circulation boomed and it became famous for such regular features as 'Noose Notes', reporting on public hangings, and the self-explanatory 'Crimes of the Clergy'. For a time Fox even became William Muldoon's sponsor.

Always a careful man with a dollar, Muldoon started to look around for a sinecure of a day job which would at the same time provide him with a chance to train regularly for wrestling. Like many other far-sighted athletes, he joined the New York Police Department, enlisting as a patrolman in 1875. It was here that he started embellishing his biography, a trait he later developed almost into an art form. To gain credibility with his equally tough fellow officers, he claimed to have served throughout the American Civil War, starting as a young drummer boy and going on to fight in a number of engagements. Muldoon even averred that he had been present when General Robert E. Lee had surrendered at Appotomax. Frequently he would reminisce sanctimoniously about the horrors of war to reporters, declaring sadly in his biography, 'The business of trying to kill one's fellow man is not a pleasant memory.'

To add credence to his claims of martial distinction, Muldoon started giving his date of birth as 1845, instead of the genuine 1851. In fact, on this estimation Muldoon would have been ten when the war started and fifteen at its conclusion, rendering it unlikely that he had first learned to wrestle in the army and then taken part in many victorious bouts against other soldiers. It was widely suspected that for the purposes of personal publicity and self-promotion Muldoon had started utilising the record of one of his brothers, who had served in the war and had been wounded in action.

The former ploughboy did, however, do well for six years as a member of New York's Finest. He co-established the New York Police Athletic Club and was allowed to train in its gym for three or four hours every day, further developing his muscles. He won the city police heavyweight grappling title and continued moon-lighting at his professional fighting career, causing a considerable stir in the newspapers when he met and defeated a formidable touring English wrestler called Edwin Bibby. Still dressed in his police uniform – Muldoon had been walking his city beat all day – he pinned the Englishman twice with little difficulty and then for good measure lifted his groaning opponent from the mat and slammed him down with tremendous force.

Bibby, who settled in the USA and kept a saloon in New Jersey, was already going through a bad patch having just been hauled up before a judge for beating his wife. The *New York Times* reported his plea of mitigation: 'He said that his wife was a habitual drunkard, that she spends from $20 to $25 a week in the gratification of her tastes, and that her habit had provoked him until he struck her.'

The *New York Times* also described the squalid background to the Bibby match, which was common to most wrestling bouts of the time, saying, with disdain, that the contest took place 'in the presence of a howling mob which represents all the lower elements of society'.

Throughout his long life, William Muldoon, within the limits imposed by his quick temper and almost neurotic demand for respect, took care to keep in with the right people. As previously mentioned, he became a protégé of Richard Fox, the influential editor of the *Police Gazette*, which backed Muldoon for some time – until, in a flash of bad temper, the wrestler fell out with the proprietor over an imagined slight.

After six years, Muldoon became well enough known to retire from the police force and open a tavern, continuing with his wrestling. He defeated the well-known Theodore Bauer, one of the many reckless hard men who frequented the rings of the era, for a version of the world's Greco-Roman title before a crowd of three thousand people. The co-owner of a New York beer shop, Bauer was once matched against a circus bear called Martin, who was muzzled and had its claws clipped. Understandably its aggressive instincts had been diluted by these handicaps and the beast was reluctant to fight. Bauer had done his best to antagonise the animal by swearing, but Martin still persisted in backing away. Finally, the wrestler managed to secure a grip on the bear's fur and threw it unconvincingly to the ground, claiming the victory.

Several of the Muldoon–Bauer matches had an over-rehearsed look to them, leading to post-match disputes between the participants and onlookers, and causing the *Brooklyn Eagle* to editorialise:

'Out of their own mouths are they convicted' is the exclamation made after reading the recent exposures of professional rottenness which has been made in the case of the Bauer and Muldoon quarrel.

There cannot be the slightest doubt in the minds of any sporting man, after a perusal of the testimony published in the case, that there has scarcely been an honest wrestling match in the country for the past two or three years.

Nevertheless, Muldoon was beginning to suspect that there was a financial killing to be made in the physical culture industry in the USA, similar to the one about to take off in Europe. In this he was assisted by the efforts of George Barker Windship, a Harvard-educated doctor.

Apart from the technically minded Belzoni, the strongman-cum-archaeologist, most of the early strongmen were not intellectuals. Few of them seemed willing or able to devote much thought to their skills. This was changed by the advent of Windship, one of the first men to devote himself to the science of the accumulation of strength and an active proselyter in its cause.

Ridiculed while a freshman for his lack of size – Windship was only 5ft 7in. tall and very thin – he was determined to improve his physique while at Harvard and spent most of his spare time engaged in gymnastics. One day, proud of the noticeable improvement in his physique, he tested his power on a commercial 'try-your-strength' weightlifting machine. He managed to register a lift of 400lbs on the coin-operated apparatus, but discovered to his chagrin that many others had scored higher on the register. He realised that, if he were to become really strong, a course of specific progressive weight training would have to be added to his agility routines.

To this end Windship undertook a rigorous course of barbell and dumbbell lifting, and developed his own dumbbell to which extra weight could be added when needed. Having qualified as a doctor in 1857, he toured the USA and Canada demonstrating and selling his patented lifting exerciser. He gave his first public lecture in 1859, but was so overcome by stage fright that he fainted onstage. Gradually, however, Windship got better and bigger, with his own physique becoming so impressive that he was soon labelled the American Samson. He preached the gospel of students exercising for no more than an hour a day but employing increasingly heavy weights when they did so. The human body should be developed as fully as possible, with no weak points.

The fact that a qualified doctor was lending his imprimatur to weight training attracted the attention of the young middle class, who followed Windship's course in increasing numbers. By the beginning of 1861, he was ready for the ultimate test. Windship announced that not only would he give a public lecture at Bryan Hall on his methods of attaining strength, he would also accept any challenges from strongmen in the audience, presenting $200 to any man who could outlift him.

The outbreak of the American Civil War in 1861 curtailed his touring activities and challenges to his audiences, but he contin- ued to teach and write about the benefits of weight training, and opened a combined medical practice and gymnasium in Boston.

Unfortunately, George Barker Windship died in 1876, follow- ing a massive stroke. His death proved a considerable blow to the advocates of training with heavy weights, many people blaming his rigorous exercising routines for the doctor's untimely death.

Nevertheless, Windship had made a segment of the American public strength-conscious and aware of the advantages of weight- lifting as an aid to health and fitness, and William Muldoon was determined to build his own physical culture empire on these foundations. First, he decided, he needed another acquiescent foil and assistant, and soon settled on a wrestler called Ernest Roeber.

Actually, Roeber was an enormously strong bartender with a day job in a tobacco factory who hated wrestling. At this time Muldoon was performing a combined strongman and wrestling act at Miner's Theatre in the Bowery. One night a group of local thugs calling themselves the Gas House Gang called on Roeber and ordered him to accept Muldoon's challenge to pay $25 to any man who could last for fifteen minutes against him in the ring. The bartender most definitely did not want to accept the challenge, but allowed himself to be coaxed into it. As he later told a writer for *Ring* magazine: 'I am not stretching things when I say I stood a good chance of being dropped off a dock with a stone around my neck if I said no.'

In the event, Roeber took a terrible beating but managed to last the distance, allowing the Gas House Gang to collect the winnings from the bets it had laid on the bartender's survival. When he got home that night, his wife was so shocked by his battered appearance that she threw his wrestling tights into a stove. Nevertheless, Muldoon was so impressed by his opponent's strength and fortitude that he recruited the bartender as an integral part of the touring stage show he was about to take round great swathes of the rural Midwest, paying him a munificent $25 a week.

The far-sighted Muldoon also had another role in mind for Roeber. The former policeman was getting fed up with wrestling but wanted to keep control of its mechanics. Accordingly, he started to build up the other man's reputation, with a view one day to handing over his title to him and maintain his influence over the championship as Roeber's eventual manager and promoter. The fact that Muldoon had no strong claim to any sort of championship at the time did not enter into his calculations.

In reality, Roeber never had a great deal of luck as a professional athlete. For a time he secured a post as a sparring partner to the world heavyweight boxing champion Bob Fitzsimmons, who would beat him up as a regular occurrence and, just to make sure that he had his attention, would set his pet lion on to the grappler. Matters were almost as bad in the wrestling ring. One night at Madison Square Garden, Roeber was matched against Hassan Noroatah in a Greco-Roman bout. After a bad-tempered contest, Noroatah was disqualified for diving at his opponent's legs and then sitting on his face. In the ensuing riot Roeber sustained further injuries, while an over-excited policeman battered Noroatah with his stick.

While he was waiting to embark upon his planned tour of the hinterland, Muldoon experienced a stroke of luck, achieving notoriety when he took part in one of the longest wrestling matches ever recorded, a monumental six hours against Clarence Whistler, a one-time foundry labourer, in New York for a side stake advertised as being $600 a-side. Their match began shortly before nine in the evening and the contestants were still at it until almost four o'clock the following morning. It was a dreadfully dull affair, with Muldoon doing hardly any of the attacking. He later claimed that his opponent had soaked his hair in ammonia and kept rubbing his head into Muldoon's eyes in an effort to blind him. After what seemed an eternity, most of the spectators had left the wrestlers to their endeavours and had retired to the bar, when suddenly all the house lights went out. The gas had been turned off. *The Spectator* of 27 January 1881 described the events that followed:

The proprietor was turning off the gas as the only means for putting an end to the protracted battle... Everyone hurried down to the bar room. Muldoon and Whistler each protested they did not want a drawn battle and that they were anxious and willing to finish the match under any condition. Finally the lights in the bar room went out and then everybody went home.

To cash in on their newfound notoriety, Muldoon and Whistler, although disliking one another intensely, left Roeber behind and went on tour together with the Muldoon and Whistler Combination, in which they gave displays of strength and posing, and wrestled each other in exhibition contests. Muldoon gave his customary imitations of famous classical statuary, while Whistler, billed as the Kansas Cyclone, simulated military rifle drill, using an iron bar 8ft long and weighing 140lbs in place of a rifle. He also lifted and walked with an iron weight, which he claimed weighed 1,350lbs. He ended his display by forming a wrestler's bridge, with his head on one chair and feet on another, while weights, which were said to exceed 2,000lbs, were piled on to his chest. Whistler was a hard man. One reporter wrote that he had once seen him deliberately pull an opponent's arm out of joint in a contest.

A further drawback to harmony on the tour was that despite his earlier defeat at the hands of the Iron Duke, the bad-tempered Whistler was convinced that he had the beating of the other grappler, as the *Sporting News* reported:

Whistler carried a small arsenal about with him. He had a seven-shooter, a wicked looking weapon, and was always poking it under Muldoon's nose, and telling the latter how he would blow him to Kingdom Come. 'Muldoon there considers himself a great wrestler,' Whistler would say, 'but he's a cub compared to me. I can lick him any way you take him: wrestling, boxing, rough-and-tumble, any way you like. And you can bet I'm running this show too. Ain't I, Bill?' And Bill would nod.

Understandably, Muldoon later admitted that it had been the happiest day of his life when the show had folded and the other wrestler had departed to Australia leaving Muldoon to return to New York.

Whistler did not last long in his new home. He died in Melbourne in 1885, soon after his arrival there. He was thirty years old. Just before his death he had defeated the highly regarded William Miller, celebrating with a three-week bender. During his monumental binge, to entertain his friends Whistler lifted heavy tables with his teeth and claimed to have drunk up to thirty bottles of champagne a day, occasionally chewing and swallowing the glasses.

On Sunday, 11 October, Whistler visited a doctor and was diagnosed with a severe inflammation of the right lung. The wrestler admitted that his rowdy lifestyle could have contributed to his ill health and contritely took to his bed. He recovered temporarily but later relapsed and died. The official diagnosis was that Whistler's heart, lungs and kidneys had all been adversely affected by his lifestyle and that a bout of pneumonia had finished him off. Rumours persisted that the glass he had chewed so vaingloriously had perforated his vital organs. Others suggested that quaffing thirty bottles of the contemporary Australian champagne could in itself be pretty lethal.

His obituary in the *New York Times* of 4 December 1885 referred to his brutality:

It is a notorious fact that all wrestlers, except perhaps Joe Acton, were afraid that in his rage Whistler, whose neck hold was terrible, might kill them.

William Muldoon was contemplating disassociating himself gradually from the hurly-burly mainstream of championship bouts in order to concentrate on his more profitable tent shows and theatrical tours. His decision to leave the ring was hastened by a series of ring scandals occurring on a tour he undertook of the western seaboard of the USA. At last the Iron Man had overreached himself – or so it seemed. Ostensibly Muldoon had gone to California to participate in a tour of Shakespeare's *As You Like It*, in which he played Charles the Wrestler in a company headed by the Polish star Madame Helena Modjeska. She and her husband spent nine months of every year touring the USA with a repertoire of classics. The company travelled by rail, road and steamship and put on eight performances a week.

As was his custom, Muldoon, who was then twenty-eight, utilised his spare time by arranging wrestling matches in which he defended his title against local hopefuls. So strong was his entrepreneurial streak that he also began to send for his cronies from the east in order to establish a mini wrestling empire on the western seaboard. Among the former colleagues and opponents he summoned were his old nemesis Clarence Whistler, soon to leave for Australia, Edwin Bibby, the Scots Donald Dinnie and Duncan C. Ross, Theodore Bauer and, in the words of the Californian *Daily Alta*, 'a Cornishman called Pasco they dug up somewhere in Arizona'.

At first, all seemed to go well. The syndicate hired halls, put on their wrestling and strongman shows and watched the proceeds accumulate in their bank accounts. As the *Los Angeles Herald* put it, 'the shekels began to pour into the coffers of this athletic constellation, of which Muldoon was the bright star'.

Then quite suddenly it all went wrong. Whether Muldoon

had allowed familiarity to breed contempt, or whether the native Californian public was not as gullible as the promoter had hoped, is not clear. Certainly a number of the imported grapplers were only putting on lacklustre performances in the ring, and were showing too clearly by their conspicuous lack of effort the contempt they felt for the marks, or punters, paying at the box office. Indignant audiences began to get restless and then openly hostile. Local newspapers took up their cause with a will, under such headlines as 'Two Tired Wrestlers', 'Whistler–Muldoon Fiasco', 'The Fatal Fiasco', 'Shameless' and 'Fraud'.

For a while Muldoon seemed to lose his hitherto sure touch. He was arrested for striking a reporter who accused him of fixing the results of the contests he was promoting. The reporter wrote that such exhibitions were nothing but 'frauds and hippodroming' and that their promoter was both parsimonious and oleaginous. Released upon bail, the wrestler was promptly rearrested when it was rumoured that he was making plans to leave the state. He also became involved in a series of public squabbles with the wrestlers under contract to him, who were alarmed at the way in which the labyrinthine scams seemed about to unravel to their disadvantage.

He fell out with Edwin Bibby, who had arrived in California with only $100 to his name. Bibby informed Muldoon that for the sake of newspaper publicity he would back himself with a sidestake against the champion, as long as he was guaranteed the return of this money after he had lost in his title challenge. He explained that the $100 was all he had in the world to get back to New York to pursue what he laughingly termed his career. He also asked Muldoon to lend him another $500, so that he could bet on those matches whose results had been preordained. Then, as the press and police closed in, claimed Muldoon in the *Daily Alta*,

'Bibby disappeared suddenly, not desiring to answer any disagreeable questions.'

Clarence Whistler was equally as demanding. Before he left New York for San Francisco, hoping to equip himself for his forthcoming Australian tour, he insisted that Muldoon send him enough money with which to purchase a new suit, so that he would look smart upon his arrival. Reluctantly the champion did so. Whistler then spent all the sartorial money on a three-day binge. He finally arrived for the fight, as drunk as ever, greeting Muldoon with the words, 'Billy, am I going to make it hot for you tonight!' In the event, the Kansas Cyclone proved to be more of a gentle zephyr and in no condition to perform his ring duties. The resulting contest was a stinker, with Muldoon being forced to hold his opponent up in case he dropped to the floor out of sheer exhaustion. The *Sacramento Daily Union* reported, 'The spectators suddenly realised that they had been duped and expressed their indignation in no gentle tones.'

Donald Dinnie then made his contribution, such as it was. He had already lost once to Muldoon in the ongoing west-coast scam and was disgruntled because the champion had hurt him to an unnecessary degree during their contest. As Muldoon later complained to a reporter from the *Daily Alta*, 'Dinnie said he was anxious for another match, if I wouldn't be so rough on him, as the heavy floors in the last match had jarred him very much.'

Muldoon agreed to be gentle with his opponent the next time around but when the Scot arrived at the Mechanics' Hall in Oregon on the night of 12 October 1883, their first bout of the three advertised lasted only seven minutes. At its conclusion Dinnie stalked out of the ring, claiming to be hurt. He refused to emerge from his dressing room for the rest of the scheduled programme. The crowd had already gathered and paid its money, which Muldoon and his associate promoter, a man called Stechhan, refused to repay. Addressing the baying mob from the ring, Muldoon shrugged and said that he was perfectly prepared to wrestle; it was his opponent who was skulking backstage. The protestors must take their grievances up with Dinnie

There was almost a riot, which was put down by the arrival of a squad of policemen. They carried the piteously protesting Donald Dinnie off with them after co-promoter Stechhan had preferred charges against him for obtaining money under false pretences. Dinnie did not have enough cash on him to post a bail bond and was forced to spend the night in the local gaol. The next morning the *Sacramento Daily Union* described the whole evening's proceedings as 'a shameless fraud and wrangle'.

Somehow Muldoon extricated himself from his problems and returned with relief to New York, but his reputation had been badly damaged by the adverse publicity in California. The Californian *Daily Alta* pointed out on 6 June 1884, 'Muldoon left this coast with his pockets bulging with the golden harvest from an over-confident public.' It was estimated that the champion had made something like $40,000 from his Californian wrestling promotions, of which about half was sheer profit for him.

Muldoon went on wrestling for a time but began to withdraw from the actual matchmaking and promotion of bouts. Both in and out of the ring the champion could still hold his own against Whistler (who later left for Australia, arriving in Melbourne in 1885) and many other tough customers in the city who kept issuing challenges. He had to in order to stay in business. Another frequent opponent among his peers was William Miller, who challenged all comers to a riot of competitive sports all on the same night, defying any man to stand up to him for ten rounds of boxing, one fall or submission at wrestling, a one-handed dumb-bell lifting contest and finally a bout with the singlesticks. It is not known if anyone was hardy enough to accept this combined challenge. The versatile Miller also at one time held the Australian deep water wrestling championship, in which the contestants grappled in 4ft of water and a bout was deemed over when one of the men had his head held under the surface until he quit or drowned.

Miller, a pragmatic character, preferred to fight only for money, but if push came to shove he was prepared to take on those who could not afford a sidestake: 'I usually ask someone who is after fighting me, "If we ain't getting paid, why should we fight?" If that doesn't put them off, I just go straight at them.'

By now Muldoon was often absent on tours, presenting exhibitions rather than actual contests. With a troupe of strongmen, wrestlers and boxers he toured the theatres, music halls and carnival tents, introducing displays of physical might to new audiences at every stop along the railroads now sweeping across the nation. In the 1880s, he toured with the song and dance men Frank B. Sheridan and Joe Flynn, in 'William Muldoon's Variety Players', which also included the boxer John L. Sullivan. As well as wrestling, a scantily clad Muldoon did a solo spot under blazing spotlights, performing a series of classical poses: the Dying Gladiator, Atlas holding up the world, and others.

From time to time, to avoid being forgotten in the metropolis, Muldoon took care to return to New York. In 1887, he appeared in a Broadway play as a gladiator in a production of *Spartacus*. The *New York Sun* of 17 April 1887 described Muldoon's entrance:

For if ever a human deserved to be likened to a splendid Bengal tiger, that human was William Muldoon. About his every movement there was something truly suggestive of the grace and classic power of the tiger.

To ensure a more permanent presence in the city Muldoon ensured that a large portrait of him was put in the entrance of Madison Square Garden.

In 1887, Muldoon gave up his wrestling title in order to concentrate on making the really big money. In the process, almost inadvertently, he cemented his reputation and set the foundations for his career as the first Father of Physical Education and the early King of the Strong Men, just two of the titles he was soon to have bestowed upon him in the USA.

He owed much of this early advancement to his acquaintanceship with John L. Sullivan, the Boston Strong Boy, the last bareknuckle boxing champion of the world, who dominated the prize ring for a decade between 1882 and 1892.

Sullivan was a boisterous, hard-drinking, pig-headed hard man, with a distinct aversion to training and a supreme confidence in the efficacy of his rushing style and tremendous right swing to make up for his lack of skill. He had just been matched to defend his title in a fight to the finish against Jake Kilrain in Richberg, Mississippi. Having already toured with Muldoon's tent show, the two men knew each other, and, with Muldoon's help, the champion bareknuckle fighter also got himself involved lucratively in the 'living statuary' or 'model statuary' posing routines, depicting Perseus slaying Medusa and other figures from the classical world. In this manner Sullivan travelled with the Lester and Allen minstrel show for the 1885–86 season. It was a lucrative gig and the fighter was not ungrateful. He received $500 a week for twenty weeks, although, bearing in mind the champion's reputation as a drunkard, a clause in his contract stated that he was to be fined $700 every time he missed a show.

Muldoon occasionally made guest appearances in these posing routines. He and Sullivan would smear their torsos with a mixture of zinc oxide and rose water, covered with white powder to bring up their muscular definition. They stood on pedestals as they moved from pose to pose.

When their man was matched against Kilrain, Sullivan's backers were at their wits' end as to how to get the champion back into shape. He was pounds overweight, his wind had gone and he was a drink-sodden wreck. Added to this, it was a well-known fact that Sullivan, whose natural habitat was a saloon, detested trainers and never paid any attention to their advice or ministrations.

To everyone's surprise, William Muldoon agreed to take on the onerous chore. He had first come across Sullivan years before when the latter had been a young fighter frequenting Harry Hill's New York bar. He knew how tough and brave the heavyweight was, if only he could be brought into shape. Muldoon informed the champion's acolytes that he would do his best to prepare him for the bout. He required a fee of $10,000 if Sullivan retained his title, but would accept nothing if the Boston man lost. There was one major stipulation. Sullivan would have to put himself completely in the Iron Man's hands and do everything that was ordered of him.

It was a sign of the apprehension in the champion's camp that all Sullivan's patrons agreed eagerly to the terms. Even the fighter himself acquiesced, however reluctantly. Thus began one of the most spartan and demanding physical development regimes recorded in the history of the prize ring.

Muldoon took Sullivan and a few sparring partners to the wilds
of a farm he had inherited near Belfast, a village in the western
region of New York state. It was a desolate spot, not improved by
its proximity to a cemetery. An *Olean New York Democrat* reporter,
trying in vain to secure an interview with the trainer and forced to
resort to penning a think-piece, said: 'It must be somewhat galling
to the brawny proprietor of the place to sit on his veranda, gaze
over at the city of the dead, and realise that even his physical perfection must finally succumb to the grim wrestler Death.'

The trainer was under no illusions about the magnitude
of the task ahead of him. On the first day of training, he described
the champion as 'a drunken, bloated, helpless mass of flesh and
bone and without a single dollar in his pocket' (*Brooklyn Eagle*,
14 July 1890).

For his part, the down-on-his-luck champion was already
wondering what he had let himself in for. He was soon to find
out. Systematically Muldoon proceeded to divest Sullivan of his
layers of fat and much of his dignity in order to begin to build
up his strength and stamina. He forced the boxer to rise early in
the morning, work out with dumbbells before breakfast, rest for a
while and then change into heavy clothing before attacking a heavy
punchbag, skip, throw heavy balls to a partner and go for excruciatingly long walks and runs across the rough countryside or swim in
the buff in flooded rivers and lakes. To assert his physical superiority, the older but much fitter Muldoon would wrestle regularly with
Sullivan, and pin the unfit boxer almost at will. They lived largely
off a diet of roast meat and stale bread, with the occasional luxury
of a glass of ale. When the journalist Nelly Bly visited him, Sullivan
complained morosely, 'I eat nothing fattening, I have oatmeal for
breakfast and meat and bread for dinner and cold meat and stale

bread for supper.' His self-pitying remarks and a few caustic asides from Muldoon were printed in a lengthy article by Bly in the *New York World* of 26 May 1889.

Not since the celebrated Captain Barclay supervised the physical rehabilitation of the bareknuckle fighter and heavyweight champion Englishman Tom Cribb, had there been such a gruelling preparation. Over a period of ten weeks, Barclay had chased his man up hills by throwing stones at him until the excess weight drained away, but Muldoon went to limits not even Captain Barclay would dream of. For a start, his period of preparation lasted for three months. To make matters even worse, he ordered both local tavern owners to refuse to serve the Boston Strong Boy with alcohol whenever the fighter attempted to break training and slip out of the camp – a frequent occurrence.

Sullivan almost went berserk. Not only was he being forced to go cold turkey when it came to quitting his beloved spirits, his physical conditioner was treating him like a dog into the bargain. Muldoon insulted his charge, humiliated him and constantly raised the bar when it came to demanding more physical output from the constantly sweating prizefighter. The urban Sullivan hated the oppressive solitude and boredom of the countryside, and, to make matters worse, was frightened of cows. But whenever the fighter deserted from the camp the inexorable Muldoon chased the boxer down and brought him back.

To the amazement of almost everyone involved, this kill-or-cure regimen devised by Muldoon worked. At the beginning of the training period, John L. Sullivan weighed 245lbs and found it difficult to perform more than a dozen consecutive jumps with a skipping rope. By the time Muldoon broke camp the heavyweight was an almost svelte 207lbs and could have scaled half a stone less if Muldoon had not taken pity on him in the days immediately before the fight and eased up on the roadwork. The champion could now execute hundreds of skipping jumps in a day.

The fight occurred in Richberg, a sawmill and lumber town about a hundred miles from New Orleans, on 8 July 1889. There were three thousand spectators. Muldoon acted as one of the champion's seconds. From the start Sullivan was far too good for his opponent. He punched the brave but outclassed Kilrain all over the ring.

At first the challenger attempted evasive tactics, only to be greeted by Sullivan with roars of 'Stand still and fight like a man!' The champion won the bout when the exhausted challenger's seconds threw in the towel after seventy-six rounds occupying a total of two hours and sixteen minutes. Afterwards William Muldoon hastily occupied the high moral ground, stating 'I am through forever with all ring fights. I never again want to see a man so knocked about and punished as Kilrain was.'

The victory did not come without its consequences. Prizefighting was still illegal in the USA and the governors of six southern states had refused to allow the championship bout to take place within their borders. Sullivan and Kilrain were first hounded out of the area and then brought back by the authorities to be tried and fined. Those considered to have aided and abetted the proceedings were also arrested, of which William Muldoon was one. In 1928, in an article written for *Ring* magazine, he described the consequences:

I had my choice of serving sixty days in Mississippi or paying a $600 fine. I paid the $600. Fortunately I had that much left and I did not go to jail. I did spend one night, and I am sorry to say it was a great benefit to me. It was just a square box, no floor in it, with seats around the edge made of logs, and there was a little slab in there with a Bible on it.

Without hesitation Muldoon chose to cash in on his newfound reputation. After facing down the mutinous John L. Sullivan for twelve weeks his stock had soared. Almost overnight William Muldoon achieved a reputation as one of the greatest conditioners of professional athletes in the country and a leading expert on the development of health and strength. It was, however, to be many years before John L. Sullivan ever spoke to his tormentor again.

Muldoon later opened a health farm, where he attracted a distinguished clientele of politicians, businessmen and show business personnel, including Elihu Root, Secretary of State in Theodore Roosevelt's administration, who grimly adhered to his creed of 'Men do not fail; they give up trying', under William Muldoon's bullying, joyless regime of early rising, supervised diets, total abstinence from tobacco and liquor, and constant exercising and horseback riding. The strongman charged his clients $60 a week for their board and training and treated them cruelly under his 'Muldooning' system of physical development, no matter how famous they might be. They took it and came back for more, giving rise to a headline in the *Fitchburg Daily Sentinel*:

William Muldoon, Professor of Regularity
Side Lights on the Builder Up of Rundown Humanity and His System Practical Preacher of All Round Temperance Who Has Been Muldooning Secretary Root. Was the World's Champion Greco-Roman Wrestler – Bitter Hater of Whisky and Cigarettes. His Guests, from Statesmen Down, Must Obey His Rules or They are Shown the Farm Gate.

He was not slow to lay down rules for his wealthy pupils: 'Life is what you make of it. If you live naturally and do not defy the laws of God, you will live to a ripe old age and be able to accomplish that which is expected of all mankind.' He was not universally popular with his clients. The novelist Theodore Dreiser emerged from a period of rehabilitation at the farm describing Muldoon in *12 Men* as 'a tyrant bullying and humiliating his clientele'. Nevertheless, the author was circumspect enough not to call his former instructor by name, but cloaked his attack under the pseudonym of Culhane. A representative of *Munsey's Magazine* also visited the health clinic and, under the heading of 'Making Men Over' in the October 1912 edition described is proprietor as 'the iron-muscled dictator of a unique autocracy'.

For all his harsh measures with his clients, Muldoon took care to make useful contacts among them, especially with senior Republican politicians. Later they were to remember him and aid his career. So many politicians and government administrators attended Muldoon's courses that in the *San Francisco Call* of 15 October 1907, a journalist wrote sardonically:

> It is rumoured that Professor William Muldoon is to become a member of President Roosevelt's Cabinet, if Congress creates the Department of Physical Culture for the repair or overworked Officers.

Muldoon certainly earned top marks for endeavour. He was prepared to use his magnificent physique and growing reputation for almost anything that might improve his bank balance and open new entrepreneurial doors. Not all his schemes came off. For a while he organised dog fights, again bringing him into contact with the law. In June 1886, the *Olean NY Democrat* newspaper said:

William Muldoon reported passing through here en route to Cincinnati where he is billed for a Graeco-Roman exhibition match with Tom Cannon of London, England… It will be remembered that Muldoon got into trouble at Olean last fall over a dog fight. He says they used him very mean in Olean, and he don't propose to go there again.

In 1887, after he had put championship wrestling behind him, a New York newspaper reported, 'The newest stage star is William Muldoon, slugger and wrestler, who is having a play built around his muscles.' Making further use of his great stage presence he also appeared on Broadway as the Fighting Gaul in *Spartacus*. He then transferred to a production of *The Winning Hand* at another theatre. This caused a writer for the *Brooklyn Eagle* to comment on the number of boxers and wrestlers becoming thespians:

Novelty Theater: There will be gloves on 'The Winning Hand' this week. Mr William Muldoon, Mr Jacob Kilrain and other celebrated gentlemen will wear them as part of their costume, for, like Mr John Lawrence Sullivan, they are actors now and their scenes in this drama of love and slugging are watched with more interest and received with more enthusiasm than the bouts in Macbeth and Richard II. The play is of a humorous sort and is enlivened by song and dancing.

Within a couple of years after the Sullivan–Kilrain title fight, Muldoon was famous throughout the land. Coincidentally, this was the period in which Eugen Sandow also became a leading member of the health establishment in Great Britain, commissioned in 1892 to devise a series of exercises for the British army. Both men were reigning supreme on different sides of the Atlantic.

In later life Muldoon became dignified and pompous and seldom deigned to talk to newspaper reporters, but during this stage of his career William Muldoon took advantage of every opportunity for publicity that came his way. He was particularly delighted when a supposed prehistoric corpse was found near Beulah in Colorado in 1877. Seven feet tall, the corpse was nicknamed the Solid Man, after the wrestler, gaining Muldoon several headlines (by now Muldoon happily answered to both the Iron Man and Solid Man nicknames as long as they garnered him favourable publicity). The find later turned out to be a hoax perpetrated by a serial jokester called George Hull, a chemist, even though the *Denver Daily Times* assured its readers: 'There can be no question about the genuineness of this piece of statuary.' The 'corpse' was made of crushed stone, clay, plaster and meat. Hull succeeded in unloading it as the Solid Man for $2,000 on showman P. T. Barnum.

Similarly, when a comic song entitled 'Muldoon, the Solid Man' became a vaudeville hit, the wrestler was not above letting it be intimated that it had been written in his honour, which certainly was not the case, as the song was a satire on big city politics:

> I am a man of great influence,
> And educated to a high degree,
> I came here when small from Donegal,
> In the Daniel Webster, across the sea;
> In the Fourteenth Ward I situated,
> In a tenement house with my brother Dan;
> By perseverance I elevated,
> And went to the front like a solid man

Chorus
Go with me and I'll treat you dacent;
I'll set you down and I'll fill the can;
As I walk the street each friend I meet
Says, There goes Muldoon a solid man.

In addition to establishing his health farm, Muldoon was simultaneously perfecting his reputation as the nation's pre-eminent promoter of strongman and physique displays. Some of these he produced in New York, enlisting the aid of his sporting cronies. They did not always meet with success. One of the flops starred Charlie Mitchell, an English prizefighter and professional hooligan, and the first major physique star to cross the Atlantic and work for Muldoon.

Mitchell was brave, tough, amoral and would do anything for money. For a time he had been the bodyguard, pimp and general fixer for a wealthy English aristocrat called 'Squire' Abingdon Baird, a crooked gentleman jockey, arranger of betting coups and general borderline psychopath, who took a delight in beating up strangers he passed in the street. If any of his unfortunate victims should dare to fight back, Baird would call for his minder. Mitchell would come running over and dutifully continue the assault. As a result, he frequently appeared in court pleading guilty to the attacks instigated by his employer. He was often fined for these transgressions and, on at least one occasion, served a prison sentence in lieu of his master.

When Muldoon came across him, Charlie Mitchell was between jobs. He had fought a courageous 39-round bareknuckle draw with John L. Sullivan at Chantilly in France, and had turned up to fight the champion in a gloved match as well. Unfortunately, true to form, Sullivan had arrived at the venue so drunk that he was unable to go through with the bout.

As a result, when William Muldoon had suggested that he arrange an engagement for the English fighter at the New York theatre, displaying his muscles in a tasteful manner, Mitchell had accepted the offer with alacrity. Unfortunately, although Mitchell was a skilful, cunning fighter, able to give away weight and hold his own with most leading heavyweights of the day, he most definitely did not possess the ripped muscular physique beloved of audiences, and was not, as billed, 'the handsomest and most symmetrically formed man living'. In fact his chest was concave and between his pugilistic endeavours he often displayed a marked paunch. His efforts to impress members of the audience at the Grand Opera House with displays of strength met with more ridicule than applause. Outside the ring he was equally mocked by reporters for his airs and graces and peacock garb, being described in one New York journal when he turned up for a court appearance as:

> …mild mannered a man who ever punched a head. He was armed, according to the strictest code of sporting fashion, wearing a drab coat of abbreviated proportion, and a derby of unusual width of brim and height of crown. A three-carat diamond sparkled in his white satin scarf, and he twisted carelessly in his hands a Malacca cane with a massive silver head.

Some of Muldoon's big city productions may have closed quickly but his touring shows continued to make his name and fortune. He started sending them out all over the country, usually starring in them himself. The acts he headed would consist of boxers and wrestlers challenging all comers, strongmen lifting weights and performing other feats of strength, and displays of the male body beautiful. In this way the cult of physical fitness and manly competitive sports honed to a spectacular degree were brought to huge areas of the USA that had witnessed nothing like them before. To preserve the dignity of the occasions the displays were always referred to as athletic shows, never sideshows.

By 1910, a typical lineup of talent in a Muldoon tent show would consist of singers, dancers and comedians, laced with boxers, wrestlers and weightlifters. They would set up on vacant land for a week and produce a number of shows each day. Most acts earned $25 a week but headliners, capable of drawing in the crowds with their names alone, could command $150 for a week's work. The lesser acts on the bill would usually sleep at night under a sixteen-foot ring pitched in the centre of the tent.

The Muldoon shows were slick and spectacular, with the emphasis on showmanship, even in the boxing and wrestling performances. Acting purely through self-interest William Muldoon made a number of permanent changes to the way in which sport was presented in the USA.

For many years he had achieved fame by participating in and promoting wrestling matches in which the moves were rehearsed and the results prearranged. By the 1890s even the less sophisticated audiences in the cities and the sticks alike were beginning to realise this and drift away from the game. The so-called sport received its death-knell as a big-time spectacle at the turn of the century, when the influential *Police Gazette* declared that 90 per cent of major wrestling bouts and many boxing matches were fixed. You never had to draw Billy Muldoon a picture. As soon as an activity ceased to be profitable he would cut himself adrift from it. It was the same with his connection with wrestling when it became discredited.

William Muldoon had already given up his championship and for years washed his hands of the professional game, although he continued to present short, usually 'fixed' bouts in his tent shows.

He continued with his interest in tent show sport, which in turn had become big business, representing as it did in the pre-silent-movie era the only sensational form of entertainment to reach the vast rural areas of the USA. In an effort to cram as many shows as possible into a day's work, Muldoon revolutionised boxing, wrestling and weightlifting in his touring shows. There were no more six-hour wrestling contests or hundred-round prizefights resulting in dull draws or no-decision verdicts.

In response to public demand, William Muldoon turned the strongman show into a popular and dramatic entertainment. His house wrestlers and boxers fought each other with mock ferocity in heavily choreographed bouts. Challengers from the audience were taken quietly aside and told that they had the choice of giving in to the booth man or suffering a badly broken limb, either during or after the display. Muldoon made another fortune from side bets on these booth matches. New 'sleeper' holds were devised by professional wrestlers to be applied surreptitiously to ultra-frisky local challengers and hasten the inevitable submissions of any foolhardy yokels before the grips caused them to lose consciousness. These shorter bouts were also popular with the tent show boxers and wrestlers as they lessened the chance of their sustaining injuries.

By this time, Sandow was also touring the USA, recruited by the master showman Flo Ziegfeld, but, while Muldoon took his health and strength displays to the sticks, Sandow kept to the main cities.

Life on a William Muldoon tent show was not easy and not for the faint-hearted. Ernest Roeber, now back in the fold as Muldoon's assistant and gofer, recalled a gifted youthful black fighter called

Joe Gans who challenged any of the boxers on Muldoon's booth. All of the tent show fighters were selected for their strength and durability and included such well-known fighters as Charlie Smith, 'the Black Thunderbolt', and Fred Morris, 'Muldoon's Cyclone'. In order not to frighten off potential challengers few of them were appearing under their real names. The sensational young Gans defeated two of the booth men with ease and was paid $2.50 for each contest. Muldoon, irritated by this turn of events, ordered Roeber to persuade Gans, now popular with the crowd, to fight once more. He insisted, however, that the wrestler persuade Gans that so far, despite his victories, he had not been boxing particularly well and that he was not worth more than the customary couple of dollars to appear. The gullible young challenger agreed and was matched with a ringer, who was really a vastly experienced fighter known as Old Pik. The contest was well advertised. Old Pik beat Joe Gans up, forcing him to retire, and earned a lot of money for Muldoon and the tent show. But the story had a comparatively happy ending for the challenger. Gans was seen from the crowd in all three of his tent show contests by a professional manager, who took him on and steered him to the lightweight championship of the world.

At about the same time that Sandow was coming to the same conclusion back in Europe (having returned from the USA in 1896), Muldoon also did away with pointless weightlifting displays by his strongmen. Instead, he sharpened up their acts, making them devise more spectacular feats of strength like lifting people and animals and bending agricultural implements, which were relevant to country dwellers working with animals and on farms.

In 1890, the movement received a healthy boost when Richard K. Fox, the editor of the *Police Gazette*, always looking for

circulation boosters, organised the first major international strongman competition in the USA. The winner was to be any man who
could lift from the ground a specially cast weight of 1,030lbs. Fox,
building on Muldoon's profitable strongman tent shows was eager
to get behind a vaudeville boom in the USA similar to the one
instigated by Sandow in Great Britain. To do this in the USA, Fox
needed to develop his own stars. By now Muldoon was too wealthy
and independent to be employed as an underling, but there was
plenty of home-grown talent to recruit.

Among the entrants were the Italian Luigi Borra, still billed
as Milo, and the leading American strongmen of the decade
Selig Whitman, Cowboy Samson and Charles S. Jefferson. The
competition was won by 29-year-old James Walter Kennedy, from
Kentucky. He straddled the weight, held it by its grips and after
several attempts managed to lift it several inches from the ground.
Afterwards, the winner admitted that he was not a professional
strongman but had been naturally strong all his life and had developed his power by rowing.

Muldoon eventually left the world of tent shows and used his
carefully nurtured Republican political connections to secure
a prestigious post as chairman of the newly formed New York
Athletic Committee, supervising boxing and wrestling in the city.
Innate showmanship, forceful leadership and attention to detail
gave great impetus to the strongman cult in the USA and were to
lay the foundations for the next and even more spectacular great
wave of strength athletes in his native country.

5

CHALLENGES, FEUDS AND
<u>MISADVENTURES</u>

On 23 April 1904, the *Football News* commented tongue-in-cheek: 'It has been conjectured by the late John Huxley, the late Prof. Lecky, and Mr Daniel Leno, sitting in Grand Council, that there are precisely 273 claimants to the title of the "strongest man on earth".'

Not a lot had changed in the last decade of the nineteenth century. Most of the original strongmen were still topping the bills and garnering acres of publicity. The shameless and brazen Charles. A. Sampson was still billing himself as the world's strongest man, despite all evidence to the contrary, and by the early 1890s had relocated temporarily to the USA. Achieving success on the vaudeville circuit, he appeared as one of the chief supporting acts at the newly opened American Theatre in New York. Featuring just below the top-of-the-bill acrobatic Frantz family, Sampson performed what were described as 'a number of remarkable feats of strength'. Also featured were the sisters Belfry, singing serio-comic songs; the two Bostons in a mock bullfight speciality act; and Mlle Anne and her performing pug dolls.

Sampson was still telling his tall stories to anyone who would listen or publish them in their newspaper columns. He claimed that only recently he had been shot in the hip at a dime museum.

Despite his wound, the strongman claimed that he had reached the assailant in Nashville, Tennessee, when Sampson had gone to the assistance of the manager who was being menaced by a thug. He had leapt upon the assailant and hit him on the chin, breaking his jaw in three places. The hooligan had been sentenced to four months' imprisonment, while Sampson had been fined $250 for hitting the man so hard.

Still on the subject of the power of his punch, Sampson told one group of local sportswriters that in the presence of Kaiser Wilhelm of Germany, the strongman had wrapped a silken handkerchief around his hand and knocked an ox unconscious with three consecutive crushing blows. Impressed by the strength displayed, courtiers of the ruler had urged Sampson to challenge the current professional heavyweight boxing champion James J. Corbett for his title. It was true, Sampson conceded, that Corbett might outbox him at first, but as soon as Sampson got close enough to deliver one of his mighty blows, it would all be over for Gentleman Jim.

He was also, he informed a press conference, in the process of preparing his most spectacular feat of strength to date. Soon he intended to lift a fully-grown elephant off the ground on his shoulders, using no mechanical apparatus at all. The only reason why he was delaying this exhibition lay in the fact that the designated elephant, specially purchased from Hamburg Zoo, had broken a leg in transit.

Certainly Charles A. Sampson had a silver tongue. By 1898 he was touring Australia with the Rickards Company. On an appearance at Melbourne Opera House in Australia, a stevedore called Adams responded to a tug-of-war challenge issued by the strongman by leading fourteen burly dock labourers up on to the stage and defying Sampson to outpull his team single-handedly. Sampson's contingency plan, should he be challenged, was to have an accomplice secure his end of the rope to a heavy object in the wings. The strongman had never dreamt that a gang of burly labourers would accept his blithely issued challenge. His tongue went into overdrive as he attempted to talk himself out of his dilemma in front of a hooting crowd. First the strongman haggled interminably over the rules that should govern the proposed contest. Then he insisted that Adams, the stevedores' coach, should leave the stage, as his presence there was giving the dockies' team an unfair advantage. After much wrangling, the stevedores and most of the audience lost interest in the whole affair and retired to the nearest bar. The challenge fizzled out, leaving Sampson to lie another day.

Eugen Sandow, on the other hand, went almost literally from strength to strength. Though not the first strongman to attract a following, he was the first to combine the activities of weightlifting, gymnastics, wrestling and out-and-out showmanship into an entertainment routine, transforming him and his more successful imitators into top-of-the-bill performers at music halls, circuses and vaudeville theatres. This led to the great influx of professional athletes on to the world's stages for a period of almost twenty-five years.

He never stopped working on his act and included an assistant in his stage routines – albeit briefly. On holiday in Aachen he encountered a massive German labourer called Karl Westphail, working in a quarry, tossing huge boulders effortlessly into the back of a cart. At a height of 6ft 3in., a weight of 370lbs and a chest measurement of 60in., Sandow renamed him Goliath and brought him back to London, hoping to train him in the arts of the strongman.

They made a well-rehearsed and gratifyingly well-attended arrival back from the Continent at King's Cross railway station, accompanied by a carefully selected assortment of boldly embossed suitcases and packing cases and other impedimenta. In front of the attendant reporters Sandow and Goliath mimed their horror when they discovered that after their luggage had been loaded there was no room inside the cab for the two strongmen. Accordingly, the pair of them walked in stately fashion behind the laden vehicle through the streets of the capital to Goliath's new digs, followed by dozens of onlookers.

Sandow worked hard to incorporate his new discovery into his act, concentrating on his charge's homeliness. A reporter from the *Sunday Times* obligingly described Goliath as 'a huge mountain of flesh and bone standing well over six feet, with a chest measurement of Heaven knows how many inches, and a huge face like a pantomime mask'.

Unfortunately, the former quarry worker showed no aptitude for his new line of work, being a slow learner and woefully lacking in the slightest vestiges of personality or charisma. The double act was not a success. Sandow described it in his 1897 book *Strength and How to Obtain It*:

> We wrestled together, and it was his business to make himself the victor. Then, in order to finish me, he took a cannon, weighing 400lbs, and placed it on his broad shoulders and prepared to fire.

Eventually Goliath ran off with his landlady and formed his own strength duo with her. Sandow was not sorry to see his protégé leave.

The Prussian's fans soon began to wonder if their hero was beginning to suffer from delusions of grandeur when billstickers started putting up posters in advance of Sandow's tours announcing that at forthcoming shows the strongman would lift a horse from the ground with one hand. Nevertheless, in the fullness of time this is what he proceeded to do.

Admittedly the horse was a small one, weighing 'only' around 600lbs, but it was still a mightily impressive achievement. However, in this case, as in so many others, the devil lay in the detail, or rather in the technical design of the apparatus used to make the strongman look so good. On the first night, Eugen Sandow used a complicated system of straps and harnesses wrapped around the docile mount, but he definitely hoisted the animal from the ground and walked a few steps with it. Alan Calvert, a bodybuilder writer, explained in *Super Strength* how the stunt was performed after the horse had been lowered by a block and tackle on to Sandow's back: 'Sandow would lean forward and allow some of the horse's weight to rest on his shoulders.'

His peers also constantly changed their acts, usually to make them appear better but sometimes in necessary cost-cutting exercises. Monte Saldo, a one-time apprentice of Sandow's, had a nice line in tearing three packs of cards placed on top of each other in half, with one revolution of his wrists. Before he reached star status, however, he discovered that purchasing three packs of cards for each performance on a twice nightly basis was proving an unsustainable drain on his pocket, so he dropped the trick from his repertoire. To make up for it, he emulated William Bankier's posing display, wearing the skimpiest of trunks, and emphasised by a full tan body make-up and a set of lights directly above his posing booth, which highlighted his writhing muscles and knowing leers at the audience.

A spectacular international act was that employed by the German Paul Spadoni, whose real name was Krause. Dressed as a Roman centurion, he would drive on to the stage at the opening of his routine in a chariot pulled by horses. He would leap out, unhitch the horses and lift the chariot and place it on his head. After a time, with audiences falling off, Spadoni decided that a complete revamp of his act was required. Accordingly, he jettisoned the centurion persona and adopted that of a prehistoric caveman, clad in skins and juggling wooden clubs. He would also juggle with six eggs and then break them into a plate to prove that they were fresh and not hard-boiled.

During his act, Spadoni also twisted iron bars out of shape. One night, after the show, a supporting entertainer took some of the crumpled bars with him to Zenke's restaurant in Brooklyn to display them wonderingly to his friends, and left them there over-night on a table. The next morning a man delivering ice casually bent them all back into shape and replaced them neatly on the table. There were plenty of naturally strong men walking about, capable of duplicating vaudeville feasts, especially when the equip-ment had been weakened in advance!

Luigi Borra, Milo, was equally pragmatic when it came to moving with the times. His particular routine was totally eclipsed by a group of Germans billed as the Saxon Trio. Whatever stunt Milo performed it could be eclipsed with ease by one of the Saxons. Fed up with the jeers of his alienated audiences and the sympathy of his fellow artistes, and beginning to suffer from a persecution complex, Milo disappeared from the music halls altogether for a few months. He reappeared rejuvenated and reincarnated as 'Brinn, the Cannonball King', in a sketch entitled 'Pastimes on a Battleship'.

Not unnaturally the action was set on the deck of a large vessel of the Royal Navy, with a transformed Luigi Borra as the epau-letted officer, assisted by members of his crew. He started the performance by juggling with several rifles. He would then attach bayonets to them and stick these into the deck before performing a handstand on the butts, taking away one arm so that he was balancing solely on the other limb. After a number of other strongman stunts based on maritime themes, Borra concluded his new act by balancing a pole on his chin – a cannon and its attendant gunner were stationed on a platform on the far end of the pole.

Even those unambitious strongmen who did not care greatly to interfere with the contents of their acts were forced to strive constantly to make them ever more acceptable to audiences. This sometimes called for a certain amount of subterfuge in what was happening onstage. Living and training as they did with heavy weights, professional strongmen possessed power beyond the wildest dreams of ordinary men. Even so, most of them reasoned that there was no point of straining to excess every night when false poundages could be painted on to the sides of weights. At the time, most strongmen were still using barbells and dumbbells with circular hollow ends. These looked impressive but were relatively light and as far as their total tonnage was concerned they could represent whatever their lifters said they represented.

Those holier-than-thou performers like William Bankier who criticised colleagues for using flimmery flammery in their performances were not well regarded by the lesser artisans in their profession. The common response to any strongman objecting to a certain amount of trickery onstage was 'Can't you give the boys a bit of a show?'

A lot of effort went into providing these displays on the road. Ingenious uses were made of apparently harmless pieces of apparatus. Professor Paulinetti, the stage name of Philip Henry Thurber, could press up into a one-hand handstand on the end of a walking stick, a great feat, but only possible because there was a small socket sunk into the floor of the stage into which he would unobtrusively fit the edge of his cane.

Similarly, packs of cards could be baked in an oven before a performance and doctored to make them brittle. The strongmen could then tear the cards in half or even in quarters with contemptuous ease. Alternatively, a tiny incision could be made across the side of the pack, which would enable the strongman to secure a grip when he started exerting pressure with his wrists.

Another staple strongman trick was to pound a boulder into fragments with one mighty blow of the performer's fist. This, reputedly, had been one of the parlour tricks of the gigantic Roman Emperor Maximus, two thousand years before. In the nineteenth-century halls the stunt was made easier if a limestone rock was soaked in water overnight. The stone would rot without changing its appearance. When it was struck the next day it would shatter most impressively.

One of the more dramatic strongman stunts was lifting and swinging a partner by the teeth. A specially designed jaw strap was used and a great deal of the strain of the weight was borne by the strongman's neck muscles.

Again and again, the more honest strength practitioners of the era insisted that the breaking of coins between the fingers just could not be accomplished by any strongman. Not for the first time, the down-to-earth Edward Aston represented the voice of reason when he wrote 'to break a penny with the hands alone was simply not possible'. This did not prevent many strongmen including such a trick in their acts, especially as a coin could be partially severed with a file beforehand, causing it to splinter most impressively when substituted for the genuine article by sleight of hand.

Hammering nails into a board with a fist was another popular trick among the first strongmen and one that could be mastered fairly easily if the nails had broad heads, were extremely sharp and the board was made of the softest possible wood. Sometimes, instead of using soft wood, a particularly meticulous strongman might hollow out a piece of wood and fill the gap with sawdust before painting over it. The great trick, however, lay in the covering used around the strongman's fists. The performer would explain that this covering was used merely to protect his hands. In fact, the cloth used was not nearly as soft as it might appear to the audience and covered much more of the fist than was strictly necessary, so that in some cases it had all the power of a muffled hammer.

Another stunt involved a strongman lying impassively on his back on a bed of nails while supporting a partner in a quivering handstand. Spectators were invited to inspect the nails beforehand but in reality the nails made no impact: packed so closely together on the board, they could not pierce the strongman's skin.

An extension of this trick was for the strongman to bend nails between his fingers and then toss them into the audience for inspection. This action could have its consequences. In the case of one unpopular performer, three professional strongmen situated themselves in the darkened auditorium for one of his shows. When the performer onstage threw the twisted nails in the stalls, the strongmen seated there merely straightened them out and threw them back on to the stage until the performer begged for mercy.

On a more mundane level, straightening out a horseshoe was commonplace among the average strongman's repertoire of tricks. In the vast majority of cases, the shoes used were specially constructed for stage use by a blacksmith out of softened metal. In his book *How to Develop a Powerful Grip*, Edward Aston, one of the more genuine music hall strongmen, admitted as much: 'There is not a man in the world who can break a brand new horseshoe … I did what all the other performers did, and that was to go to a blacksmith and get the "right kind".'

Another popular trick consisted of a strongman writing his name on a wall chart while supporting a weight attached to his little finger. The secrets were to choose a very short name and to hold the chalk and weight in such a way that most of the weight was resting on the forearm, taking the strain off the little finger.

A strongman lifting a man above his head would always select a light victim, except in the case of Arthur Saxon, a genuine strongman who scorned such deceptions. A diminutive volunteer, or preferably an assistant planted in the audience, would be called up on to the stage. A heavy leather belt would be fastened about his waist and secured under his shoulders. The strongman would grasp the belt at the level of the other man's chest, bend his legs and then straighten up. If the strongman's arm was then straightened and locked into place, it was possible for a trained, muscular professional to lift the other man above his head, because most of the weight would be taken on the lifter's legs. It then remained only for the strongman to march triumphantly around the stage holding the other aloft.

Many similar tricks of the trade could be performed with a little practice and ingenuity on the part of the strongman concerned. Breaking a chain was not difficult if one of the links had been specially weakened and then camouflaged over. Other chains could be torn asunder with the teeth when the strongman bit into them, especially if one of the links had been replaced with a duplicate of soft lead with nickel-plating, or had been eroded with prussic acid and then cleaned.

When a strongman placed his head on one chair and his feet

on another, while an assistant smashed a stone to smithereens on his chest with a sledgehammer, great care would be taken by both men to ensure that the weight of the stone equally balanced across the strongman's torso. The bigger and heavier the stone used, the greater was the amount of impact absorbed, especially as the assistant was not driving the sledgehammer viciously into the other man's chest, but only using enough force to break the stone.

At the same time, interwoven with the inevitable duplicity, a number of strongmen seemed to possess powers that did appear to be out of the ordinary. A case in point was the American William Le Roy. Billed variously as the Nail King and the Human Claw Hammer, Le Roy displayed enormous strength in his jaws, teeth and neck. He could push a nail held between his teeth through a board 1in. thick and withdraw with his teeth a nail hammered through a 2in. plank. He could also twist a 2in. screw into a hardwood plank with his teeth, withdraw it the same way, screw it back in again and then offer a prize to any man in the audience who could get it out with a pair of pliers. Even that professional sceptic and debunker Harry Houdini was forced to admit, 'I saw no chance for trickery in Le Roy's act.'

Over the years, on the outer fringes of some of the more reckless strongmen's presentations, a number of the routines intended to impress audiences seem to have been based more on optimism bordering on recklessness than an excess of technical knowledge on the part of the performers. For years one of the fraternity, billed simply as the Bulletproof Man, toured the halls claiming that his strength was such that no bullet could kill him. He would conclude his act with an assistant shooting at him from point blank range. After this artiste's death, surprisingly from natural causes, his costumes were examined and it was revealed that his sole source of protection from the one-man firing squad was a concealed jacket packed with tightly ground glass. It had been a miracle that over the years no bullet had been able to penetrate such a relatively flimsy covering.

Martin 'Farmer' Burns's act was dangerous to the point of bordering on the macabre and manic. The burly American wrestling champion was very proud of the strength of his massive 20in. neck and from time to time he would migrate from the grappling ring to the vaudeville circuit with his infamous 'Long Drop' moonlighting feat. His props consisted of a six-foot trapdoor drop and a standard hangman's noose. Burns would stand on the platform with his hands tied behind his back in the traditional attitude of a condemned man. A lever would be released and Burns would plunge into the abyss below. He would remain there, twisting and turning for a timed three-minute span, before being hauled back up to the platform. If the wrestler was feeling in a particularly entertaining mood or wanted to milk the applause he would also whistle 'Yankee Doodle Dandy' as he twisted and turned on the end of the rope.

It became a part of burlesque lore that one night, a comedian waiting in the wings to go on witnessed the sight of a twitching Farmer Burns dangling onstage through the trap door, whistling manfully. He remarked with scorn, 'All that because he's too lazy to learn a comic song!'

The sheer outrageousness of Burns's act was rivalled only by that of another failed American strongman of German origin. His real name was Leonard Borchardt, but he performed professionally as Oofty Goofty. Failing to make the grade as a weightlifter and muscle-flexing exponent, but determined still to carve out a vaudeville career for himself, this man reinvented himself as yet another Wild Man of Borneo in a San Francisco freak show. Covered in tar, upon which were stuck handfuls of horsehair, he was wheeled on to the stage in a cage, gibbering, rattling the bars and shouting 'Oofty Goofty!' at the audience.

Unfortunately, the artiste became ill when he found that he could not perspire through the coating of tar on his skin. Taken to a local hospital in this sad state, the attending physicians and nurses could not remove the layer of tar which had congealed, despite their efforts. They did their best by dousing their patient in a solvent and laying him out, as he groaned softly, on the roof of the hospital, until the sun had melted some of the tar. It took the performer another five months of semi-permanent residence in a Turkish bath before he was completely free of his matted covering.

Oofty Goofty, however, had the heart of a trouper. He was determined to secure some sort of work as a performing strong-man and, as he pondered over the problem, he took temporary employment as a song-and-dance performer. He learned one song and persuaded a proprietor called Bottle Koenig to allow him to sing it at the latter's Barbary Coast beer hall.

So horribly did Oofty Goofty perform that in a very short time he was thrown out of the stage door into a cobbled alley. It proved to be a eureka moment for the would-be strength athlete. As he landed on the ground with sickening force, Oofty Goofty convinced himself that he had experienced no pain from his collision with the stones.

Oofty Goofty decided to put his newfound 'ability' to good use. He devised another act in which he would sit on a stage without moving and allow himself to be hit or kicked, for a suitable fee. Ten cents would allow a patron to kick him, while for a quarter any member of the audience could strike Oofty Goofty with a stick of his own choice. Fifty cents would allow a wealthier onlooker to belt the performer with a baseball bat. Throughout his new career, Oofty Goofty's only coherent line of dialogue was a hoarse 'Hit me with a bat for four bits, gents!'

For a brief period Oofty Goofty even experimented with allowing spectators to hit him with baseballs hurled from any part of the house, often at the same time. This gave him the chance to upgrade his billing temporarily to that of the Human Skittle. After a time, however, he removed this from his act on the grounds that it was proving too dangerous, even by his standards.

Sadly Oofty Goofty had to admit that his performance was not being talked of in the same breath as those of Sampson or Sandow, but he was in show business and earning a living of sorts. It all came to an end, however, when the performer grew too ambitious. In an attempt to publicise his act he had the temerity to challenge the irascible boxer John L. Sullivan. At the time the Great John L. was preparing to defend his title against the urbane former bank clerk known professionally as Gentleman Jim Corbett.

As was his custom, Sullivan was undertaking this particular stage of his preparation in a billiards hall. When Oofty Goofty approached him and challenged the champion to hit him, Sullivan, enraged at being disturbed while he was plotting a shot, swung round and delivered a crushing blow to the entertainer's body with the thick end of his cue. It was later claimed that the force of the blow shattered the stick into three pieces.

It was the end of Oofty Goofty's vaudeville strongman act. Sullivan's swipe had been so fierce that the entertainer sustained a permanently damaged back. Even worse, his spirit had been crushed when he realised that he could after all be hurt, even if the man delivering the damage was one of the fiercest punchers in the business. Oofty Goofty retired from the stage and took up alternative, less onerous, employment cleaning out saloons and stables.

Even in the best regulated of acts things could still go wrong with any performance involving the use of heavy weights and intricate – and sometimes primitive – machinery. Catching a cannonball was an exploit that only the bravest or most foolhardy included in their strength acts. A Danish ex-sailor called John Holtom was one of the first music hall strongmen to attempt it, beginning to perform the trick in 1870. He would stand directly in front of what looked like an ordinary artillery cannon placed a few yards away onstage. For the occasion Holtom wore gloves with a pad affixed to his chest. An assistant would load the weapon and fire it. There would be a deafening explosion. Holtom would catch the flying ball and throw it to the ground. There were rumours that the cannon was all noise and no substance, but no one ever attempted to claim the three thousand francs Holtom offered to anyone duplicating his feat. Perhaps the rumour that the always begloved Cannonball Man had lost two fingers during the early days of his act helped to deter prospective challengers.

One of John Holtom's few competitors with the cannonball stunt was a Frenchman called Louis Vigneron, known as the Cannonball King. Vigneron was a savate or French kick-boxing expert and was also well known on the strongman circuit for his spectacular but undeniably dangerous stunt of hoisting a cannon onto his shoulders and firing it. He claimed that the gun weighed 180 kilos, but this was almost certainly an exaggeration.

One evening, at the casino at Boulogne-sur-Mer, Vigneron was going through his performance. It was a trick that he had accomplished with no problems at least eight hundred times over the previous few years. As usual, he heaved the cannon on to his right shoulder, lit the fuse and then crouched slightly to minimise the effect of the weapon's recoil as it exploded. On this occasion the weapon did not fire. Vigneron began to place it back on the ground. As he did so, inadvertently he swivelled the piece round so that it was facing his body. Suddenly it exploded, killing him instantly.

A newspaper editorial of the time deplored the constant demand for increasingly dangerous stunts in the world of entertainment: 'The fate of this well-known performer is in strict accord with that of the majority of individuals who have habitually accomplished feats which strain the ordinary courses of events to the utmost limits of possibilities.'

The Saxon Trip also tended to be a little accident-prone, although on at least one occasion this was fortified by their habit of going off on beer-drinking binges from time to time. One afternoon, all three of them got drunk in a London club. Staggering out of the establishment they hired a cab to take them back to the music hall for the first house that evening. The cabman was doubtful but allowed himself to be persuaded to allow the three burly Germans into his vehicle.

Once inside, the largest of the three, Arno, had to sit on the knees of his brothers. Undeterred by the cramped conditions, all three of the strongmen started singing 'Deutschland Über Alles'. At the appropriate times in the refrain they also stamped with their feet on the floor of the cab. The tortured base of the cab splintered and collapsed under the pressure. The three inebriated strongmen refused to leave the vehicle and insisted on walking the cab – still inside – to the theatre, while the bemused driver steered his horses. Soon the partly dismantled carriage was being followed by a large crowd.

The inebriated strongmen reeled into the music hall and continued singing raucously in their dressing rooms while the other acts tried to go through their performances on the stage. When the time came for the top-of-the-bill act to appear, the distracted manager begged the happy Germans to calm down and hustled them on to the stage. Somehow the curtain rose to the usual opening martial music. The three men should have been standing rigidly to attention in a gladiatorial tableau – instead, all three men were swaying like trees in a high wind. Arthur stood with a 100lb kettlebell in his upraised arm, while Oscar (the latest addition to the line-up) sank to the floor and lay soporifically at his feet. Meanwhile, Arno looked on with a meaningless beam on his broad face.

They should have moved smoothly into their opening scene. Instead, Arno dropped the kettlebell, destroying several of the stage boards. Vaguely remembering what should happen next, Arno staggered across the stage to commence a teeth grip. He managed to put the leather protective mouth shield mouth into place and secured the appropriate leather strap around a terrified assistant. He kept revolving as the assistant was propelled round and round in the air. Unfortunately, Arno became dizzy and opened his mouth to gasp for air, releasing his grip on the strap. The assistant, still in a leather cradle, went sailing out over the orchestra pit into the audience, where he remained motionless, groaning. The spectators, unsure whether this was meant to be part of the act, but suspecting otherwise, by now were helpless with laughter.

Next in the running order, Arthur Saxon was scheduled to balance a 100lb kettlebell on top of his head and gracefully stoop to pick up two other kettlebells of a similar weight, one in each hand. In his inebriated state, somehow he succeeded in perching the first weight on his head. As he bent to grasp the others the first weight slipped and fell into the orchestra, shattering the piano. The members of the orchestra fled. Arno watched the players disappear and shouted indignantly, 'Where's the band? We can't perform without music!'

Operating on the principle that the show must go on, Arthur then picked up a heavy barbell but lost control of it and dropped the weight, wrecking another section of the stage. A courageous stage manager appeared and begged the three strongmen to abandon their performance. It was too late; the Germans were now beginning to feel quite comfortable. After a brief discussion, they decided to move on to Arthur's big set piece. This consisted of his lying on his back and supporting a number of men and weights on his hands and feet. After much swaying and manoeuvring, the other two managed to place a 267lb barbell across the prone Arthur's legs and attach a 100lb kettlebell to each raised foot. After a great deal of vocal persuasion and many appeals to the innate courage of true-born Englishmen in the audience, six volunteers were finally persuaded to sit astride a barbell held aloft at arm's length by the doughty Arthur. He promptly lost control and dropped the complete load. What was left of the stage was now littered with sprawling bodies and damaged equipment. Finally the curtain was brought down.

As it happened, the resultant publicity did the Saxon Trio nothing but good. The three Germans embarked upon a lengthy, successful and relatively sober provincial tour of an act entitled 'Strong Men of Today'.

Some time later, the Saxons were involved in another mishap. This one was much more serious than their previous drunken escapade and brought about a temporary halt to their career. Two of them, Arthur and Kurt, were concluding their act by lying on their backs under a large trestle table, extending their legs and supporting the wooden structure as it lay across their feet. A motor car carrying several passengers was then driven along the length of the table. They called the stunt 'Brookland on Four Legs', after the famous motor racing venue.

The anatomical principle behind this stunt was based on the fact that the strong bones of their legs would support the table, not the muscles of their thighs and calves. However, the positions they adopted meant that their legs could not be extended fully and had to be reinforced by the two strongmen clasping their knees with their hands.

This night their efforts were not enough to support the weight of the car. Their legs were not braced sufficiently firmly and the table collapsed, bringing down the car with it and injuring both men badly.

Another major casualty among the leading strongmen was Bobby Pandour, the stage name of Wladyslaw Kurcharczyk, a Polish gymnast who arrived in London at the turn of the century to tour the halls with his brother Ludwig in an acrobatic horizontal bar- and hand-balancing act. Pandour was relatively light but very muscular. He aroused the suspicions of fellow strongmen by claiming never to train with heavy weights. He said that his main forms of exercising consisted of constantly flexing and tensing his muscles and running up two flights of stairs carrying his brother.

Another cause of jealousy among the strongmen was the fact that the handsome Pandour was very popular with women. Visitors to Pandour's dressing room before a performance reported that he was usually surrounded by a bevy of nubile admirers. In 1907, he and Ludwig went on a successful vaudeville tour of the USA. He took advantage of his superb physique by adding a posing routine to the act. The curtain rose to reveal Bobby Pandour balancing precariously on a narrow Roman column about 10ft above the ground. While a bright spotlight shone down on him, Pandour would go through his muscle-flexing act. One night, while appearing at a Cincinnati hall he lost his balance and fell to the ground. Pandour was so badly injured that he was never able to perform again.

In most cases, however, in the closing decade of the nineteenth century and at the start of the twentieth, a dexterous strongman with a modicum of common sense, a good stage presence and a ready wit to deal with mistakes and hecklers, could usually rely on himself to sail through most of a well-rehearsed performance with a minimum of effort and few repercussions from disgruntled patrons or faulty equipment.

Unfortunately, matters became a little more borderline when it came to issuing and accepting challenges. A good, robust confrontation from the audience was a staple part of a performance and all the top-of-the-bill strongmen were expected to include one in their routines, with any challenges heavily advertised outside the theatres.

At a certain point during a performance by any of the well-known strength athletes the strongman would usually perform a particularly impressive feat of strength. He would then challenge any man in the audience to duplicate the lift or stunt for a cash prize. As a rule there would be no shortage of local amateur would-be strongmen eager to climb upon to the stage and compete for such a prize.

Even the high and mighty Sandow felt obliged to include a perfunctory confrontation or two of this sort in his act, although secretly he considered this part of the proceedings to be a little below his dignity, ignoring the fact that he had achieved fame by challenging both Cyclops and Sampson. He would produce his famous challenge dumbbell, weighing only 5lbs, and defy all comers to lift it from the ground, at the same time squeezing the handle as hard as possible. Built into the handle of the weight were grips of different strengths, each one of which could be activated if squeezed. Each successful exertion of power caused a small bell to ring, giving off a cacophony of sound as challengers struggled with the bar, at the same time holding the weight overhead.

Usually a professional strongman would have enough power and technique to defeat any amateur. Occasionally, however, something could go wrong and the performer would find himself with a challenger patently strong enough to become a nuisance. As a matter of professional pride as well as economics, such a threat plainly could not be tolerated and there were many stratagems to be employed to safeguard the precious cash prize.

Sometimes the challenge consisted of lifting a heavy barbell or dumbbell previously hoisted to a great fanfare by the strongman. Most of these special weights had very thick handles. As a matter of course the majority of strongmen spent years in training, practising to make sure that they could encompass such handles with their hands. They would start by lifting ordinary weights, and then, every week or so, make the handle thicker by wrapping another layer of tape around it. Eventually they could cope with massively reinforced handles, far beyond the grip of ordinary men.

If a particularly dangerous challenger should appear on the scene, powerful enough to succeed in lifting the weight, a number of ploys could be brought into play by the suddenly alerted staff onstage. The principles of balance and concealment were often instigated to make challengers look stupid and reinforce the supremacy of the professional. It was not uncommon for the stage to be littered with apparatus towards the conclusion of a display of strength activities, and to have assistants and assorted stage-hands milling about in front of assorted curtains and drapes. Once the principal strongman had lifted his champion barbell, with its weight almost certainly greatly exaggerated, some time would elapse before the amateur was allowed to have a go. In the subsequent confusion the piece of apparatus would have been switched for a replica, identical in appearance but unobtrusively doctored.

The difference between these two barbells lay in the fact that the one now being presented to the tyro from the audience to lift was completely out of balance. Either one of the globes at the end of the bar was up to 20lbs heavier than the other, or a few drops of mercury had been surreptitiously inserted into one of the globes, increasing its density to a remarkable extent. In either case, even if the aspirant could heave his weight up from the stage it was now so unwieldy that not even the most powerful of men could get it overhead. The sight of the challenger staggering wildly and help-lessly about the stage was usually the signal for wild hilarity among the fickle crowd.

A lot could and did go on behind the scenes to ensure that a sucker never got an even break. Arthur Saxon, the strongest of the Saxon Trio, offered £150 to anyone who could lift his challenge barbell. If would-be challengers were thin upon the ground the strongman would place the weight in a prominent position in the foyer of the music hall at which he was currently appearing and encourage passers-by to lift it. Many tried and a surprising number were successful. This impelled a number of the marks to challenge the strongman on the stage at an evening performance. This time hardly anyone ever succeeded in getting the barbell overhead. It was not surprising, as the reinforced weight on the stage was now at least 100lbs heavier than the one which had been on view in the foyer.

The most famous of all the challenge dumbbells was that owned by Thomas Inch, the Scarborough Hercules. Inch was a flamboyant, astute businessman who developed a huge empire with his physical culture postal courses, modelled on those of Sandow. At one time he employed seventy-two people to send out his postal bodybuilding lessons from a suite of offices bearing the slogan 'Here we make men!' For years he roamed the halls with his vaunted piece of apparatus, defying all comers to lift it from the ground to arm's length overhead as easily as he could. As an inducement he offered to pay a mind-boggling £200 to anyone who could accomplish this. The dumbbell was a masterly contraption. It weighed 172lbs, with a very short, thick handle only 4in. long. This meant that no one with large hands could secure a proper grip on the handle and hoist it overhead. As most amateur strongmen had fingers like bananas, hardly any of them could even hold the challenge dumbbell, let alone heave it off the ground. The handle was also designed so that it almost seemed to roll from the hands of those trying to lift it. This secured the Scarborough Hercules, who had remarkably small hands for his size – his wrist was a little over 6in. and he could slip a lady's ring over any of his fingers – a comfortable, undefeated living for decades. In time he grew so confident that he enlarged the scope of his prize and offered all comers £5 for every inch they could lift it from the floor.

As always, among the fraternity of strongmen rumours spread that Inch was practising a certain amount of jiggery-pokery in his stage act. It was claimed that the Scarborough Hercules had four identical challenge bells and that even the strongman could lift only one of them. The other three were 'ringers'. An assistant of the strongman claimed that it had been his task before a stage exhibition to test each of the four dumbbells by hitting them with a spanner to ensure that only the one which gave off a particular reverberation should be offered to Inch to lift. The other three were for the use of the hapless challengers.

Before long, Inch had extended his challenge to include professional strongmen, and there were many who sought to collect the £200 now on offer. Thomas Inch always enjoyed tormenting his rivals with his challenge dumbbell, writing: 'I used to smile to myself often when I saw strong men stooping down and peering beneath the handle, turning my bell from side to side for the "secret".' The challenge was a particular source of irritation to Edward Aston, who worked on Thomas Inch's touring show for a time and was irked that the sum being offered in newspapers to any man who could lift the Inch challenge weight equalled Aston's wages for a considerable period of time. But even Aston could not lift the challenge dumbbell. Like others he suspected that Inch took care only to lift the one carefully selected weight, leaving the impossible replicas to all comers. At one matinee, while he was struggling in vain yet again with the challenge weight, he called out sarcastically to his employer standing in the wings: 'Which one is this, Mr Inch?'

'The one I'm going to lift tonight!' came the complacent response.

Apart from Inch himself, no one lifted the challenge dumbbell more than a few inches from the ground in its owner's lifetime. Towards the end of his long career he was claiming that no one had ever shifted it at all, although this does not seem to be accurate. Certainly he was the only man of his time able to lift it overhead. Many seeking to probe the secret of the weight in question put forward a number of theories but none were ever proved. Some noticed that a small hole had been bored in the centre of the handle. Could it be that Inch placed a pin through the thin hole, attached to a thin rod tied to his wrists and concealed by the gloves he wore when he performed his lifts? If this was the case, this might balance the handle and prevent the dumbbell from writhing and squirming in his hands. The designer of the dumbbell always denied this.

On one occasion in 1907, there was a major wrestling tournament held at Hengler's Circus in London. Most of the major grapplers of the day were there, including the Russian Ivan Padoubney and Louis Uni. Inch left his dumbbell at the circus for a few days. Most of the wrestlers tried to lift it but none succeeded. On the final day Inch turned up, claimed his dumbbell, ostentatiously lifted it and marched out with the weight to a waiting hansom cab.

In addition to orthodox weights, other strongmen spent a great deal of time in preparing more complicated diabolical contrivances with which to torment mugs from the audience and prevent their winning the prize on offer. A common implement was a specially constructed chest expander with a number of short rubber strands. On this occasion the challengers were allowed to compete first in an effort to draw the expander out to its full extent. As usual, few succeeded. There would then be a short comedy interlude in which two of the strongman's assistants would come forward. Each man would take a separate end of the expander. Between them, with much huffing and puffing and falling over, they would draw the piece of equipment out to its full extent a few times. What they were really doing was making the rubber strands more malleable. When the waiting strongman finally strode forward, he was able to manipulate the freshly weakened strands with apparent ease.

The Scot William Bankier, performing as Apollo, defied anyone to lift his challenge sack of flour and some heavy weights, offering a prize of £10 to anyone who could lift the bag. It weighed a considerable 280lbs but its almost total immunity to being lifted by anyone but Bankier lay in its shape. It was packed very hard into quite a small compass, so that anyone attempting to lift the sack had to lie down next to it and squirm around in an attempt to drag the bag on to his back, causing it to roll off time after time. It was also very greasy and difficult to hold.

When Bankier issued his challenges he showed himself to be less grasping and a better businessman than many of his competitors. He was always prepared to give a challenger an even break and allow him to have a chance to win a prize. If a contender looked a capable lad and his supporters had bought an encouraging number of tickets, Bankier would sometimes substitute the challenge sack for a lighter one, which the amateur would be able to lift. This would send the aspirant and his fans home in happy frames of mind and perhaps encourage them to return and try again later in the week. This time the sack on offer would be the original almost unliftable one.

Arthur Saxon also included a sack of flour, weighing about 300lbs, in his act. Constant practice allowed Saxon to hoist the package into the air quite easily and walk around with it. However, it was filled so awkwardly and covered with layers of slippery chalk to such an extent that few approaching it for the first time could hope to lift it because it was so slippery for the uninitiated.

While challenges to all comers drew in a steady number of patrons to music halls on a regular basis, the occasional grudge matches taking place between professional strongmen were huge successes at the box office. A number of them were undoubtedly fixed but every so often two rival strength athletes, prompted by greed or animosity or even a genuine desire to find out who was the more powerful man, would meet onstage in a genuine competition, starting with the Sampson–Sandow match of 1889, which kicked off the whole strongman craze. These events gathered so much newspaper publicity that on the nights in question it would usually be a case of standing room only, no matter how capacious the halls.

From an early stage in his career, Eugen Sandow did his best to eschew challenges from his peers. This was probably due to an unpleasant experience he had early in his reign as the world's strongest man. In 1890, despite his reservations about public challenges, Sandow allowed himself to be inveigled into a strength contest against the veteran Louis 'Hercules' McCann, who stood 5ft 11in. tall, weighed 219lbs and had a chest measurement of 40in., with 17in. biceps. Sandow had just dispensed with the services of the wily Professor Atilla, who surely would never have allowed his relatively inexperienced protégé to become involved in such a shambles.

The match took place at the Royal Music Hall at Holborn in London on 10 December. It quickly degenerated into a farce, with mutual recriminations, accusations of cheating, refusals to attempt certain challenges and even threats of legal action. At the end of the shambolic performance it seemed as if Sandow had succeeded in four out of six strength challenges, while McCann had triumphed in only three. It came as something of a surprise, consequently, when the ubiquitous Marquess of Queensberry, befuddled by all the claims and counter-claims made by the protagonists, declared McCann to be the winner *and* made a hasty exit. The *Morning Post* of 11 December described the confusion:

The judges then retired to draw up their decision, which was considered by the vast majority to be almost a certainty for Samdow. Whose splendid proportions and modest bearing, coupled with the fact that he had undergone far greater exertion than his opponent, made him a strong favourite. After an absence of about a quarter of an hour the judges returned and the Marquess of Queensberry announced that Hercules had won the competition.

McCann, along with his brother, was able to return to the strongman circuit with an enhanced reputation, and could display the specially struck commemorative medal presented to him. In part, its inscription read 'For defeating Sandow and sustaining the prestige of Englishmen as athletes.' One jingoistic newspaper report commented that 'Hercules's victory is regarded as the apotheosis of English bull-beef over German sausage.' A more balanced view was taken by another newspaper commenting on the propensity of strongmen to squabble like prima donnas whenever they met in opposition: 'Win, tie or wrangle seems to be the order for all strongman competitions.'

The disputed defeat had no effect on Sandow's popularity or status, although he claimed to have lost £5,000 in side bets over the result and threatened to take out a legal injunction against the decision. The Prussian made a mental note in future to avoid counter-productive strength challenges as far as possible – but only a few years later he found himself embroiled in yet another confrontation.

This time his adversary was Arthur Saxon, who had been issuing public challenges to the Prussian for some time using posters and billboards.

Arthur Saxon challenges Sandow or any other man in the world for any amount. A match can be ratified at 'The Sporting News' office. Man and money ready.

Such challenges were nothing new; Sandow had been receiving them from various upstarts for some time. But on this occasion his pocketbook was being threatened. His lucrative contracts with the various music hall chains all stated that should he ever lose his title of the strongest man in the world his engagements could be terminated. With the phrasing of his challenges, Arthur Saxon was actually intimating that *he* was the champion strongman. It was time for action.

One February evening at the Grand Theatre in Sheffield, in 1898, Eugen Sandow put on an old coat and a pair of dark glasses and took his place among the audience. When Saxon issued his customary challenge, Sandow went up on to the stage, stripped to his shirtsleeves and accepted the offer to attempt to duplicate Arthur Saxon's impressive routine of lifting, especially using the bent press, a gruelling one-handed lift which involved using a strange crouching position.

Saxon succeeded in bent pressing the weight at the second attempt. At first, Sandow could not lift the 264lb weight but he refused to leave the stage until he had hoisted the weight to his shoulder overhead at the fifth effort. However, he could not complete the technical demands of the lift, which called for the arm to be extended and locked above the head.

Subsequently, a jubilant Saxon started jeering at Eugen Sandow in his advertising matter, claiming to be the stronger of the two men. To safeguard his livelihood as a top-of-the-bill artiste, the Prussian had no recourse but to sue his German rival. It took three

years for the case to come for judgment before Mr Justice Bigham
at the Birmingham Assizes. It is plain from the court transcript
that Eugen Sandow had the time of his life at his appearance before
the judiciary. At one stage, before anyone could stop him, he had
divested himself of his upper garments with practised ease in order
to reveal his torso. On another occasion, when the strongman
was asked if he had been ill on the night of his appearance on the
Sheffield stage Sandow had boomed, 'I have never been unwell in
my life!'

The result centred on the evidence of a former member of the
Saxon Trio, Arno Saxon, who seemed to be bearing a grudge against
the others. Arno, no blood relation to the others, had originally
formed the trio but had left it. This man testified that Sandow had
never had a chance of bent-pressing the challenge weight. When
it was the Prussian's turn to lift it, the witness swore, a member
of Saxon's troupe had surreptitiously performed the old trick of
pouring quicksilver into one of the orbs, rendering it completely
out of kilter and impossible to control. The former member of the
troupe stated that Arthur Saxon always held the weight level when
he performed the bench press, but that he had noticed that Sandow
usually tilted the weight when he performed the lift. This would
cause the quicksilver to run into one of the globes.

Sandow declared that subsequently he had been able to purchase
the weight in question and that when he had examined the globes
it was revealed that they certainly could have been tampered with
in the manner described.

The Prussian was also aided by the obvious ignorance of the
finer points of weightlifting on the part of Mr Justice Bigham. The
judge was bewildered by the technical issues at stake and confused
by the contradictory evidence given by different witnesses.

Misunderstanding the technicalities of the complex bent press lift, he ruled in favour of Sandow, saying 'he handled the bell in exactly the same bodily attitude as Arthur'. This was manifestly untrue, but even in the august eyes of the law Eugen Sandow was still semi-officially the strongest man in the world. The jury found in his favour and decreed that £25 in damages should be paid to the strongman by Arthur Saxon. The Tivoli theatre company, which owned the Sheffield music hall, had to pay £2.

In another 'meeting of the titans', Thomas Inch would come face to face with his former employee, Edward Aston. Edward Aston was a subdued, down-to-earth Yorkshireman who had joined a Bradford weightlifting club at eighteen and had soon developed an impressive physique. He was so keen on his new hobby that he undertook extra training at home with a set of weights formed from large paint tins on the ends of a broom handle. He had to stop this, however, when one of the tins became dislodged and fell on his foot, breaking a bone.

Aston turned his mind to embarking upon a paid career when he started visiting touring strongman displays at music halls in neighbouring cities. As a challenger from the audience, he soon developed a reputation among the professionals as a youth to be avoided, especially after he succeeded in shouldering the challenge flour sack presented by Arthur Saxon.

For a time he toured the smaller halls in a strongman act with his brother, but then settled down in Westmoreland for a time, earning a steady living giving weightlifting exhibitions at summer country shows. During this time he was noticed and commended by such famous strongmen as Hackenschmidt the wrestler and Louis Uni. It was not long before Aston started receiving invitations to join established troupes. After some thought, he started touring with a mixed group of wrestlers and strongmen headed by Madrali, the Terrible Turk. Perhaps foolishly, Aston allowed himself to be persuaded to become involved with the grappling side of the displays, despite the fact that there was some animosity between the wrestlers and the weightlifters. One night his kneecap was smashed in a bout. He still managed to throw his opponent into the orchestra pit, but was put out of action for some time.

In 1911, two years after he had turned professional – and still irked by the challenge weight debacle – Aston challenged Thomas Inch for the title of Britain's strongest man. It was a sign of Sandow's pre-eminence among his peers that even the brash Inch did not dare to claim that the contest was for the Prussian's title of the world's strongest man.

A few years before, Inch had virtually awarded himself the national strongman championship, but he was so strong and famous that few of his rivals sought to dispute his claim. Inch had never made any attempt to conceal the extent of his success in all realms of the physical culture world and a number of his peers were happy to back Aston when he challenged Inch for his championship. As Aston weighed a few pounds over eleven stone to the Scarborough Hercules' fourteen stone plus, the bigger man was a strong favourite to win.

The contest was held at the grandiosely named International School of Physical Culture in the Tottenham Court Road in June. At the end of a series of wins, Aston pulled off a surprise by taking Inch's title from him with a total weight lifted of 1,215lbs to Inch's 1,167lbs. Inch was not a good loser. On subsequent occasions he put up heavier totals than the one accomplished by Aston and each time claimed that he had regained his championship *in absentia*, but this did not deter Edward Aston from billing himself as Britain's strongest man for the next twenty years.

Throughout his long career Aston maintained his popularity with audiences and his peers, if not with Thomas Inch, because he always seemed to maintain a sense of proportion. Once, when he had been shown round a steelworks in Barrow on a publicity jaunt, he watched the labourers pushing wheelbarrows loaded with iron ore up steep inclines, and emerged from the factory commenting that he had no business calling himself the strongest man in the country, as he could never do what the steelworkers accomplished day in and day out.

Those bodybuilders who had patented even the most bizarre of their own particular devices still kept a very strict eye on any efforts by rivals to copy them. Even the mighty Eugen Sandow, who generally kept away from less successful strongmen, swooped hungrily on a competitor when he sued a Hungarian hairdresser called Joseph Szalay who ran a gymnasium in the basement of his London business premises. Sandow accused Szalay of copying Sandow's Grip Barbell with his own smaller hand gripper. The court found in Sandow's favour and the court judgment cost 'Professor' Szalay a great deal of money. In a rare example of solidarity, a number of strongmen who did not like the way in which Sandow hounded other strength athletes banded together to give a benefit performance for the stricken Hungarian in Camberwell in 1912. Edward Aston and a number of others turned out for the occasion, and all the ticket proceeds were given to the 51-year-old Szalay.

Throughout his career, there was one rival strongman Sandow would never contemplate meeting in competition: the American Andrew Hall. Hall's speciality lay in having rocks broken with a sledgehammer on top of his head. For this purpose he wore a close-fitting metal helmet with a flat surface. The boulders were placed on top of the helmet, while an assistant hammered away at them enthusiastically. Optimistically Hall suggested Sandow meet him in a six-event match. Sandow could select any three weight-lifting feats for their challenge, while Hall would then ask the Prussian to stand quietly while three stones were smashed on top of his head. Sandow ignored the suggestion and continued to say no.

Despite his selective attitude to challengers and their challenges, Eugen Sandow soon redeemed himself in the eyes of the public – and his fellow strongmen – if such rehabilitation was needed. Only a month after the petulant claims and counter-claims at the Birmingham Assizes, in September 1901 Sandow organised the finals of his 'Great Competition' at the Royal Albert Hall in London. It was a nationwide bodybuilding competition and had been three years in the making. The contest had been designed to find the best built of all Sandow's physical culture pupils in the United Kingdom, 'to afford encouragement to those who are anxious to perfect their physiques'. Sandow's gymnasia, with specially selected instructors, were now in operation in most major British cities and were well attended. Writing in the *Harmsworth Magazine* in 1898, one pupil described his initiation:

I imagined I should be passed into the gymnasium to swing a dumb-bell for an hour or so, and be invited to drop in again when I was next that way. I was mistaken. Had my object been to enlist in Her Majesty's forces, the examinations and tests I was subjected to could not have been more extensive or peculiar. I was sounded, measured, weighed, pounded and questioned, the results being solemnly entered into a big ledger, as though it might all be used as evidence against me should the need ever arise.

Sandow first mooted the competition in the opening issue of a new magazine he issued in 1898. It was called *Physical Culture*, although the title was soon changed to *Sandow's Magazine of Physical Culture*, in order to cash in on its founder's growing fame. In its pages Sandow announced that a series of provincial contests would culminate in a great final, to be held in the capital. There would be a total of a thousand guineas in prize money, with £500 and a gold statuette going to the eventual winner.

The final was held on Saturday 14 September. Although the tournament was held at the height of the Boer War and on the same day as the American President William McKinley was assassinated at the Pan-American Exposition in Buffalo, New York, the hall was packed to its capacity of 15,000 people, with hundreds turned away. It was announced that all proceeds were to be donated to the Mansion House Transvaal War Relief Fund.

At eight o'clock in the evening the crowd rose to its feet as the band of the Irish Guards played Chopin's funeral march as a tribute to the dead President. Then, the house lights went out, twenty spotlights were switched on, and fifty boys from the Watford Orphan Asylum marched on. They were followed by displays of wrestling, gymnastics and fencing. Then the sixty finalists from all over the country marched on in leopard skins and tights, and lined up to be assessed.

The judges of the competition were the sculptor Sir Charles Lawes and the author Dr Arthur Conan Doyle. Sandow was on hand to act as a referee in case of differences of opinion. Slowly the judges walked up and down the lines of muscular men and picked a dozen finalists. There was then an intermission.

When the curtain rose after the break, Sandow went through a curtailed form of his act, posing, lifting weights and tearing packs of cards in half. He was applauded appreciatively. Next, the twelve finalists came on for the final judging section. Each one stood on a pedestal in turn, giving an exhibition of muscle control for the judges. Finally the winner was announced. He was William L. Murray of Nottingham. Billy Murray was quite a well-known sportsman in the Midlands, having played football as a full-back for Notts County.

The Great Competition secured enough publicity to satisfy even Sandow. Billy Murray promptly turned professional, touring the country billed as 'the most perfectly developed athlete of modern times'. With his supporting company he presented a simulated Roman gladiatorial display, with marching, weightlifting, mock fights and posing displays, ending with the whole company presenting a spectacular tableau.

The only sour note to the whole Great Competition was that the so-called solid gold statuette of Sandow presented to the winner turned out to be made of bronze with a layer of gold plating.

Even at the height of his career, however, not everyone was a fan of Sandow and his efforts to improve the physiques of the British nation. The playwright George Bernard Shaw, having attended some of the overdeveloped strongman's displays, put the case for all the wimps and weaklings of the world:

> Whenever I go to hear him lecture he is always
> saying, 'Why don't you get to be like me? and I
> look at him and I see a magnificent man, so
> muscular that he can hardly walk. Well, I want
> to walk!

Such attacks, no matter how famous and waspish the man launching them, were mere pinpricks to Sandow by this stage. With his magazine, postal courses, bodybuilding equipment, other commercial offerings and sold-out stage shows, the Prussian was indisputably pre-eminent among bodybuilders and strongmen in Great Britain. Others, however, were acquitting themselves well enough in the scramble for crumbs from the Prussian's table.

6

SEX, ADVENTURE AND ROMANCE

Like many strongmen, including old adversary Charles Sampson, Eugen Sandow spent some time in the USA. In 1893, he was recruited by an American impresario called Henry S. Abbey of the firm Abbey, Schoeffel and Gru, and appeared as a supporting act in a show called 'Adonis' at the Casino Theatre in New York. He performed his usual act of posing and allowing horses to run over a reinforced plank balanced across his chest. At first, things did not go too well for the strongman. The show was a dreary one and the strongman's act was wedged in between two dull and uninspiring sketches. To make matters worse, a heat-wave kept the New York audiences away. Sandow also incurred the jealousy of his leading man, an actor called Henry E. Dixey, who was unfortunate enough to appear semi-nude onstage immediately before Sandow's entrance. The *New York World* of 18 June 1893, made much of this fact:

> New York has come to look upon Dixey as a fairly well-made young man. When New York has seen Sandow after Dixie, however, New York will realize what a wretched, scrawny creature the well-built man is compared with a perfect man.

Then, as happened so often in Sandow's life, he experienced a stroke of luck. In this case it was to transform his future and lead to the second great physical culture renaissance in North America.

The good fortune came in the shape of Florenz 'Flo' Ziegfeld, a young entrepreneur, who hitched his wagon to the strongman's star and as a result saw his own career take off. He was born in Chicago in 1867, the son of the founder of the elite Chicago Musical College, a private establishment. Flo Ziegfeld did not share his father's lofty tastes and caused trouble at an early age when he started charging his friends to see what he swore were invisible fish in a bowl of water. A born and highly accomplished liar, he was sent off to a Wyoming cattle ranch by his parents for stretching the truth once too often. He returned chastened to help his father at the college, but was much more interested in ballroom dancing and going to shows than in further refining the musical taste of his father's pupils.

At an early age, he was able to come to his father's assistance in an unusual manner. Ziegfeld senior, revealing an unexpectedly skittish side to his nature, had opened a Chicago nightclub called the Trocadero, hoping to cash in on the crowds attending the city's recently opened World Fair. The Columbian Exhibition was designed to celebrate the four hundredth anniversary of the discovery of America by Christopher Columbus in 1492. The show received its official opening ceremony in 1892, but it was a year later before the first paying customers were allowed in. From this unpromising start the exposition gathered strength and was the largest display of its kind so far witnessed, covering six hundred acres of land, lasting for six months and welcoming over twenty-seven million visitors. The emphasis throughout was on exoticism. Forty-six different countries were represented by stands or displays, and there were hundreds of unofficial sideshows, all lit by millions of Thomas Edison's new electric light bulbs, powered by generators, turning night into garish, noisy day

The exposition was crammed with great performers, to such an extent that it came to be defined by the number of talented acts that were denied permission to exhibit their wares on the sprawling site. Young Scott Joplin, soon to be the ragtime king, had to be content with fronting his first band at a saloon (some said brothel) outside its boundaries. The great Buffalo Bill Cody was not allowed to bring his Congress of Rough Riders within the walls. Acting on the principle that if you can't join them, beat them, he set up his tents on the fringes of the fair and made a fortune.

Despite the crowds, Mr Ziegfeld senior soon realised that he was out of his depth even in such shallow waters of popular entertainment and hastily handed over the management of his failing club to Flo, begging him to get it running at a profit again. His son responded to the challenge with alacrity. Touring Europe, he booked up acts and transported them back to Chicago. Even with these new acts, he soon decided that his club needed a charismatic headliner to draw in the crowds, preferably one who would work cheaply.

One night, the young impresario caught Sandow's poorly attended act in New York. Ziegfeld was not particularly impressed with the strongman's weightlifting displays, but he noticed that as soon as Eugen Sandow went into his muscle-flexing display, the women in the audience were riveted. Never mind the chain breaking and card tearing; here was the perfect male body to be exploited.

Acting at once, the showman signed Sandow and bought his contract from the promoter who had imported him into the USA. Disillusioned with his artiste's lack of success, Henry S. Abbey let him go willingly. Ziegfeld could not afford the salary demanded by the Prussian, so he offered him 10 per cent of all ticket sales, assuring the other man that this sum would far exceed any steady wage that Sandow might have in mind. He was soon proved to be right.

Before Sandow could open at the Trocadero, Flo Ziegfeld embarked upon a whirlwind publicity campaign to make his charge famous at the Columbian Exhibition. Billstickers pasted hundreds of posters of a semi-nude Sandow on all available walls. As well as newspaper interviews, Sandow casually performed feats of strength in public places to draw attention to both himself and his act.

Eugen Sandow made his debut at the Chicago Trocadero on 1 August 1893. Ziegfeld's publicity blitz had worked; the house was packed. The show began at eight o'clock in the evening and meals and drinks were served throughout each performance. Flo Ziegfeld's talent-spotting tours were reflected in the eclectic form of the performances on offer. The showman was firmly of the opinion that any popular show should contain sex, adventure and romance. All three ingredients were presented on the stage of the Trocadero during the run of Eugen Sandow's show.

An acrobat called Astarte performed aerial revolutions, to be followed by Gustave Marschner, 'the champion trick cyclist of the world', who was said to be the possessor of a medal valued at £150, won at the Leipzig world championships in the previous year. He claimed to have a repertoire of two hundred cycling tricks. Next came a musical interlude, with Russian dances performed by the Ivanoff Imperial Troupe. There was a gymnastics display from Marko and Dunham, then, at 10.45 p.m., Eugen Sandow, the top-of-the-bill act appeared and went through his routines for an hour. At Ziegfeld's request he opened with what was to prove the highlight of his performance – the posing routine. He displayed himself in a large upright cabinet lined with black velvet, with spotlights from above emphasising his musculature. His body hair was shaved and he was dusted with white powder, to provide the effect of a living marble Greek statue. An orchestra conducted by Sandow's friend and companion Martinus Sieveking provided music specially composed by the conductor as Sandow posed in the form of famous classical statues. He constantly flexed and relaxed his well-defined muscles and even made them dance in time to the musical accompaniment. At the end, Eugen Sandow hurried off the stage to tumultuous applause to change for the strongman section of his act, which followed at once. This had not varied much since his British music-hall tours of the last three years, except that he now also opened a safe with his teeth and claimed that the weights he was tossing about weighed in excess of 300lbs. To justify this claim, at the climax of his act the Prussian hoisted an odd-looking barbell overhead. Instead of the usual orbs, there was an enclosed wicker basket at either end. When he lowered the contraption to the stage the baskets were opened to reveal a man crouching inside each one.

The first night was a great success, but Flo did not ease up on his publicity blitz. While constantly fine-tuning the strongman's act, Ziegfeld also sold thousands of photographs of Sandow wearing only a fig leaf – with Sandow's full approval and cooperation. He also initiated a newspaper discussion as to how the fig leaf might have been kept in place. The general consensus of opinion was that either it was suspended from a wire around Sandow's waist that later had been airbrushed out of the photographs, or that it had been pasted on.

For weeks Ziegfeld and Sandow existed in a state of permanent mutual delight at the way in which events were unfolding. At last the inventive 25-year-old Ziegfeld had a suitable and amenable subject for all the publicity stunts he had been dreaming of for so long. Sandow, for his part, realised that in the flamboyant American he had a showman of genius to guide him and transport his performances to the highest levels.

Ziegfeld had been right about the handsome Sandow's appeal to the ladies, playing a trump card to enormous effect quite early on in Sandow's run at the Trocadero nightclub. One night Ziegfeld himself appeared at the end of the strongman's performance to make a surprise announcement. He declared that if any lady in the theatre was prepared to donate the sum of $300 to charity then she would be invited to a private interview with Sandow in the strongman's dressing room after the show.

It was a risky gimmick and could have gone wrong. But to the showman's relief, two prominent society ladies, Mrs Potter Palmer and Mrs George Pullman, neither a shrinking violet, accepted the offer at once. Mrs Potter Palmer, the wife of a real estate baron, was the Chairman of the Board of Lady Managers of the Chicago Exposition, and was game for most things. The *Chicago Herald* wrote of her 'Society – even Chicago society – which Mrs Potter Palmer loves, is but a vast and merry whirl and she craves more.' Mrs Pullman, whose wealthy husband devised the improved railway sleeping car bearing his name, was equally outgoing.

Both ladies signed their cheques and visited the Prussian in his dressing room after the final curtain, chaperoned by a covey of reporters who made frantic notes as the two visitors sat demurely listening to a lecture on the basic principles of health, delivered in Sandow's guttural German accent. Afterwards, they were both allowed to touch the strongman's quivering biceps.

The attendance of these two society doyennes opened the floodgates. Soon, after each performance the strongman's dressing room was as busy as Piccadilly Circus as eager, wealthy female fans crowded in to see the strongman. A piece of doggerel in a Californian newspaper summed up the situation in which women of all ages and backgrounds flocked to see the strongman at his afternoon performances:

> Oh dear, how the ladies did hustle to see
> The perfect man pose at his great matinee...
> The ladies from most of our Art Schools were there,
> The 'old' and 'homely', the young and the fair.

The Chicago Exposition ran for six months and, as long as Eugen Sandow continued to perform at the Trocadero, Ziegfeld kept his one-man publicity-machine turning. He even made a point of publishing Sandow's measurements in the public prints as often as possible:

Weight: 199 lb   Height: 5 ft 8.5 in. Waist: 29 ins   Chest: 48 in.
Neck: 18.5 in.   Biceps: 18.5 in.   Thigh: 26.5 in. Calves: 18 in.

He also took every opportunity to have the strongman examined by publicity-seeking doctors, who would declare afterwards that Sandow almost certainly was the most perfectly developed man in the world.

It was on this aspect that Flo Ziegfeld concentrated his publicity efforts. He no longer declared that his man was the strongest in the world; there were in fact by now a number of shapeless, shambling human gorillas performing in the circuits who could lift heavier poundages above their heads than Sandow could. But who cared? What the impresario was intent on putting over was the sheer shapeliness and sex appeal of the strongman. For a start he discarded the Prussian's trademark leotards, tights and singlets and had him performing his posing exhibitions in skimpy briefs. He succeeded to such an extent that in 1893, as Sandow's bandwagon started to roll in the USA, one newspaper declared that if the strongman's display had been attempted in a theatre by a woman, it would have been banned by the authorities.

Ziegfeld also made it plain that, as well as being as handsome as a Greek god, Eugen Sandow was a very strong man. When Amy Leslie, the drama critic of the *Chicago Daily News*, arranged to interview the Prussian in a public park, the lurking showman bribed a guard to reprimand the strongman for picking flowers. Sandow held the official in the air until Miss Leslie begged him to lower the guard to the ground. The guard pocketed his $5 and the journalist had her exclusive story.

After three months at the Trocadero in Chicago, Flo Ziegfeld decided that the rest of the country was ready for Sandow or at least that the section that lay along the coast of California was ripe for exploitation. He put together a variety show, headed by Sandow, and headed west with it.

It was a significant moment in American vaudeville. Flo Ziegfeld was to become the leading showman of his era and, more or less by chance, Eugen Sandow was to become the first fortunate recipient of the American's enthusiasm and burgeoning expertise. He even had the distinction of having his name included in the title billing.

The company was called 'Sandow's Trocadero Vaudevilles'. The tour, which was a smash hit from the start, was to occupy seven months. In that time the supporting acts changed from time to time but Ziegfeld, who travelled with the show, put the bill together as carefully as a jigsaw puzzle.

At first Ziegfeld did not tamper with the traditional pattern of the vaudeville bill. Most of them opened with a 'dumb' act, perhaps dancers, to give the audience a chance to settle down. They would be followed by a reliable singing act, or something similar. Then it would be time for a 'name' act, someone who would be recognised, at least by reputation, by most of the spectators. Next would come a comic sketch, which led in turn to a spectacular display by a magician or a troupe of animals. After the intermission there would be another dumb act, possibly a troupe of acrobats. There would be time for another comic sketch, and then the star of the show would appear. Finally there would be another dumb act to clear the theatre before the second performance of the evening.

All these staple ingredients were present in 'Sandow's Trocadero Vaudeville Follies'. Among the constantly changing supporting acts, the principal comedian was veteran Billy B. Van, who went back as far as the blackface minstrel shows and had appeared with James J. Corbett in the former heavyweight champion's monologue performances. Nick Kaufmann introduced his cycle ball routine, playing a form of polo on two wheels with an assistant. Tom Browne was a *siffleur*, billed as 'a rival to the mocking bird: the most remarkable and brilliant whistler in the world'. The versatile Browne could also imitate tunes being played on the cello and the trombone, although presumably not at the same time.

Miss Scottie introduced her almost-human dog, a collie able to play cards and solve mathematical calculations. There were five trapeze artistes, collectively known as the Flying Jordans, 'performing the most graceful and daring aerial acts ever witnessed'. Amann, an impersonator, travelled with the show for most of the time, depicting different characters from history. The closing dumb act was often Herr August Dewell, a Scandinavian gymnast.

Above all there was Eugen Sandow, the Monarch of Muscle and a promoter's publicity-conscious dream. Sandow was up for anything that would advertise his show. Tirelessly he gave inter-view after interview to local reporters wherever he was appearing, performed feats of strength in public to attract the crowds into the theatres, and was never afraid to trade upon the drawing power of his good looks. His blonde curly hair, upturned moustache and symmetrical build were to be featured on posters everywhere.

And always there was Flo Ziegfeld, preparing the way for his main event, making sure that the strongman's name was seldom out of the newspapers. One of them, the *San Francisco Call* of 14 April 1894, described Sandow's triumphal entry into the journal's city:

> Eugen Sandow, the perfect man, will arrive in the City tomorrow morning to commence his engagement at the Vienna Prater. He will be escorted to the Palace Hotel, and on Sunday will receive fifty specially invited newspaper men and physicians.

Gathering converts to his cause all over North America, Sandow soon found many men determined to imitate his success. One man of particular annoyance was a competitor who went by the name of Sandowe. His real name was Irving Montgomery, although in some contemporary law court accounts which littered his career he appears as Montgomery Irving. He was naturally big and strong, and hailed from Birmingham in the UK, drifting into the strongman business when Sampson and his partner Cyclops visited the area with their act. The impressive-looking Irving had accepted Cyclops's challenge from the stage for a wrestling match. To deter potential opponents and gain a psychological advantage over them, it was announced before the exhibition that no champion professional grappler would take Cyclops on unless the latter agreed to omit certain lethal holds and throws from his repertoire. Actually the coin-breaker was not nearly as rugged as he appeared. When Irving materialised with his challenge, both Sampson and Cyclops were worried. They were considerably relieved when, as he was getting changed backstage for the bout, Irving intimated casually that for a trifling consideration of a £5 note he would throw the bout to Cyclops.

As it happened, when they entered the ring Cyclops discovered, somewhat to his surprise, that he could defeat the Birmingham strongman without resorting to bribery. Nevertheless, Irving's pragmatic approach to victory and defeat had impressed Cyclops. When he and Sampson subsequently parted company he invited Irving to join him in a new professional pairing and accompany him on a tour to the United States.

In order to boost Irving's reputation before they left the UK, in 1895 Cyclops arranged a public trial of strength between his new partner and his former one. Irving met Sampson at the Grand Theatre of Varieties, Liverpool. Sampson defied Irving to duplicate a series of feats. As the younger man looked on with growing trepidation, Charles Sampson lifted a barbell from the floor to his chest, then overhead, back to his shoulders and then to the floor. He then bent a series of iron bars out of shape by smashing them against his arms. Finally the man from Alsace-Lorraine stood on a chair with his feet strapped to the seat, bent over, picked up a heavy dumbbell from the stage and lifted it overhead. Irving tried in vain to duplicate the feats but left the stage admitting failure.

Soon after, Irving and Cyclops were on the other side of the Atlantic, with Irving adopting the professional nomenclature of

Sandowe, hoping to use this alias to pick up theatrical bookings in more remote areas of the country. It did not work. Soon Irving was being referred to scornfully in newspapers as 'the false Sandow'. The *New York Dramatic Mirror* of 5 March 1894 wrote: 'Sandow has not only a rival but a fraudulent imitator in a person calling himself "Sandowe" who recently appeared at the Buckingham Theatre in Louisville.'

Nevertheless, the spiky and notoriously litigious Eugen Sandow could not allow this passing off to proceed unchallenged. Earlier he had pursued the imposter all over Britain in order to make his imitator desist, with similar writs and injunctions. Now he was suing Irving in the USA and was to be successful. The Birmingham strongman was fined $100 and costs, and ordered to stop billing himself as Sandowe.

As would be expected Sandow made the most of these court hearings, held on 21 April 1894:

> Arrayed in a glossy plug hat, white hands encased in Parisian gloves, and otherwise dressed to kill, he looked strangely out of place among the busy crowd of legal practitioners. Sandow took a seat, raised his hat, smoothed his glossy curls and beamed on the throng.

As it happened, Irving did not fare too badly from the resulting publicity. So pronounced was the strongman cult in the USA that he was recruited by a producer to play the part of Ursus, the strongman, in a touring production of the sex-and-sandals play *Quo Vadis*, based on the novel. A contemporary newspaper account, however, was quick to remind readers of his attempt to copy Sandow and went on to say of his stilted acting performance that Irving 'was

physique conscious throughout the play, and his appearances were
a series of poses'.

Back on tour no opportunity for plugging the act was lost by the
Prussian or his promoter. Reporters were even invited into Sandow's
dressing room after performances to witness the strongman taking
ice-cold baths in a portable bath and then enjoying a cigar and a
glass of malt whisky before going off in search of a game of billiards.

Before the tour was over, Sandow was famous and Flo Ziegfeld
had made a quarter of a million dollars. Obviously not every stunt
attempted came off. On a brief visit to Chicago, Flo had the bright
idea that Sandow should emulate the Biblical Samson and wrestle
with a lion. Unfortunately, eager to preserve his star attraction,
Ziegfeld took too many precautions. The elderly lion was heavily
muzzled and over sedated, as was reported by the *Brooklyn Eagle*:

San Francisco, Cal. May 23. Over three thousand people assembled
at Central Park last night to witness a wrestling match between
Sandow, the perfect man, and Colonel Daniel E. Boone's tame lion
Commodore. Commodore was muzzled, his paws being encased
in boxing gloves, and he was so handicapped that free action was
almost impossible. When Sandow entered the iron cage the lion
was lying on all fours and no amount of teasing could get him to
stand up or lose his temper. Sandow lifted him from the ground
and swung him around and around, but it was of no avail. After ten
minutes of this farce the match was given to Sandow.

Indeed, the show and Sandow were not without criticism. Sandow
was sometimes accused of being a trifle too smug and pleased
with himself. One newspaper reported in 1893 that after he had

supported a team of footballers on his chest, 'the big fellow is able to spring up and make his particularly self-satisfied bow'. There were also persistent annoying whispers about the strongman's sexuality, with Sandow suffering another minor professional setback when a report was circulated from the manager of one vaudeville hall. The manager commented on the performance of one of Sandow's latest rivals, Al Treloar (Albert Toof Jenkins), who had once been employed to clear surplus weights from the stage after Sandow's performances at the Chicago Exhibition. The theatre manager said that Treloar's performances had been much more successful than those of Sandow's because the American was obviously the manlier of the pair.

In an effort to deflect accusations that his leading man was homosexual, Flo Ziegfeld began to emphasise the less obvious physical measurements of the Prussian. Much play was made with the design and placement of the fig leaves that Sandow wore in his photographs. Some were designed to draw attention to the size of the strongman's penis, or even to hint at the presence of an erection. Stories of ersatz romances between Sandow and various actresses and music hall stars were planted in the newspapers. At the same time the promoter did his best to discourage rumours that the strongman was greatly admired by such well-known gay poets as Edmund Gosse and John Addington Symonds. The former, it was said, had even taken some nude photographs of Sandow with him to the 1890 funeral of Robert Browning in Westminster Abbey, in order to alleviate any possibility of boredom.

But these were minor niggles and largely ignored by Eugen Sandow's growing army of fans. During this hectic period, Sandow took time off to return briefly to Britain to marry Blanche Brookes, the daughter of a well-known Manchester photographer. Little is known about their lives together. Sandow was notoriously secretive about his private life and, although there were two daughters of the union, the marriage does not seem to have been a happy one. The marriage perhaps came at a convenient time to lay to rest rumours of the strongman's real sexual prowess and it was probably no coincidence that the ever-watchful Flo Ziegfeld was the best man at the ceremony, held at Manchester Cathedral on 8 August 1894.

When Sandow returned to the USA with his bride to fulfil a nunber of contractual appearances, Martinus Sieveking moved out of the home they had been sharing. Eventually he was to secure a minor reputation as a musician, but at first he did not find it easy to pursue a solo career. After one solo performance at Carnegie Hall in New York in 1896, the music writer for the *Brooklyn Eagle* complained that other critics had been too hard on the young pianist: 'It is quite true that Sieveking is no such pianist as Paderewsli or Rosenthal. He lacks the magnetic charm of one and the sensational facility of the other, but there is no reason why he should be jumped upon so furiously.'

Back in the USA, Sandow was still on the crest of a wave, even if the newly installed Mrs Sandow did make her husband give up his practice of providing private performances of muscular development after his shows. As the Trocadero troupe moved from city to city, Flo Ziegfeld continued to keep the publicity drums beating. Everything was grist to his particular mill. Even when an unfortunate resident of Flatbush went mad in September 1894 and was committed for suffering from delusions that he was Eugen Sandow, Ziegfeld saw to it that the delusions were fully reported in the newspapers:

He nearly scared the wits out of his wife a few weeks ago by piling all the parlour furniture on the piano and compelling her to take a seat on the top of the pile while he dropped on his hands and knees, crawled under the piano and attempted to balance the whole business on his chest. When he had, as he believed, accomplished the feat, he flew into an insane rage because his wife was unwise enough to tell him he had not budged the piano.

Finally the troupe was dissolved. It had been an outstanding success, but both Ziegfeld and Sandow wanted to move on to other things. Slow horses at too many track meetings had lost Ziegfeld much of the money he had made out of Sandow, but all his life he was to bounce back from such reverses. His was now already a name to be reckoned with on the American theatrical scene. The young American, still under thirty, wanted to put on musical shows in New York. He was to succeed in this aim and become a major player along the Great White Way, with his constant ostentatious search for stars and stated aim of 'glorifying the American girl'. The spectacular 'Ziegfeld Follies' became an annual event on Broadway between 1907 and 1931.

For Sandow, there was first a little local difficulty to overcome. While he had been milking the applause from his American stage appearances, Sandow had been forced to return to New York periodically for yet another appearance in a court of law. The reasons for his visit were described in the *New York Times*:

Eugene Sandow, the strongman, came to town from Boston yesterday to press his charges of assault and blackmail against Sarah E. White, known as 'Lurline, the Water Queen'.

The case and its antecedents took the Prussian on a journey into the past, all the way back to the night when he had launched his career by challenging and defeating Sampson at the Imperial Theatre in London for the title of the strongest man in the world.

Sarah White, or Lurline as she was better known, had been the woman sitting in the theatre. It was claimed that she had substituted the genuine arm bracelets for doctored ones when they were passed among the audience. She and Sandow had once been friends but were now bitterly opposed and the cause of the dispute was money. Lurline claimed that the strongman was in her debt financially. In the original court deposition, the Water Queen, as she was sometimes billed, claimed that a down-and-out Sandow had borrowed the sum of £11 from her in Brussels when he had been appearing there with his acrobatic act with Françoise. Subsequently, she asserted, the strongman had left the city without repaying the money.

Some time later, when Sandow was waiting in London to challenge Sampson, he had approached Lurline again. She had been on a music hall tour of England. On this occasion, claimed the Water Queen, Sandow had visited her in the capital on several occasions and had borrowed another £400 from her. She had also fitted the poverty-stricken Prussian out with some new clothes.

When Sandow had achieved success in vaudeville in the USA, Lurline had written to him, asking for repayment of the debt. The strongman had ignored her. Lurline had written again, calling Sandow a blackguard. Eventually she had caught up with him outside the Casino Theatre in New York. There had been a sharp exchange of words, culminating in Lurline raising a riding crop she had been carrying. Sandow said that if she attempted to strike him he would seize her hand and crush it. The Water Queen then hit him across the face several times with the crop, before the pair had to be separated by onlookers.

All this and more came out in court. At first, Sandow denied that he owed his accuser anything. Then he heard that Louis Atilla, his former stage partner and trainer, was crossing the Atlantic to give evidence on behalf of Lurline. Sandow began to have second thoughts but, as it happened, Atilla arrived too late to appear in the witness box. The case was postponed and then abandoned when Sandow paid Lurline a sum of money in an out of court settlement.

It was a sour note on which to end what had been a triumphant three years. Sandow quietly left for London, leaving behind quite a legacy in the USA. He had achieved personal fame and fortune. He had given the national physical culture movement a considerable fillip. He had set thousands of men and quite a few women on the path to improved health and strength. He had taken the Grecian ideal of physical perfection out of museums and archaeological digs and on to the accessible music hall and vaudeville stages and into people's homes.

He also left behind him the seed corn for a revival of the professional strongman cult in the USA. His writings and stage displays encouraged others to develop their bodies. He also inspired entrepreneurs who went on to build on his work. Louis Atilla settled in New York, slowly renewed his previous friendship with Sandow and developed a highly successful gymnasium catering to the needs of athletes, businessmen and politicians. The Harvard-educated Al Treloar, who had once been an assistant working in the background of Sandow's stage act, won the first major American physique contest at Madison Square Garden in January 1904, and used it as a springboard to a lucrative stage career and then a long term as

LEFT Described as having the perfect male body, Eugen Sandow was one of the most successful strongmen of his time. His challenge to Charles A. Sampson in 1889 kick-started the age of the professional strongman and earned him the title of world's strongest man.

BELOW Sandow showing some of the poses that made his postcards sell in tens of thousands. He was the first strongman to highlight 'body beautiful' posing displays in his act.

LEFT Defeated by Sandow, Charles A. Sampson continued to call himself the strongest man on earth, despite all evidence to the contrary.

BELOW Cyclops, Sampson's partner. His claims to be able to break coins between his fingers and to be able to incapacitate opponents with his wrestling holds were treated with derision by his fellow strongmen.

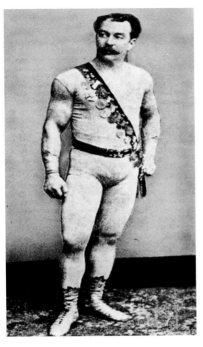

ABOVE LEFT Louis Atilla (Louis Durlacher) was Sandow's first trainer and had a claim to be one of the pioneers of modern physical education.

ABOVE RIGHT The Saxon Trio, from left to right: Herman Saxon, Adolf Berg and Arthur Saxon. The personnel of the act varied but, when they were sober, they were the strongest conglomeration on the halls.

LEFT Handbill displaying items from Sandow's stage act. The strongman did his best to avoid weightlifting stereotypes and always strove to include more spectacular acts, culminating in supporting a horse on his shoulders.

Advertising poster for the enormously popular 'Sandow Trocadero Vaudevilles', which toured the USA for seven months in 1894. The show cemented Sandow's fame and made the producer, Florenz Ziegfeld, a wealthy man.

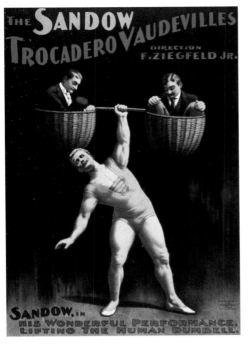

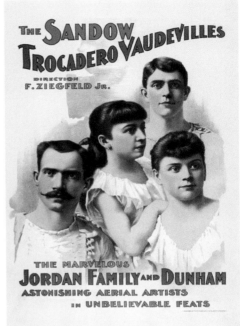

ABOVE LEFT Sandow lifting the 'human barbell' on his tour of the USA in 1894.

ABOVE RIGHT The Flying Jordans supported Sandow on his tour of the USA. A well-known trapeze act, they claimed to have been the first performers to bring off a double somersault into the arms of a waiting catcher.

LEFT Originally billed as the 'Wild Men of Borneo', Hiram and Barney Davis were a pair of very strong dwarfs from Connecticut. They toured with circuses for decades as Waino and Plutanor, exhibiting feats of strength and wrestling all comers.

LEFT Georg Hackenschmidt, 'the Russian Lion', the first freestyle wrestling champion of the world and a genuinely strong man. His producer, C. B. Cochran, had to persuade him to go easy when he wrestled challengers on the halls.

RIGHT Advertising bill for Hackenschmidt. Cultured and well-read, and a friend of George Bernard Shaw, he wrote a number of books on philosophy after his retirement.

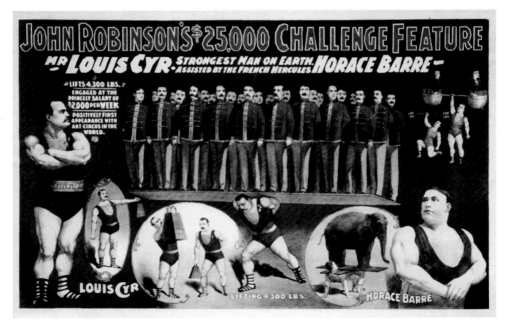

A circus poster from 1898, advertising the mighty Louis Cyr and his partner Horace Barre. Included in the strongman stunts illustrated is Cyr's documented feat of supporting on his shoulders a platform containing twenty-five men.

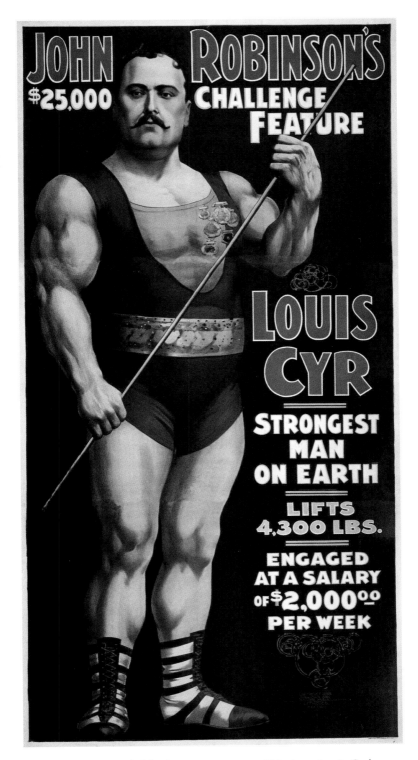

Although he was probably the strongest man of his time, Louis Cyr's act tended to be repetitious and uninteresting. He set weightlifting records but hated touring and retired early.

ABOVE LEFT Launceston Elliot took first and second places in weightlifting competitions in the 1896 Athens Olympics. Four years later he was unsuccessful in the Olympic discus event and ventured into the world of professional strongmen.

ABOVE RIGHT From 1911, Edward Aston held the title of Britain's strongest man for twenty-three years. He was the first Briton to lift 300lbs above his head with one hand and later retired to become an adagio dancer on the music halls.

LEFT Sandow the businessman. In addition to designing and selling bodybuilding equipment and postal courses, he produced his own magazine, advertised various products and manufactured cocoa, cigars and corsets.

an influential physical culture coach. Having witnessed Sandow's shows several times in Chicago, Bernard Macfadden took himself from practically slave labour to become a great guru of popular physical excellence in the USA, publishing a string of magazines and books on the subject, including the influential magazine *Physical Culture* (not to be mistaken with Sandow's own *Physical Culture*). The newly named Bernarr (a name more resembling the macho roar of a lion) built a bodybuilding empire and became a wealthy if controversial strength and health guru. Inspired by Sandow's fame in Europe, Richard K. Fox, editor of the *Police Gazette*, organised the first national strongman contest in the USA.

Before this there had been a few strongmen touring the vaudeville halls in the USA and writing about the advantages of exercise before Eugen Sandow ever entered the country. The Prussian's publicity efforts were to elevate them even further. One of these strongmen was Adrian P. Schmidt, a tiny but fiercely muscled Frenchman domiciled in the USA. He had made his reputation on the halls with demonstrations of the strength of his fingers. Schmidt was able to hook his index digit around a chain above his head and by sheer controlled power haul himself up steadily until he was level with the chain. In 1901 he wrote the bestselling *Illustrated Hints for Health and Strength for Busy People*.

Another bodybuilder whose severe visage glowered down from hundreds of American newspaper advertisements at the beginning of the twentieth century was 'Professor' Anthony Barker. He had toured the halls billed as the Herculean Comedian with a slapstick strongman duo but had retired from this to found his postal course, under the slogan 'Why Not Be a Perfect Man?' He also published a bodybuilding book a year before the arrival of Sandow, under the title of *Physical Culture Simplified*.

Perhaps inadvertently Schmidt and Barker had stumbled across a vein that was about to be exploited widely on the other side of the Atlantic: the profitable sharing of their knowledge with the man in the street.

ELABORATE NONSENSE

When Eugen Sandow returned from the USA to found his physical culture empire he discovered that many of the professional strongmen that he had left behind him had similar ideas, if on a smaller scale. The strongmen had no idea how long their fame and drawing power would last, so they did their best to cash in on the moment. They sold signed photographs at the stage doors after their shows, some of which depicted them nude in 'artistic' poses and had a ready sale among the gay community. They wrote fanciful autobiographies, or had them written for them. Above all, they offered to pass on their secrets of strength to others. Newspapers were filled with advertisements for these mainly spurious bodybuilding courses designed for little men who desired to become big. There was an eager uptake of such printed sheets by members of the public.

There were reasons for such a large potential market. Most men of the time were physically weak and had poor diets. By the time of the Boer War, England was primarily a nation of town-dwellers. Army recruiting figures for the period, released in 1903, described the condition of those would-be volunteers who had passed a preliminary test and had been forwarded for further physical checks. Over six hundred thousand men were processed through to this second stage. Of this total more than two hundred thousand were rejected as being physically inadequate. Among the men accepted and recruited, another five thousand could not cope with the training. After two years in the ranks another fourteen thousand had been medically discharged.

Yet there were encouraging signs and stirrings of interest in physical development, especially among the middle classes. Following upon the example of Hippolyte Triat, a retired music hall strongman who opened a gymnasium in Paris in 1847 and charged a fee for membership, others began to open gymnasiums in the larger cities of Europe. Organised sport, with its requirement of physical fitness, started to encourage men and sometimes women to exercise. The Oxford–Cambridge Boat Race became established in 1856 and athletics clubs began to spread. The Matterhorn was scaled in 1854, encouraging mountaineering as a hobby for those who could afford it. By 1863, the first professional football clubs had been formed and matches were being well attended.

Increasingly there was the example of the Greek Ideal. In the eighteenth century, two Englishmen called James Stuart and Nicholas Revatt spent two years studying architecture and art in Greece. In 1762, they published *The Antiquities of Athens and Other Monuments of Greece*, showing the muscular symmetry favoured by ancient Greek sculptors. This started an interest in the artistic depiction of the well-developed gods, as men began to compare their own bodies with those of the marble deities. At the beginning of the next century, Lord Elgin brought the Elgin Marbles to the British Museum, bribing the Ottoman custodians to release some of the statues of the Parthenon in Athens. This helped spread the philosophy of the Greeks, who believed that the human body could reflect the ideal beauty of the gods, symmetrical in form and heavily muscled. Artists and sculptors of the Renaissance took this up in their idealised depictions of the human form. By the nineteenth century, photographs of heavily muscled models could also be produced.

The advent of the Young Men's Christian Association also helped in the promotion of health and strength. In 1841, Sir George Williams created the movement in London and by 1854 there were almost four hundred of these institutions in different countries. Originally intended 'for the improving of the spiritual condition of young men engaged in the drapery and other trades', the aims of the movement soon widened. Sir George emphasised the importance of using these institutions for improving the health and strength of their members, saying at an 1864 conference, 'We must add physical recreation to all YMCAs.'

These factors, allied to the performances of Sandow and his peers on music hall and vaudeville stages, led to thousands of would-be athletes toiling away to the point of exhaustion in the privacy of their homes over barbells, dumbbells, chest expanders, the long-handled wooden swing implements known as Indian clubs, and many other esoteric forms of apparatus in order to develop the body beautiful. Even when they did not succeed, still they enhanced the fame and bank balances of those supplying their courses and apparatus.

Most of these publications were catchpenny items designed to part the credulous from their money. Despite the flamboyant public claims for the efficacy of their exercise routines and their insistence that once they themselves had been mere pigeon-chested weaklings, most professional strongmen were aware that the most effective way to develop an outstanding physique was to have been born robust, preferably of big parents, to have developed an above-average bodyweight and mass naturally, and have nurtured it by hard manual work from an early age. A large number of these potential strength athletes were not, however, particularly tall; many of them were only of average height or below. The more fortunate among them would have developed a local reputation for their crude feats of strength in the workplace at an early age and have attracted the attention of an experienced and knowledgeable trainer at a well-run gymnasium. They would have then embarked upon a long-term system of progressive training with heavy weights, often lasting for years, making sure to increase the weight of the barbells and dumbbells being used at regular intervals. At the end of this process of progressive weight training, a few aspirants would emerge with enough strength and savvy to be taken under the wing of an agent or manager and then embark upon careers in travelling circuses and on the music halls and vaudeville theatres.

Throughout their careers, when they were not travelling, most professional strongmen spent hours every day improving their physiques and increasing their strength. The Russian Pyotr Kryloff, (the King of Kettlebells), a former sailor, who performed regularly on the halls until he was sixty, described a typical day's training, undertaken when he was at the peak of his music hall career in an edition of *Hercules* magazine in 1914.

After waking up, I breathe deep fresh air for 10 minutes, then I practise with rubber bands (chest expanders). I pull them in front of me,
overhead, from the back, with each arm, etc. Then I do push-ups on
palms or fingers for no more than 100 reps. I run for 12–18 minutes.
Jump like a frog: short jumps on toes with deep squat. I take a hot
or cold shower. In half an hour I have breakfast: eggs, 2 cups of milk
and 1 cup of liquid very sweet tea. I go for a walk. I have dinner at
5 p.m. After 2 hours I train with heavy kettlebells: clean and press

or clean and jerk (on alternating days) a 5-pound barbell (80 kg) standing and lying for 50 times (5 sets of 10 reps). Then I press two 32-kg kettlebells for 50 times (5 sets of 10 reps). I squat with 5-pound barbell for 100 times. Then I take stairs with a heavy man on my back. To finish my training I exercise with 20 pounds (8 kg) dumbbells, take them both in one hand when training biceps. After training I take a shower and go for a walk.

Edward Aston, the British physical culturist, was equally straightforward about the amount of effort needed to build up an impressive physique. In his instructional book *Modern Weightlifting and How to Gain Strength*, he described his own training regime, especially before a challenge contest. He would spend the morning walking, have a good lunch and then engage in weightlifting activities throughout the afternoon. After another stroll in the evening he would go to bed early.

Needless to say, the prospect of such arduous and daunting full-time daily routines would not have attracted the attention and shillings of most novice physical culturists. They wanted to believe that they could develop bulging biceps and swelling chests without having to spend too much time on the process, nor having to buy expensive and hard-to-store cumbersome barbells and dumbbells, the stock-in-trade of genuine professional strongmen.

Those postal courses which did advocate the use of weights usually concentrated on exercises consisting of repetitions with light weights, whereas what was needed for a professional strongman's musculature were regular training sessions involving lifting progressively heavier weights.

The providers of postal courses were only too willing to reinforce their misconceptions. Most of the operatives of the courses were hack journalists or freelance writers. The majority of the strongmen themselves paid little attention to the flimsy duplicated pages being issued in their names, except to take a cut of the profits. Some of them later admitted to having absolutely no idea what strange theories of physical awareness were being propagated under their name. The main selling points of the brochures issued by their writers were to keep the costs down and make the exercises seem easy. Accordingly they were delighted to assure would-be clients that massive bodies could be developed without the assistance of any apparatus, or if special equipment was needed it would be unobtrusive and easy to use.

One such huckster, Otto Arco, ('Official Title Holder: The World's Best Developed Man') who at 5ft 2in. in height and 138lbs in weight must surely have been one of the smallest of all the muscle men, was at pains in his book *How to Acquire Super-Strength* to inform potential purchasers that he eschewed the use of barbells and dumbbells in his pupils' routines. 'Rest assured I will not try to force the use of them on to you.' However, Arco (born Nowasielsky) must have appreciated that punters would hesitate to pay the required thirty shillings for a haphazard set of freestanding exercises like push-ups and deep-knee bends and the rest. He assured his pupils that he was in the process of developing a piece of apparatus with which to supplement his course 'which is absolutely unique in the line of exercising apparatus. Something which enables anyone to master the basic feats – the first principles – of tumbling and hand balancing.'

A later strongman, J. C. Tolson (Apollon: 'In All the Wide World No Course Like This'), from Dewsbury, claimed hopefully that 'My system is beyond ordinary Physical Culture, it is really the Science of Living.' Tolson, who had copied his stage name from that of the original French Apollon, too, pushed the advantages of his specially designed muscle-building contrivances in his mail-order advertising pamphlet 'Strength Secrets by the Mighty Apollon': 'The appliance I supply with my course conserves energy – it's the Finest Bodybuilding Appliance of All Time. It can easily be fitted into the pocket and lasts for EVER.'

In fact, the Apollon apparatus consisted of a number of small steel rods of varying lengths, thickness and pliability. Pupils were requested to attempt to bend these bars, developing the muscles and strength of their arms in the process. Tolson did indeed possess great natural strength in his upper body. He had broken into show business by going up on to the stage when a professional strong-man called Samson (no relation to C. A. Sampson) had challenged any member of the audience to bend an iron bar. Tolson had done so and won a cash prize. Reckoning that this was easier than work, the Dewsbury man had followed Samson from town to town, winning his challenge prize at each hall in which the professional appeared. Eventually Samson had dropped the challenge from his act, leaving Tolson to turn professional. His postal course and the accompanying lumps of metal lasted much longer than his stage career.

Alfred Danks, called the great unknown bodybuilder because he seldom appeared in public and never courted personal publicity, devoted a long life to promoting a physical development course based upon the use of the chest expander under the headline of 'The Danks System Can Transform Physical Wrecks Into Robust Individuals'. An expander consisted of two grips joined by a number of steel or rubber springs, which could be contracted or expanded by exerting pressure on them. Danks did not invent the contraption but he specialised in its development to such an extent that at its peak he claimed that his course and the accompanying equipment were selling at the rate of a thousand a month. The expanders fetched between four shillings and six shillings each. Danks's tariff for his instructional manuals varied according to the degree of skill and strength possessed by each student enrolling:

Average man: 8 shillings
Advanced Physical Culturist: 12 shillings
Strong Man: 21 shillings

Like many other similar course providers, Danks also offered a supplement to his course, in this case a bottle of the Danks rubbing liniment for two shillings and sixpence.

Other strongmen were fortunate enough to be sponsored by established food and drink manufacturers. Almost inevitably Eugen Sandow led the way. After he had expanded his original act of balancing horses on a plank across his chest to his even more spectacular stunt of appearing to carry a horse across the stage, his ever-present business acumen kicked in. For a pecuniary consideration he allowed Murphy's, a major Irish brewing firm to use photographs of him carrying the horse in an advertising campaign to publicise their strong stout. Other strongmen were quick to emulate him. Before long Edward Aston was writing:

One preparation which I can conscientiously recommend is that known as 'Bovril'. It is a fact that most leading athletes recommend 'Bovril' and nothing can be better either before or immediately after practice than a cup of hot 'Bovril'. It prevents and dispels fatigue.

By the end of the nineteenth century, club swinger Tom Burrows had secured a contract to advertise the tonic drink Phosferine. Everywhere he appeared, advertisements for the tonic, accompanied by photographs of the strongman swinging a pair of clubs, would appear. This was the case with the Singapore *Straits Times* of 21 October 1907, in which he attributed his recent recovery of form to the drink:

> I chiefly attribute this recent improvement to the wonderful beneficial effect which Phosferine has already exerted, both before and after any one of my feats. I must confess that there were times when I should certainly have broken down but for a few timely doses of Phosferine.

Arthur Saxon 'after years of experience of diet in general and Hovis in particular', recommended the inclusion of the brown bread in any athlete's diet, while the Scottish strongmen Donald Dinnie and Alec Munro for many years advertised the drink Irn Bru. Not to be outdone, Thomas Inch, the Scarborough Hercules, recommended both 'the valuable properties of Hovis' and Bovril, 'the athletes' stand-by'.

Most of the apparatus and supplements offered by strongmen and their agents were harmless enough, if not particularly effective, but the implement offered by William Bankier (The Scottish Hercules) would probably have attracted the censure of a modern health-and-safety representative:

> I have a great faith in electricity for keeping the muscles in condition, especially after any hard work. I have invented what I call 'a muscle developer' which is useful to anyone who really wishes to go for the sole subject of building up muscle.

Bankier's muscle developer was in reality a dumbbell containing electric batteries. These were activated when the user exerted a certain amount of pressure and gave the lifter a mild electric shock, or, as Bankier put it, 'a stimulation'.

As an adjunct to his stage performances, the ubiquitous C. A. Sampson did his best to plug what he called 'massage rings' as an aid to the development of the muscles of the upper arm. He claimed to have come up with the idea after being wounded while serving in the Franco-Prussian War, although he would only have been eleven years old when it started and a year older at the conclusion of hostilities in 1871. According to this particular old soldier's account, he had been lying in pain on his bed in a hospital ward when he had had occasion to hoist himself into a sitting position by pulling on two steel rings suspended from ropes dangling from the ceiling. Idly he had slipped his wrist through one of the rings and pulled it up over his biceps. The rubbing of the ring against his injured arm had an amazing effect upon the development of his semi-paralysed limb. As a result, the future strongman had included this system of massage into his training system and kindly shared the knowledge for a fee to anyone attending his exhibitions of strength.

Later, the always-industrious Sampson started advertising his 'Roman Column' apparatus. This was a vertical board on to which the exerciser was strapped and stabilised by wires. Basically the exerciser carried out normal exercises but while dangling from an upside-down position.

Launceston Elliot, the former Olympian, advocated the use of his spring grip apparatus, two bars separated by a spring which were squeezed in the hand to exert pressure.

The Contractem

An Anatomical, Pneumatic, Weightless Dumbell

Can be carried in the pocket whilst travelling

As used by Launceston Elliot,

World's Amateur Weightlifter

British Amateur Weightlifter

No Weight?

Why????

Because resistance equals the weight required and is always in harmony with strength

3s.6d medium order 4 shillings large

With chart of exercises

The Anatomical Contractem Hand Grip Co. Ltd.

The Contractem Company was dissolved in 1907, presumably before it could make the fortune of the strongman advertising it.

It was definitely safer and more profitable to produce postal courses in which little apparatus was used. The trick lay in finding some sort of a hook that would distinguish the lessons from the others in a crowded market. Australian Don Athaldo made his bid for commercial success when he based his *Health, Strength and Muscular Power* course around a series of aphorisms to be repeated daily by his students. These included such gems as 'I am now as fearless as anyone, and I fear nobody'.

Other home fitness courses were based on deep breathing, carrying small rubber balls which had to be squeezed continuously all day, lifting sandbags, wafting in the air a rod with a weight at one end, and extending at arm's length a wooden pole with a piece of metal dangling from a length of chain. The pole had to be held in both hands at arm's length and then turned to wind up the lump of metal.

An optimistic purveyor of a health and strength course was Joe Price of Gloucester, holder of the title of the Champion Blacksmith of England. His muscle-building technique was based on the use of a sledgehammer, which had to be swung in a variety of ways, according to the instructions provided by Price. Whether the sledge-hammer was provided or whether the pupil had to find his own implement was not made clear.

Adrian P. Schmidt, the pioneer of American bodybuilding postal courses advertised what he called his 'automatic exerciser'. This consisted of a long lever, with a weight attached to one end. The person using the exerciser could select the point at which to hold the bar and lift the weight. The farther away from the weight the point was held, the greater the effort required to lift it.

Freestanding exercise courses, employing the body's own resist-ance, were more popular than those demanding the use of weights. These resistance courses were cheaper and easier to carry out in a confined space. Until the arrival of the much-hyped Dynamic Tension course supplied by the American Charles Atlas from the 1920s, the most popular non-apparatus course was the one adver-tised by a diminutive German called Max Sick.

Only 5ft in height, the Continental music hall strongman arrived in Great Britain in 1909 to cash in on the strength craze, which was still flourishing. Sick used weights in his training but was also an advocate of muscle control, developing individual muscles and muscle groups by tensing and contracting them. After years of practising, he reached a stage where he could isolate any one muscle or group and make them appear to dance across his heav-ily defined body. He linked up with another strongman, Sandow's one-time apprentice Monte Saldo. Between them they issued the Maxalding bodybuilding course. This consisted of freestanding exercises without apparatus, in which the practitioner adapted the use of his own bodyweight and contraction of individual muscles and groups of muscles in order to develop his musculature.

A few professional bodybuilders would have nothing to do with issuing courses that promised to reveal hidden methods that would make men out of weaklings. The Scot Donald Dinnie, content enough to advertise Irn Bru, would recommend no fancy training systems. When asked the secret of his success as a strongman and wrestler he replied that it was all due to hard work and oatmeal porridge: 'I kent nothing about what you call your scientific preparation of athletes. It may be well enough in its way, but I think a good deal of it is elaborate nonsense!'

8

<u>LOUIS AND LOUIS</u>

By the start of the twentieth century, two men stood out as the strongest of the professional music hall and vaudeville stage performers. Unfortunately, one was a dour, shambling, uncommunicative character and the other was so lazy that he could make a sloth look energetic, so neither ever drew the crowds that flocked to see Eugen Sandow's performances.

The two men were Louis Uni, who performed as Apollon, and Cyprien-Noé Cyr, who changed his first name to that of Louis because he or his associates thought it would look better on his posters. Both men were born within a year of each other, Uni in 1862 and Cyr in 1863. Sandow was a few years younger, although he achieved international fame long before the other two.

Louis Uni was born in Herault in France and grew to be a strong youth who looked older than his years. When he was fourteen, he ran away from home and joined a travelling circus. Before long he was rounded up by the police and returned to his parents. Uni persisted in his efforts to become a professional strongman until finally, and with considerable reluctance, his father put him in the charge of a couple of professional wrestlers, who did their best to harness the burly youth's strength and turn him into a grappler. However, Uni did not like the rough and tumble of struggling with an opponent on canvas and concentrated on weightlifting, developing his strength and physique still further.

The plodding strongman did not seek excitement, but out-of-the-ordinary events tended to seek him out. A story he told many times over his long life related to the months he spent in the South of France as an army conscript. One day, the strapping young private was approached by a stranger and asked if he would like to earn a large sum of money for a night's work. Strapped for cash like most recruits, Uni eagerly agreed. He claimed that the following night he was placed in a cab, blindfolded, and driven for many miles across the countryside. With his eyes still covered, Uni was led inside a house. There the blindfold was removed and Uni found that he was in the bedroom of an elegant, scantily dressed middle-aged woman.

The woman quickly made it obvious to the young soldier why he had been summoned to the chateau. He spent the night doing his best to respond to the demands of his companion. He was roused before dawn, paid off, blindfolded again and sent back by coach to his army camp.

When he retold this story over the years that followed, Louis Uni always insisted that he was certain that the lady he had been hired to service so vigorously must have been some childless wife of the owner of the estate, eager to secure an heir for her under-performing husband. Uni, the strongman believed, had been selected for the task because of his outstanding physique. He never attempted to discover the location of the chateau or whether his heroic efforts over the course of the long night had been successful.

Released from his military service, Louis Uni returned to his strongman routines with travelling circuses. One of these catch-penny institutions went broke in Italy, forcing Uni, who had not been paid off, to walk all the way home. Fortunately there were plenty of other tent shows looking for husky young strength athletes and the Frenchman was soon back in the business. By this time he was happily immersed in this irresponsible, nomadic form of life and even married several times into circus families. His first wife represented a move up the social scale, being a member of a family of lion tamers. His new bride even tried to promote the strongman to the rank of lion handler. Uni enjoyed wearing the gaudy accoutrements of his new trade's uniform but was extremely apprehensive of the fierce beasts he was supposed to be controlling. In the end he abandoned life with the lions and returned to the comfort and comparative safety of his strongman act. The story issued to outsiders was that Uni's physique had been so imposing that the cowed lions under his command had refused to perform for him and merely slunk whimpering to the four corners of the cage. Louis Uni's marriage and his demotion to the lower echelons of circus performers both ended soon afterwards.

His strongman act, on the other hand, prospered. By the time he was twenty, Uni was beginning to secure a reputation and break weightlifting records. Before long he had remarried and had developed quite a spectacular act. He was invited to appear at the Folies Bergère in Paris, where he used the stage name of Apollon. His act opened on the dramatic outline of a fortress at night, illuminated only by moonlight, and patrolled by the silhouettes of sentries. In front of this stronghold was a door, with heavy iron bars running from the top to the bottom. Suddenly the massive figure of Apollon appeared at the bars in the gloom. He was clad in a cloak, bound by chains and was plainly trying to flee from the castle. He crouched to avoid the sentinels. Suddenly an alarm sounded. Vigorously the sentries started searching the stronghold for an escaped prisoner.

Desperately Apollon broke the steel bonds about his body and began wrestling with the iron bars of the door. Slowly he pulled them apart and escaped through the aperture, to roars of approbation from the audience. Apollon discarded his cloak, bounded to the front of the stage and went into a posing routine. From this he moved into a weightlifting display involving barbells and dumbbells, juggled with a fifty-kilo block weight, tossing it from hand to hand and over his shoulder, before arching his body and planting his head and shoulders and feet on two chairs, while a piano was lowered with a block and tackle on to a platform supported across his chest and a pianist played a tune on the instrument.

Apollon then climbed on to a high table and performed a number of balancing acts with heavy weights, while several assistants lay on their backs beneath them. If the strongman were to make a misjudgement or falter with the weights, which he never did, they would crash down on to their heads. He ended his performance by lifting his celebrated Railway Wheels barbell, an enormous pair of train wheels advertised as weighing 36lbs, joined by a thick bar. The strongman had noticed them in a junkyard and included them in his act. Apollon claimed to be able to lift them overhead, but there was no record of his ever doing so. To hoist the contraption to his chest was an impressive enough feat of strength, although there were rumours that for many performances a substitute set of railway wheels, weighing much less than the original ones, were used by the strongman.

It was always a popular performance and secured for Apollon top-of-the-bill status all over Europe. Only once did it go wrong. After each performance of his opening stunt, in which Apollon pulled apart the iron bars of the fortress door with his bare hands, a blacksmith had to be called in to fix them back into shape. On one occasion the man called in to do this tempered the bars too firmly. Try as he might at first, at that night's performance Apollon could not move the iron rods. He struggled mightily, while the orchestra vamped and the audience grew restless, while his quick-tempered second wife stamped her foot and hurled insults and fierce exhortations at her husband from the wings.

Only after a titanic effort did the strongman manage to pry the iron bars aside and slip through them. However, he had exerted so much energy in the process that he was utterly exhausted. Apollon collapsed on to the stage and his act had to be abandoned for the evening.

Occasionally the strongman overreached himself. A combined music hall and restaurant in Paris soon proved him to be a poor businessman and administrator. His 'Concerts Apollon' did not do well, and he was forced to close up.

He was soon back on the road at the head of a company, presenting a series of sketches set in Ancient Rome, representing gladiatorial displays, exhibitions of strength and even a titillating visit by the victorious warriors to a Roman brothel.

Uni was always handicapped by his inherent indolence. He had to be roused before he could be persuaded to perform to the limits of his considerable strength. One night in 1892, he was appearing at the Varieties Theatre in Lille when he was tipped off that a rival strongman group, the Rasso Trio, headed by Godfrey Nordman, intended jumping on to the stage to challenge the Frenchman. Determining to give his rivals no quarter, Apollon asked a friend and fellow strongman, Batta, to load up his special thick-handled challenge barbell until it attained a weight of 198lbs. When this had been accomplished, Apollon tested the weight speculatively and declared that it was still not heavy enough. Leaving the stage he ordered Batta to add more weight to the orbs.

At this stage a wrestler called Paul Pons, who was also appearing on the bill, mischievously suggested that they give Apollon a real workout onstage that night. Accordingly the two overgrown schoolboys crammed the globes with extra iron packing, until the weight reached a staggering 341lbs. Batta and Pons then made themselves scarce.

At the evening's performance, the Rassos Trio watched Apollon going through his usual routine and then left their seats and demanded to compete with the Frenchman in lifting his challenge barbell. Unaware of its true weight, Apollon strode over to the piece of apparatus, grasped it with both hands and hauled it up to his chest. He then proceeded to lift it overhead and hold it there. Concealing any shock he must have been feeling at the unexpected increase in the weight he was bearing, the strongman took away his left hand and held it aloft with his right arm alone. Finally, still maintaining his balance, he stood defiantly on one leg only. When Godfrey Nordman made his attempt, he could only just lift the barbell off the ground before dropping it with a clatter.

Louis Uni had a long career as a top-of-the-bill strongman in European theatres. In an almost obligatory requirement for contemporary strongmen, almost like the National Service obligations of later generations, Uni came to London and performed at the Royal Aquarium. During his visit he was openly contemptuous of the lifting abilities of his rivals, stating publicly and with some truth that audiences wishing to witness real feats of strength should attend only the performances of Apollon.

In a lower key, Uni also maintained his wrestling career but at this he was no match for the best of the professionals. At an international tournament held in Vienna, he was disqualified in consecutive contests against Aimable de la Calmette and former fellow performer Paul Pons. In each case Uni protested hotly that he had been cheated, but his complaints were ignored. He lost another match to Ivan Padoubny at Hengler's Circus in London. Again he refused to accept the verdict and was hustled off the stage by the veteran Tom Cannon on behalf of the management. Uni continued to earn a good living from his appearances as a professional strongman, but as time passed his natural indolence took over. Unless he was fired by circumstances usually he did just enough to get by on the stage, but his natural strength was sufficient for him to retain his top-of-the bill status for decades to come. He was still touring with small strength shows when he was past sixty years of age.

There was another giant with just as much potential as Louis Uni's. His staple stage act was a display of almost unrelenting power. Night after night he started his performance by using one hand to lift a 273lbs weight from the floor to his shoulder and then above his head. Next he lifted a 300lbs barbell with both hands in the same way. He then hoisted 174lbs with his right hand straight from the floor to an overhead position. Pausing only to lower the weight to the ground, he repeated the lift with his other hand. He moved on to holding out a 100lb weight at arm's length, perpendicular to his body. He lifted a barrel of sand, said to weigh 314lbs, from the ground to his shoulder with one hand. Using only his middle finger, he pulled 551lbs from the ground. He went on to perform a few more strength feats before ending his performance by supporting across his back a platform containing eighteen seated men.

It was a display fitting of a man who called himself the strongest athlete in the world. The only drawbacks were that the performer was a shapeless, 300lb uncharismatic giant peering out at the world through a mass of facial hair. And, apart from the final platform lift, the display was basically pretty dull.

The man's name was Cyprien-Noé Cyr, later known as Louis Cyr to fit on the advertising bills. A French Canadian from St Cyprien, near Quebec, he was born on a farm in 1863, the eldest of seventeen children. His father was of average size but his mother stood over 6ft tall and could manhandle 200lb sacks. Cyr was an enormous child who grew to be a huge teenager. From an early age he showed signs of possessing great strength and was soon doing a grown man's work in the fields and forests. His mother encouraged him to grow his blond hair to shoulder length, to emulate the Biblical Samson. He had three years of full-time education, between the ages of nine and twelve, and then left school to go to work, finding employment as a lumberjack in the winter and on farms during the summer months.

When he was fifteen, the family emigrated over the border, to Lowell in Massachusetts, but returned to the province of Quebec in Canada. A local blacksmith who had worked as a part-time strongman taught the young Cyr a few tricks of the strength athlete's trade and the teenager was soon performing at local fairs. It was an age and an area containing few written records, so the feats of strength claimed on Cyr's behalf as he was growing up were almost certainly exaggerated. It was certain that the young giant could lift heavy barrels, bales of straw and large agricultural implements beyond the capacity of most men. As he developed his act, however, stories were spread of the young farm labourer and lumberjack lifting barrels of cement, pushing a freight car up an inclined railway track, lifting a farmer's cart from a rut, and carrying an injured lumberjack for seven miles on his back to find help.. When he was still a teenager he was said to have lifted a horse from the ground at an athletics competition in Boston.

That he was enormously strong is certain, although even in his teens he possessed a great deal of excess weight around his middle which made him cumbersome and reluctant to attempt feats requiring speed and dexterity. Normally a shy, reticent man, he also had a quick temper from an early age, which led to his walking out of public displays if he thought he was being mocked. His fame spread throughout the province. At the age of eighteen he engaged in a stone-lifting contest with David Michaud, who claimed to be the strongest man in Canada. Cyr outlifted the other man by moving from the ground a heavy boulder which his adversary could not even budge. Whether the stone in question really weighed the 480lbs claimed for it is less clear.

With the development of the strongman cult in the USA, impresarios were always on the lookout for young men who could draw in the crowds. It was not long before a local showman called Mac Sohmer had signed Cyr up and taken him on tour of Quebec and the Maritime Provinces. The young strongman managed to raise his wage from $25 to $35 a week, but it was the last success he was to have. Sohmer proved to be a hard taskmaster and a drunk. He made Louis Cyr undertake a series of two-hour performances on a gruelling tour, neglected him and finally abandoned the youth far from home, taking all the box office receipts with him.

It was a traumatic start to the French Canadian's professional career, but he persevered. For a time his father took over the strongman's management, taking Louis around the countryside with several companions, billed as the Troupe Cyr. This did not work out either, and for a time Louis Cyr joined the Montreal Police Force, stationed outside Montreal in the village of St Cunegonde.

He served from 1883 until 1886. The highlight of his service occurred when he attracted more attention by arresting several wrongdoers and carrying them back to the police station.

He was no happier upholding the law than he had been touring the sticks with his shows and by this time he was married and had several children. He resigned from the police force and opened a tavern with an adjacent gymnasium, hoping that his local fame would bring in the customers. For a time he was successful in his aim. He would attract publicity to his hostelry by staging well-managed stunts. He would carry 300lb casks of ale from the brewer's cart into his saloon and would lift his wife over the bar by seating her on his outstretched palm on one side and depositing her on the floor on the other side.

During this period, Cyr rejected a number of offers to turn professional. Eventually the bar failed and for a time Cyr was back on tour with a small troupe of boxers and wrestlers. The American-based promoter and magazine editor Richard K. Fox soon persuaded the strongman to embark upon a tour of the USA, and in March 1891, Louis Cyr gave an exhibition of his strength to journalists in the offices of Fox's *Police Gazette*.

Again the strongman was not happy with a touring life, but at first made conscientious efforts to lift heavy weights in his act. In 1895, in Boston, he pulled off the greatest feat of strength of his whole career: he lifted an inch or so from the ground a platform containing eighteen seated men. His burden was estimated to have a total weight of 4,327lbs.

The *Boston Herald* wrote that Cyr retained a self-satisfied smile as he motioned the men to the lifting platform, supported on trestles. Then he stooped beneath it and placed his back firmly against the oak board. So silent was the crowd in the hall that the gibbering of a monkey in the eaves could be heard. Cyr strained, the board did not move. He braced himself for a supreme effort. 'A mighty tugging was heard, the muscles of the strongman creaked like a door upon a rusty hinge, and slowly did the platform rise with him.'

Cyr was a considerable glutton. As a sideline, he and his partner Horace Barre engaged in eating contests with challengers. On one occasion he and Barre were reputed each to have eaten a whole suckling pig. As a result of these indulgences his weight ballooned. Soon he scaled over 400lbs and his health began to suffer.

He continued to tour, however, and over the years developed the dubious reputation of being a strongman's strongman; other strength athletes were in awe of the French Canadian's power but his stage act continued to be less than gripping. For some time his main offering was to hoist a sack of pig iron on to his back. Compared with the sparkling displays of Sandow, Launceston Elliot and others, it was pretty low-key stuff. Cyr tried to spice up the act and included a feat in which, wearing a piece of apparatus consisting of straps and hooks, he stood between two horses pulling in opposite directions without being torn in half himself. The theoretical principle of the act was that as long as the pull from each horse was equal Cyr merely acted as a human link in a chain.

He also balanced a ladder on his chin while his wife Melina stood on top of the contraption. He sometimes included a stunt in which three men gripped his long hair while he revolved and spun them round and round. In addition to balancing men on a platform, sometimes he would end his act by lifting a heavy barbell on to his shoulders. Four men would hang from each side of the barbell and another would sit on his shoulders. Carrying the nine men, Cyr would then walk off the stage. He issued an open prize of $100 to anyone who could duplicate any of his major feats.

On his tours of North America he engaged in a number of public challenge matches with other strongmen. On these occasions even the normally meticulous Cyr was prepared to conform to the accepted practice of fixed results, if he could be persuaded that the resultant publicity would be good for his career and bank balance. In October 1891, he competed publicly against the distinctly dodgy partnership of Cyclops and Sandowe – the false Sandow – in Montreal.

The whole affair had a dubious ring to it. While the French Canadian was away touring the USA, the duo challenged Cyr from the stage of the Lyceum Theatre during their act. They followed this up with posters claiming that Cyr was frightened of them and should accept their challenge or for ever keep his silence. 'Why does he not come forward?' they demanded.

For the next few nights the two strongmen continued to denigrate Cyr during their Montreal appearances. They were so successful in their aim that supporters of the local hero stormed the theatre one night and the police had to be called out. Towards the end of the week, as Cyclops and Sandowe were going through their act and issuing their customary jeers at Cyr, the French Canadian strong-man lumbered down the aisle, shouting 'Je suis ici! Je suis arrivé!' ('I am here! I have arrived!').

To the delighted cheers of the audience Cyr climbed painfully up on to the stage, seized a pair of challenge dumbbells and lifted them easily above his head. Cyclops prudently disappeared from sight. Sandowe moved forward as if to challenge Cyr, seemed to think better of it, turned and bolted from the stage. After a few moments Mr King, the manager of the theatre, appeared from the wings and addressed the audience: 'I have spoken with Sandowe and Cyclops,' he shouted, 'and told them that they owe it to you and themselves that they meet Cyr in a contest!'

Mr King went on to announce that the proposed contest would take place on the stage the following evening at eight o'clock. The hall was full at the appointed time. Cyr took his place to an ovation but the other pair did not turn up. Mr King appeared to explain that Cyclops and Sandowe knew that there was no point in attempting to compete with the mighty Louis Cyr.

The event caused an enormous stir in Canada and the USA, and Richard K. Fox put up a sidestake of $5,000 to back the French Canadian in a contest against any strongman in the world. The more cynical, however, suspected a publicity stunt, especially as it was known that both Fox and Cyr were eager to broaden the strongman's public appeal and boost his international reputation. To this end Cyr even put an advertisement in the *Boston Globe*:

> Louis Cyr is at all times ready and anxious to meet any of the alleged strong men from any nation – Sandow preferred – and will cheerfully forfeit the sum of $1,000 to any of them who can duplicate his feats.

Soon afterwards Cyr left for a tour of Europe. During this trip he spent a day on the estate of the Marquess of Queensberry. The peer promised to give one of his horses to the strongman if Cyr could repeat his feat of resisting the pull of two horses. The French Canadian was up for the challenge and was attached to two of Queensberry's strongest dapple-greys. The horses were quite unable to shift the giant. The Marquess did indeed hand over one of his own favourites and Cyr kept it on his farm for many years. He also included a fanciful drawing of the Marquess of Queensberry looking on in awe as part of a poster advertising his act.

Cyr's arrival in London was greeted with interest by his fellow strongmen but was an artistic and financial disaster. He appeared at the Westminster Aquarium on 19 January 1892. Among the crowd were the aristocracy of those strength athletes currently earning their livings on the British music hall stages: Eugen Sandow, C. A. Sampson, the McCann Brothers, Launceston Elliot, Monte Saldo, Charles 'Professor' Vanisttart, Louis Attila and many others. While they were impressed by the sheer strength of the French Canadian, they all agreed that Cyr's powers of presentation and showmanship were practically nonexistent and that the big man would never make a name for himself outside North America.

A tour of the major provincial cities followed and was equally unsuccessful. His stage performances continued to be dreary, none of the leading strongmen would accept his challenges and he was cheated financially by his European agents. Nor did he adapt well to local customs. A popular music hall song of the day was called 'Get Your Hair Cut'. When Cyr was appearing in Liverpool he became convinced that passers-by were abusing him. He stalked into a hairdresser's and had his locks trimmed, which meant that he had to remove from his act the stunt in which he swung men clinging to his hair.

At this stage in his career, Cyr was still taking some pride in the integrity of his act. Once, when he was appearing at a London hall, the strongman was lifting a dumbbell when a man in the audience complained that the weight that was being hoisted so easily could not possibly be as heavy as the strongman asserted. His jibe touched a nerve. The infuriated Cyr stalked down to the footlights and engaged in a heated exchange with his heckler. At the time, still arguing, he idly tossed the dumbbell from hand to hand as if it were a light book. Fellow strongman Charles Vanstittart, who was in the audience, later said that it had been the most amazing feat of unconscious strength that he had ever witnessed.

Cyr returned from Europe with his record as a strongman intact but having failed to become an international celebrity. However, for the next three years, between 1893 and 1896, Louis Cyr was probably at his peak as a strongman. It helped that the lordly Richard K. Fox arbitrarily bestowed upon the French Canadian the title of the strongest man in the world. Under this heading he found plenty of work touring with shows in North America, and joined up with the Ringling Brothers' circus while spending the winter months appearing as a leading act at Austin and Stone's dime museum in Boston. The latter proved to be hard work. The establishment was open for over twelve hours a day, with a fresh show starting every hour. Admittance, as always, cost ten cents.

Cyr did not enjoy the grind of touring with the circus, although he was a featured act. A bonus of his itinerant life was that he made a steady income on the side engaging in various challenges. Once he even defeated John L. Sullivan, the former heavyweight boxing champion. Sullivan was still frequenting saloons and laying down the law to fellow drinkers. He would bet that no man could emulate his trick of being able to blow a silver dollar out of the bottom of a glass with a single exhalation of breath. Cyr beat the former boxer with ease.

After a few years, including a spell running his own circus, he grew tired of life on the road. He continued to eat too much and took little exercise. His weight continued to balloon and he grew depressed. His health started to deteriorate. He had once been meticulous in his behaviour onstage, even to the extent of keeping a set of scales on the platform so that the accuracy of the weights he was lifting could be checked. One day the scales disappeared for ever. It became common knowledge on the strongman circuit that Louis Cyr, *le homme le plus forte du monde*, was cheating.

A friend asked him why he, of all people, was dissembling in such a manner. The world-weary Cyr shrugged and replied cynically: 'What's the use? I make the people think I am working. They would believe I lifted 480lbs if I said so … what's the sense of lifting 240 if I can get by with eighty?'

Soon afterwards he retired to his farm near Montreal, where he lived as a virtual recluse, too shy to appear in public because of his increasingly ungainly and unkempt appearance. He continued to eat voraciously and took to drinking heavily. He spent much of his time sleeping at night in a large rocking chair, a lonely, embittered man, reduced finally by his doctors to a milk-based diet. Towards the end of his life he made a comeback of sorts, in 1906, defending the title of the world's strongest man against Hector Decarie at Parc Sohmner. Cyr was forty-four years old and had to leave his sick bed in order to compete. He could still bring in the crowds in his home country and it was estimated that an audience of four thousand people came to see his swan song.

It is possible that the match was fixed in order to give Cyr one last payday and to allow him to pass on his title to the younger man, of whom he approved. Out of eight lifting events, each competitor won four. By the end, Louis Cyr was panting for breath after any exertion on the stage and was forced to sit down between each lift. Cyr made one last public announcement: 'I have decided to retire forever. I pass on my crown as the world's strongest man to Hector Decarie.' The newspaper *La Presse* summed up the feelings of many of the strongman's compatriots: 'Louis Cyr, beaten by age, is no more than a shadow of himself, a remnant of his past glory, a relic of his former power.'

9

THE ELECTRIC GIRL
AND OTHER LADIES

Few strongwomen appeared as single acts until the eighteenth century. Some appeared as adjuncts to male strength artists, but their jobs were usually to fetch and carry the lighter pieces of equipment and to look on admiringly as the male members of the troupes strutted on the stage. By the eighteenth century, however, the first solo strongwomen were beginning to put on displays of their own.

In a handout entitled *The Parlour Portfolio*, dated 1724, one woman was described thus:

To be seen at Mr John Symes, peruke-maker, opposite the Mews, Charing Cross, the surprising and famous Italian Female Samson, who has been seen in several courts of Europe with great applause. She will absolutely walk barefoot on a red-hot bar of iron; a large block of marble of between two and three thousand pounds' weight she will permit to lie on her for some time, after which she will throw it off at about six feet distance, without using her hands, and exhibit several other curious performances, equally astonishing, which were never before seen in England. She performs exactly at twelve o'clock, and at four, and six in the afternoon. Price: half a crown, servants and children a shilling.

Thirty years later, another female strongwoman appeared on London's entertainment scene. She performed in an acrobatic act with her husband, the Frenchman Anthony Jacob Duger, perhaps of mixed blood. He was a tightrope walker, performing on both slack and tight wires, and also carried out acrobatic feats on the backs of different chairs.

Mlle Duger, like many of her predecessors, appeared on posters as the Female Samson. She performed in the intervals while her husband recovered backstage from his wirewalking exhibitions. She was presented to the audience as an entertainer who had given much satisfaction to HRH the Princess Dowager and the royal family of Great Britain. To warm up the crowd and whet its appetite for what was to follow, she started by arranging herself on her hands and feet, with her back arched, while stones were broken with a sledgehammer on an anvil laid across her stomach. Her handbills gave some idea of the pleasures to follow:

I. She lies with her body extended between two chairs and bears an anvil of 300lb on her breast, and will suffer two men to strike it with sledgehammers. II. She will bear six men to stand on her breast lying in the same position. III. She will suffer a stone of 700lb to lye on her breast and throw it off six feet from her.

At this stage M. Dugee, presumably much refreshed after his rest, returned to the fray and executed a dance with iron fetters chained to his legs. To end the performance, husband and wife combined to demonstrate a dance called the Drunken Pheasant.

Some of the female strongwomen had a number of strings to their bows. In 1896, the *Strand* magazine playfully described one of these performers appearing in London:

Miss Darnett, 'the Singing Strong Lady', extends herself upon her hand and legs, face uppermost, while a stout platform, with a semi-circular groove for the neck, is fixed upon her by a waist-belt, which passes through brass receivers on the underside of the board. An ordinary cottage piano is then placed by four men on the platform and presently the lady's callous spouse appears, bowing, and calmly mounts upon the platform also presumably in order that his execution might carry greater weight with the audience – and with his wife.

As Miss Darnett phlegmatically bore the weight of the piano and her husband, the latter then played a series of soothing waltzes by Strauss. Towards the end, without shifting her position, the strongwoman would aid the accompanist by singing a love song.

Miss Darnett had a rival on the London halls at this time in the shapely form of Mlle Arniotis, who embarked upon a long run at the Alhambra Theatre. Unlike the musically inclined British strongwoman, Mlle Arniotis was an out-and-out strength athlete, although her publicity matter made it clear that she definitely was not over-muscled. Her closing display consisted of lifting a barrel with her teeth, with two ten-stone men perched on the lid. A versatile artiste, she was always prepared to expand her act – if the price was right. When a group of young bucks out for a night on the town bet her £10 and offered to pay for the price of the piano being used in her act, she shrugged, lifted the instrument, carried it to the edge of the stage and threw it into a previously cleared space in the aisle in the stalls.

Another French strongwoman who was touring the halls of London and most of Europe during this period was Madame Elise. Born in Neuilly near Paris, she later married a strongman and formed a double act with him. Madame Elise was capable of standing on a platform with a 700lb barbell across her shoulders and a man hanging on to each end of the weight. She was said to be able to carry eight men on a bridge placed across her shoulders. This strongwoman was also capable of putting her power to practical use. Once, when travelling through Cornwall in a caravan containing five other female circus performers, the horse drawing the vehicle baulked at the foot of a particularly steep hill. The strongwoman took the beast's place and used a rope to tow the caravan to the brow of the hill. There is no record as to the whereabouts of Madame Elise's husband during this particular emergency.

Several muscular female performers combined acrobatics with feats of strength during their circus displays. One of these was a German-born performer of mixed race who usually appeared under the name of Miss La La, although she was sometimes billed as the African Princess, Olga la Negresse, the Cannon Woman, the Human Gun Carriage and the Venus of the Tropics. Her real name was probably Olga Kaira. Her displays included a high-wire act, performing feats of strength including dangling from a rope and even holding a cannon by her teeth above the arena. She appeared at the London Westminster Aquarium in 1879, but already had become famous with her dazzling displays at the Cirque Fernando in Paris in January of that year, where she had attracted the favourable attention of the artist Edgar Degas, who painted her hanging from a rope by her teeth above the heads of the spectators. A critic in *The Era* magazine, reviewing Miss La La's act, made much of her colour at a time when black performers were relatively rare, and speculated dismissively that black men and women were probably 'superior in the matter of strength to whites'.

A number of female circus performers used a trapeze as an

integral part of their acts to display a combination of suppleness and strength. Madame Ali-Braco balanced a cannon on her shoulders and then performed a little preliminary trapeze work before lifting the cannon from the ground with her teeth while dangling from the trapeze. Even more impressive was the routine of the tiny but extremely tough German Lillian Leitzel, who was a circus acrobat. No one messed with this diminutive waif. She could swear like a trooper and was inclined to strike any tardy stagehand who did not prepare her apparatus to her complete satisfaction.

Well-educated and cultured, from an early age she nevertheless decided that the circus life was one that she wanted to embrace. Her mother and two aunts had been trapeze artistes and although her grandmother did her best to educate the girl and encourage her to take up a classical music career, Lillian made her own trapeze at home and practised on it daily. When she turned professional, using a rhythmic swinging motion she would hang from a bar high above the ring and pull herself up by one hand, encouraging the crowd to shout out the number of repetitions she could manage in this way. Her record was twenty-seven pull-ups with her right arm and seventeen with her left. She also performed on the rings, impressing the crowds as she plunged and swooped. The onlookers would have been even more impressed if they had known that every time Lillian performed one of her spectacular revolutions she temporarily dislocated her shoulder in the process.

The trend of strongwomen to move from the circus arena to the music hall and vaudeville stages began in the 1880s and 1890s, when the appearance of the forerunners of 'laddish' magazines such as the *Police Gazette* hit the shelves. This promotion of female flesh transferred itself to the performances of some of the female artistes. There had been exhibitions of semi-nudity onstage since the 1860s, with posing displays of *tableaux vivants* and *poses plastiques*, although much of the titillation involved was heightened by the tactful use of lighting and all-embracing body stockings. In 1869, the British dancer Lydia Thompson had taken her troupe of scantily clad British Blondes to the USA and helped to widen the rift between vaudeville and much racier and bawdier burlesque performances. A year later the Folies Bergère had opened in Paris, with its displays of female beauty.

There was a sudden craze for the forerunner of striptease performances when variations of Salome's Dance of the Seven Veils started being performed on many music hall bills. This glorification of the female form was emphasised even before Flo Ziegfeld instigated his upmarket displays of female fresh, known as girlie shows. The beautiful Australian swimmer, Annette Kellerman, was so famous for her form-fitting one-piece bathing suits cut well above the knee that she was actually arrested by the Boston police for appearing in public wearing one. She had retired from active competition to headline vaudeville and music hall bills, protesting that the voluminous costumes of the day hindered her chances of breaking fresh world records: 'I might as well be swimming in chains!' Even so, she set a world record for swimming a mile in twenty-eight minutes. There was no doubt, however, that it was the swimmer's shapely form that vaudeville audiences wanted to see, not her expert demonstration of the new-fangled trudgeon stroke.

Billed as the Diving Venus, the Australian appeared at a London music hall to perform her Mermaid Show in a glass-sided tank. The manager had placed a dozen large mirrors around the tank. When asked for the reason for this action, he had replied trenchantly, 'What are we selling here? We're selling backsides, right? So, if one backside is good, a dozen backsides are even better!'

Few if any of the circus strongwomen making the transition to the halls in the wake of the bare flesh movement could boast the attractive lines of Annette Kellerman and Lydia Thompson, but the admittedly rather bulky new arrivals did their best to make their shows sexy as well as awe-inspiring.

Kate Brumbach, who performed as Sandwina, after Eugen Sandow, was born in Vienna in 1884, one of fourteen children of a professional strongman and woman act.

Although she was a hefty lady, she was quick to point out that at a weight of 200lbs all her measurements were in proportion. Performing as Sandwina (her publicity material on posters claimed that she had once outlifted Eugen Sandow in a weightlifting contest, but there is no evidence of this) she was soon being billed as the strongest and most beautiful woman in the world and made much of her physical attributes. On one well-advertised occasion she arranged for a group of doctors to examine her at Madison Square Gardens in New York. They declared Sandwina to be the perfect physical specimen. At a height of 5ft 9in. tall, her chest measurement was 44in. and her waist 29in. She had a hip measurement of 43in. and her flexed right bicep was 14in.

As a child she worked in her parents' travelling act, performing acrobatics and twisting steel bars and horseshoes out of shape. By the time she was a teenager her father had given her featured billing, offering any man who could defeat her at wrestling a prize of one hundred marks. In this way Kate, who was a romantic at heart, met her much-loved husband Max Heymann. He was nineteen at the time and a professional acrobat, while Kate was sixteen. In their contest, Kate threw Max so hard that he bounced off the ground before lying prostrate. It was a case of love at first sight. As Max slowly recovered and started twitching on the floor of the circus ring, he looked up at his conqueror, who was gazing down solicitously at him. As Max wrote in later years, 'I knew that never before had I been in the presence of such loveliness… Then she lifted me in her arms as though I was a toy doll and carried me inside her dressing tent.'

After a time, the pair formed a double act. They were married in 1910 and split from Kate's parents' troupe. They left Germany for the USA where, with two assistants they toured as the Sandwinas. Eventually they were spotted by bookers and joined the Ringling Brothers' Circus, with Kate billed as the Iron Queen. She lifted weights and juggled with cannonballs. Forty pounds heavier than her husband and partner, she would throw him overhead and then catch him, holding him aloft in one hand. Their theatrical bills, which may have lost something in their translation from the original German, read 'she tosses her husband about like a biscuit'.

Josephine Schauer was even stronger than Kate Sandwina but did not possess the German's charisma or striking looks. It is not sure whether she was born in Hoboken, New Jersey or in Germany but she married a professional strongman in Paul Blatt, the Hoboken Hercules. Blatt had been looking for a partner for his act and had heard of the feats of strength of the large neighbourhood girl and deliberately set out to find her. They rehearsed their new act, fell in love and married, touring Europe and the USA together from 1899 until 1910, when she retired.

Josephine took the name of Minerva for her professional appearances. She went through the usual routines of breaking horseshoes and chains with her hands and even catching cannonballs after they had been fired, although the firing mechanism of the gun being used had been considerably modified and the velocity of the projectiles was not quite as explosive as Minerva would have her audiences believe. Her *pièce de résistance* lay in lifting a man who was seated in a chair, and holding him out at arm's length ahead of her.

It was as a lifter of heavy weights that she excelled. At the Bijou Theatre in Hoboken in 1895, using a harness lift she succeeded in hoisting a total of 3,564lbs from the ground. Challenging and defeating another strongwoman, Victorine, in 1893, Minerva achieved great fame, with Richard K. Fox, editor of the *Police Gazette*, presenting Minerva with a belt embossed with golden dumbbells and seventeen silver plates. The magazine also bestowed upon Minerva the title of the world's strongest woman.

Neither Sandwina nor Minerva concealed their appetites for food and drink. Kate Sandwina admitted that there was nothing to beat a good bottle of beer or a fine bottle of wine. Minerva was even more candid about her regime in an interview published in the *San Antonio Daily Light* of 15 August 1892:

> Eating is about the principal part of my existence, and I always have the best I can possibly procure. For breakfast I generally have beef, cooked rare; oatmeal, French-fry potatoes, sliced tomatoes with onions and two cups of coffee. At dinner I have French soup, plenty of vegetables, squabs and game. When supper comes, I am always ready for it, and I then have soup, porterhouse steak, three fried eggs, two different kinds of salads and tea.

Most of the leading strongwomen came from the USA or Continental Europe. Only one strength athlete from the British Isles made any sort of impact on the music hall circuit. Her name was Kate Williams, although sometimes she was known as Kate Roberts. She was born in Abergavenny in Wales in 1875, the daughter of an Irish preacher who had settled in Wales. Kate showed early talent as an athlete and when she left school at the age of fifteen to work in a local tannery she enrolled at a local gymnasium in order to keep fit.

The gymnasium was run by a small-time music hall strongman called William Roberts, whose stage name was Atlas. Under his tutelage, Kate Williams began to specialise in strongwoman tricks and was soon appearing at local fairs. The costume that she wore was scanty enough to be described as shocking for its time, although her male audiences grew with every performance. Causing a local scandal, she and William Roberts fell in love and ran away together – Roberts was already married, with a young family.

At first, Kate appeared in Roberts's music hall troupe, 'The Society of Athletes'. Soon, however, the girl had developed such a reputation for her strength and good looks that she and Roberts joined together as a double act on halls in London and the provinces, appearing as Atlas and Vulcana. It soon became clear that Roberts employed many tricks in his act, earning the contempt of his peers and audiences. But no one disputed the ability of his partner. A pretty, normal-looking woman, she was still able to lift heavy weights and carry a small organ on her back. She could lift a weight of over 120lbs over her head with her right hand. She was possibly the first strongwoman to perform the Tomb of Hercules stunt, hitherto the exclusive province of male strength athletes. She would lie backwards on the stage supported on her hands and legs, staring at the roof, while a platform was placed across her stomach. Then, at her command, two horses would be led onto the platform and left standing there.

She was also adept at publicity stunts. In 1901 she gathered a large crowd in London's Strand when she lifted one end of a carriage stuck in the mud, while policemen replaced a shattered wheel. Genuinely courageous, she once stopped a runaway horse in Bristol, saved two children from drowning in the River Usk and in a blaze at a music hall rescued a horse belonging to an equestrian act.

Though never starring on the halls, there were a number of other strongwomen acts, most of whom had their own impressive specialisations onstage. Athleta, a Belgian girl, paraded around the stage carrying a bar upon which clung four men dressed as soldiers. She came from a circus family and handed on the tradition when her daughters Brada, Louise and Anna continued the act after their mother's early retirement. Sasha Padoubney, the sister of the famous Russian wrestler, Ivan, claimed to be the women's world wrestling champion and challenged all comers in the 1880s and 1890s.

Charmion, whose real name was Laverne Vallee, performed the usual strongwoman act but opened her performance with a startling stunt which made her name. In a variation of Salome's Dance of the Seven Veils, she dressed in ordinary Victorian clothes and swept backwards and forwards above the stage on a trapeze, stopping at the end of each graceful arc to remove an item of clothing. The curtain would be lowered before the final garment could be discarded and dropped.

One who did have great success, and who undoubtedly became the most famous strongwoman of all time was just fifteen when she commenced her music hall career. Her performance was genuinely sensational, at least at first. Later she suffered considerable obloquy at the hands of audiences and the press, halting her career after only two years.

Her name was Lula Hurst, although for stage purposes she usually appeared as Lulu Hurst, the Georgia Magnet. She was born in Polk County, Florida, in 1869, the daughter of a farmer and church deacon, a wounded veteran of the Civil War. Later, to heighten the drama of her feats of strength, writers and illustrators depicted her as a mere slip of a girl, although she seems to have grown to a fair size as a teenager. One newspaper report described her both tactfully and accurately as a typical country girl, approaching 6ft in height, with lovely hair growing down to her shoulders. Less gallant observers referred to her as stout.

One night, while an electric storm raged outside, Lula was sharing a bed with a visiting cousin. Suddenly there was a strange popping noise in the room and some items of furniture and clothing started to move. The next morning, the girls told Lula's parents what had happened. As confirmation of this, for the rest of the week heavy articles in the house seemed to move of their own volition without anyone being near them.

News of the phenomenon spread around the neighbourhood. A committee of local dignitaries, including Lula's father, was formed to investigate the strange occurrences. It was generally agreed that all the bizarre goings-on seemed to centre around Lula Hurst. A theory was formed that during the storm Lula had been struck by lightning and now possessed electrical powers which she could harness to do her bidding.

Other, larger committees of scientists and doctors were brought together to ponder over the matter. Steadfastly, Lula Hurst was able to demonstrate her powers to all of them. By this time she even appeared to have widened her range, effortlessly lifting from the floor a chair containing a large, heavy man. Starting with a demonstration of table rapping at a local spiritualist meeting, she began to appear nervously at church and civic social gatherings to exhibit her newfound gifts.

Inevitably, the story reached the newspapers. Equally inescapably, the showmen followed. Lula's parents were persuaded to accompany their daughter on a tentative tour of the vaudeville halls. Paul Atkinson, a stage manager taken on to mastermind the tour, proved to be efficient and loyal, and later married Lulu, as she was now known.

The initial tour was a great success. Lulu was promoted to top of the bill and her itinerary was expanded. She appeared in Washington, Boston and New York, to considerable acclaim and packed houses. In two years she travelled more than 20,000 miles by train. She even visited Great Britain. Everywhere she went, audiences agreed that her act was a strange one. Nothing like it had been seen on the halls before, which may have accounted for the act's success. At the beginning of her brief stage career, Lulu owed a particular debt of gratitude to Henry Grady, the editor of the *Atlanta Constitution*, who took up her cause and made Lulu front-page news.

A typical show would start with Lulu waiting onstage with her father and Paul Atkinson. The young girl always wore a colourful dress. The stage manager doubled as a slick compère and was described in one newspaper as 'he of the perennial smile'. Atkinson introduced Lulu and asked for male volunteers from the audience to come up on to the stage to assist with the demonstration. By the time Lulu was well known there was no shortage of would-be helpers. If a celebrity in the audience could be induced to come up and take part, that only added to the fun.

Once sufficient men had gathered nervously around Lulu, the show could begin. The first scene usually consisted of Lulu holding one end of an ordinary umbrella and one of the male volunteers clutching the other, with instructions to cling on for dear life and prevent Lulu from attacking him. Atkinson would then give the word to commence. The umbrella at once seemed to take on a life of its own. While Lulu seemed to exert only the gentlest of pressure on her end, the umbrella started writhing furiously. The volunteer did his best to maintain his grip but within seconds he was being belaboured by the umbrella and knocked to the floor, while the parasol continued to thrash him. An endearing part of the act was Lulu's habit of giggling happily as she demonstrated her superiority over her male challengers.

When the audience had finished laughing and cheering, Atkinson urged another man to take the place of the one now cowering on the ground. Again Lulu touched her end daintily. This time the umbrella gave a great leap. While the volunteer clung on to it, the girl released her hold and the umbrella seemed to send the man flying halfway across the stage, where he fell down with a crash. Sometimes Paul Atkinson would call out 'Behold the power of the electric umbrella!' or words to that effect.

These were only the preambles to an evening of female dominance. With one man gripping a walking stick horizontally between two hands, Lulu would place her open hands on the centre of the cane, without seeming to push at all. The cane would start jerking uncontrollably, tearing itself from the man's hands and sometimes felling him.

Stunt after stunt followed. Lulu would hold a heavy man effortlessly above the ground in a chair. She then repeated the performance standing on a set of weighing scales. Although Lulu weighed 140lbs and the volunteer was often in excess of 200lbs, the needle on the enlarged scale showed only around 175lbs instead of the 300lbs-plus it should have displayed.

One volunteer recounted his experiences when he picked up a chair and held it firmly in both hands, with the back of the chair against his chest. Lulu then placed her hands calmly over the volunteer's. In the *New York Times* (6 July 1884), the man wrote:

> I have wrestled and sparred and worked hard in the athletic way on many occasions, but I never struggled so desperately in my life as I did with that chair. I found it impossible to control it and was thrust backwards and whirled around… During all this time I did not feel any undue pressure from Miss Hurst's hands, although the chair felt positively bewitched.

Lulu defied large men to lift her from the ground, lifted a chair while four men pushed down on it with all their might, balanced on one foot while a man endeavoured unsuccessfully to push her over, held a broomstick and defied anyone to push it through her hands, and performed many other stunts which seemed to prove that she was either incredibly strong or possessed of strange powers. It was all so overwhelming that the *New York Times* wrote with mock severity on behalf of the beleaguered male population:

> This must be stopped, or there will be no such thing as safety outside a monastery.

Lulu Hurst even performed her tricks before the inventor Alexander Graham Bell at his home and then in his Washington laboratory. The erudite inventor of the telephone was at a loss to explain the reasons for her accomplishments. On another occasion she gave a private demonstration to the actress Lillie Langtry at New York's

Madison Theatre. The game English actress must have tried to engage with Lulu in some of her physical endeavours, because she emerged from the theatre with her dress torn and her lip cut, complaining of bruising and stiffness. The only other thing she would say in response to the questions of waiting reporters was 'That is the result of wrestling with the Georgia Wonder!'

Perhaps Lulu's greatest feat occurred at the Brooklyn Theatre in New York, when she took on the famous former sumo wrestler Matsuda and other athletes before a full house. Altogether there were twenty men on the stage, led by the wrestler, all determined to beat the Georgia Magnet, the title under which she was almost always billed (although she was also known as the Georgia Wonder and the Georgia Marvel). Lulu started with her usual challenges with umbrellas, walking sticks and billiard cues, sending the volunteers flying in all directions. Finally she was faced by Matsuda and four other men. Matsuda sat gingerly in a chair, held aloft with both hands by Lulu, while his four associates pressed down hard on its arms. Desperately the four men tried to force the chair from Lulu's hold and down on to the stage. They might as well not have bothered. Within minutes, as the crowd screamed its approval, the chair, together with its occupant and helpers, was bucking and rearing all over the stage.

Finally an exhausted Matsuda gave up, jumped down from his seat, bowed stiffly and led his helpers off the stage with as much dignity as they could muster, leaving Lulu, still holding the chair, to accept the audience's rapturous applause. A newspaper reporter present noted:

The audience went wild in their wrought-up enthusiasm over this wonderful and exciting scene.

For almost two years the Georgia Magnet could do little wrong. Then, almost abruptly, Lulu's act began to disintegrate. Suddenly she was no longer the golden girl. Sharp-eyed newspaper correspondents and disloyal stagehands began speculating on the causes behind the Electric Girl's apparently almost supernatural abilities. A plethora of imitators began to flood the halls, also claiming to be Georgia Magnets. Some of them even called themselves Lulu Hurst, though most of these did not have the original Lulu's dexterity and stage presence. Unfairly, audiences grew disillusioned, feeling that the Georgia Magnet had been overrated.

The tide, once it had turned, was inexorable. A killer blow to Lulu's future was struck when the august *New York Times*, once her ally, gave her an excoriating review on 13 July 1884:

> 'The Phenomenon of the Nineteenth Century', which may be seen nightly at Wallack's, is not so much the famous Georgia Girl, with her mysterious muscle, as is the audience which gathers to wonder at her performance. It is a phenomenon of stupidity, and it only goes to show how willingly people will be fooled, and with what cheerful asininity they will help on their deceivers.

On an appearance in London, Lulu was particularly plagued by the attentions of a local engraver called Thomas Johnson. He seemed to have studied her act in forensic detail and to have worked out how every stunt was accomplished. He harassed Lulu by constantly appearing onstage and challenging her.

The Electric Girl suffered her reverses with surprising level-headedness. After all, she had had a good run for her money – or rather for other people's box office contributions. It was estimated that over two years in those happy income-tax-free times she had accumulated a total of at least $50,000 and perhaps as much as double that amount. Additional income had been earned from advertising soap, cigars and even farm equipment, the last appearing under the slogan of 'as strong as Lulu Hurst!' She had also attracted the love of a good man in the devoted Paul, whom she had married on tour. And she was still only seventeen.

The Electric Girl, now plain Lula Hurst again, cancelled a proposed tour of Europe with few regrets, dissolved the act and returned home with her new husband and her parents. She and Paul bought a house in Madison and settled down. There followed twelve years of contented silence. Then, in 1897, when she had almost been forgotten, Lula published her autobiography. It was a sensation and went into a number of editions. The account of her life and theatrical tours was an anodyne and airbrushed enough version of history, but for some reason, perhaps in order to purge her conscience, Lula added a section in which she was amazingly frank about the so-called 'secrets' behind her stunts.

According to Lula or Lulu Hurst, the whole extended episode had been an improvised amalgam of a bored, bright, self-confident girl of above-average physical strength stumbling almost unconsciously upon a stream of events which at first she had hardly understood, then had merely gone with, finally realising that she had a chance to achieve fame and fortune. Added to that, she had been fortunate in obtaining the assistance of a shrewd father and boyfriend, both practical men devoted to her. There had been no supernatural aspects to her gifts; she had merely adopted what she termed 'unrecognised mechanical principles'.

It turned out that practically the only genuine thing about the events which initiated Lula Hurst's strange and lucrative journey to fame was the electric storm raging on the night that the girl's visiting cousin was sharing her bed with her. Most of the other events were prompted merely by Lula's mischievous imagination and a desire to torment her cousin, who was plainly terrified by the storm outside.

As the other girl cowered sobbing under the bedclothes, a smirking Lula did her best to increase her terror. Discovering that the headboard of their bed was loose, Lula squirmed round and started rocking it against the wall with jerking movements of her feet, producing the strange popping sound that was soon to intrigue the earnest investigating committees. She was aware that her cousin had turned her head away and closed her eyes tightly to ward off any evil spirits. This made it easy for Lula to hurl pillows and cushions and small items of furniture about the bedroom, at the same time screaming that they were being moved without any physical assistance. By the end of the storm, the cousin was convinced that she had seen everything that Lula had claimed to witness and backed up Lula's story with complete conviction. With devilish ingenuity, for several days Lula continued her persecution of the credulous other girl, by taking her clothes from her trunk and hanging them on picture rails and other projections around the house, all the time asserting that they had been moved by some supernatural force.

When it came to demonstrations of her apparently outlandish gifts to the local investigators, Lula was motivated by a wish to avoid getting into trouble for playing such cruel practical jokes on her cousin. At the same time the easily bored farm girl living in an isolated area was also intrigued to see just how far she could go before her interlocutors discovered the truth, as she was sure they would. She must have been an utterly convincing actress; when she talked of the 'power' that was taking her over, most of her listeners believed the wide-eyed, outwardly straightforward and ordinary lass appearing before them.

From spiritualist acquaintances she heard about the process of table rapping, in which an unseen presence beats out a message on a surface. Lula was an intensely practical girl. She investigated the table in her parents' lounge, subjecting it to a detailed scrutiny. By a process of trial and error she ascertained that a table could be encouraged to produce the effect of raps at an intersection of joints and mortices, where there might be gaps to be exploited, especially if the wood should be dry and thin in this area. If she could just find the right spot to press, the table could almost seem to come to life under the slightest pressure she exerted, giving off reports of sounds as loud as a pistol shot.

It was the same when Lula started putting her first act together. By chance she had stumbled across the principle of resistance techniques. With her intelligence and ingenuity, and allied to the practical assistance provided by her father and Paul Atkinson, she soon developed these techniques into a most original vaudeville routine. In effect, like performers going back to Thomas Topham and John Charles von Eckenburg, and even earlier, she based her performance on utilising the principles of the fulcrum and the lever, cleverly disguised.

In her autobiography, she also explained how she had carried out the feat of lifting a heavy man in a chair with two more men seated on his lap. For a start the chair was constructed to give the lifter every advantage, with a round edge and a curved and rounded back. Automatically, the man seated in a chair would grasp the arms of the seat and place all his weight on his feet. Lulu would then exert a horizontal thrust, without doing any lifting, using her knees as points of support for her elbows. As soon as a slight movement was exerted, the hardest part of the work was over. When Lulu stopped pushing, the chair would move, the equilibrium being destroyed. Before it could be established again the chair was relatively easy to lift some 6in. off the ground.

In this candid fashion Lulu explained effect after effect in her book. Everything depended upon getting the volunteers onstage into the right state of mind and the correct bodily positions. Once they were worked up to a suitable state of excitement their imaginations took over. With the Georgia Magnet's unobtrusive prompting, the positions of their bodies were so strained and unnatural that they could rarely exert their full force in the direction they wanted throughout the different tricks. She quoted the words of a perceptive panel of doctors who had witnessed one of her performances: 'It is the experimenters (i.e. the volunteers), not the subject, who knock themselves, the chairs, canes, umbrellas, etc., about.'

Lulu provided examples. A man holding a billiard cue horizontally above his head in a manner dictated by the girl could be pushed around by the girl's open hand because the volunteer was then in a state of unstable equilibrium. Again, once a subject started struggling with the umbrella he was holding, the force of the air beneath its folds was enough to drive it into all sorts of positions, often appearing to be belabouring the panic-stricken volunteer. All that Lulu had to do was utilise the power of leverage and release her contact with the umbrella or stick when she felt the volunteer pushing, and increase it when she saw that he was giving way in the other direction.

In every stunt the volunteers did the Georgia Magnet's work for her by losing their balance after they had been placed in contorted and unnatural positions. This applied in particular to Lulu's celebrated trick of appearing to hold a chair casually aloft while four large men, straining frantically, could not push it back down on to the floor. The volunteers were all off balance and were devoting all their strength to regaining that balance, although they believed they were endeavouring to get the chair back down on to the stage.

Lulu Hurst's strongwoman act had many imitators. One of the most successful was Dixie Annie Jarratt, who was born in 1861. It is likely that she and her husband saw Lulu Hurst's act in Milledgeville, Georgia, where they lived in 1884, and between them were able to work out the stratagems behind the Georgia Magnet's tricks. Within a year Dixie, aided and abetted by her husband Charles Haygood, was touring locally with a pirated version of the Electric Girl act. She was using the stage name of Annie Abbott and, to heighten the resemblance with her predecessor, was calling herself the Georgia Magnet while advertising that her performance was based on the supposedly mysterious propensities of electricity.

Soon she was on her own. One day in 1886, her husband Charles, a deputy town marshal of Milledgeville, got into an argument over prohibition with a man who accused the deputy of having insulted his brother. Without warning, the man produced a revolver and fired two shots at Charles Haygood at point blank range, killing him at once. The killer was later tried and acquitted.

That left the newly named Annie Abbott, still in her twenties, with three children, one of them only recently born, and no form of subsistence except what she was earning from her occasional local stage appearances. In an effort to make ends meet she stopped performing only in Georgia's halls and started appearing all over the country, wherever anyone would employ her. She had selected the right moment. Her performance became a polished and entertaining one. Young Annie Abbott filled the vacancy left by the recently retired Lulu Hurst. In addition, she had the sense to play upon her sex appeal. Unlike Lulu Hurst, who looked capable of flooring a man with a single punch, the slight Annie concentrated on femininity onstage and off. For her performances the fragile girl wore skirts so short that they almost revealed her calves, and blouses with bare arms. A contemporary report on her act in the *Minnesota Star Tribune* of 15 October 1890 stated:

> It was the most wonderful and utterly inexplicable exhibition – a genuine phenomenon – ever witnessed in this country.

Annie polished and enhanced the original routines of Lulu Hurst and added her own slant to them. As well as performing Hurst's lifting the chair and controlling the umbrella stunts, she would also challenge anyone to take a stout stick – held across the palms of her hands extended horizontally before her, with just two thumbs over the stick – away from her. Annie stipulated only that the volunteers used no sudden jerking movements, nor could they lift her from the floor in order to claim the stick.

She made a feature of her small stature and centred her act on a stunt in which she defied any man to be able to lift her from the ground or move her in any way against her will. Later she polished this trick, claiming that she could transfer these powers to any boy in the audience, making it impossible for the child to be lifted even by the strongest of men. In an interview with the *Midgeville Union Recorder* in September 1893, she said:

> I take a small boy and he places his hands in mine gently and after having him look me in the eyes for some moments the gentlemen find it impossible to raise him from the floor.

She would take the hand of a selected boy and make him look her in the eyes steadily. It was at this stage, Annie claimed, that she transferred her power to the boy. She then released him. As long as the boy kept his attention on her, he could not be lifted from the ground.

Her show went from strength to strength. Soon Annie had another manager and her own touring revue, 'The Mistress of Mysterious Power, and Powerful Company'. Her posters continued to concentrate on her apparent vulnerability.

Tonight!
Annie Abbott
The Georgia Magnet
Will Perform Miracles
She Weighs Only 97 Pounds
No One or Two Men Can Lift Her
No One Can Throw Her Off Balance
She Has Baffled the Scientists of the World,
Who Cannot Explain It
What is the Power or Force?
Absolutely the Most Wonderful Woman of the Age

Annie did so well on her tours of the USA that she allowed herself to be booked to perform at the Alhambra in London in 1891. This did not go as well. Annie was seasick all the way across the Atlantic. Her opening nights at the Alhambra were successful enough, causing a British magician, John Nevil Maskelyn, who, as a sideline had invented the pay toilet, to write sourly in an appendix to his book *The Supernatural* in 1892:

There has appeared in our midst a young lady hailing from the land of the new religions and wooden nutmegs, professing to possess abnormal powers, in the form of some occult magnetic influences enabling her to perform feats of strength out of all proportion to her physical development. To say that this young lady has set the Thames on fire is a very mild way of putting it.

The Georgia Magnet was even presented to the Prince of Wales. By November of the same year, however, Annie Abbott was in trouble. Her act was exposed as a series of tricks by an inquisitive and persistent reporter from the London *Star*. This writer claimed, with the aid of diagrams, that many of Annie Abbott's feats were performed not by the girl but by a team of perspiring stagehands behind the scenes taking the strain by operating hoists and pulleys connected by concealed cables to apparatus on the stage.

Audiences at the Alhambra dwindled, but Annie was resilient and persistent. She continued touring Europe for another two years and returned to the USA as popular as ever. She did, however, display a certain lack of local knowledge by appointing as one of her European stage assistants the bellicose Charlie Mitchell. Charlie was a useful man in a street brawl but his association with any venture did not automatically convince onlookers of its honesty.

Throughout her career Annie Abbott manipulated newspapers and any other publicity sources that came her way. Like Lulu Hurst she claimed that she was possessed by a power that she could not explain. This force, she went on, sometimes caused her excruciating headaches. She gained more attention when she advertised in newspapers, offering a reward to anyone who could rid her of the headaches brought on by her strange gift.

In 1896, Annie Abbott married her manager, Frank B. Baylor,

and retired from show business. It was not the end of the Georgia Magnet, however. For many years after the death of his wife in 1915, Baylor trained and sent forth a stream of Annie Abbotts, in a weird show business human franchise.

Unlike Lulu Hurst, none of the Annie Abbotts ever divulged the secrets behind their communal act. Other magicians and strongmen who studied the principles behind the performances of the various electrical girls were convinced that the original Annie Abbott and her successors used the laws of physics for their strength tricks. She certainly adopted Lulu Hurst's knowledge of realigning the stance and bodily positions of her challengers so that they were at a physical disadvantage without realising it, but there may also have been a more mundane reason for her success.

Annie's celebrated apparent inability to be lifted from the ground, a number of newspaper exposés claimed, could be traced back to one of the routines of a French illusionist called Robert Houdin, who had been born in 1805.

Like Houdin, Annie Abbott, said her detractors, placed metal plates in her shoes. Beneath another metal plate on the stage was placed a powerful electromagnet. When Annie was about to be lifted by a strongman, she would drift over to the plate and stand on it. An associate hidden below would activate a switch and the girl would be firmly anchored to the stage for the duration of the would-be lifter's efforts.

The transference of her powers by osmosis to a child in the audience was explained away by the fact that the child in question was almost always Annie Abbott's son Charles who travelled with her, even as far as Russia. On these occasions he too had metal plates inserted in his shoes and always knew exactly where the corresponding metal plate was situated on the stage.

At the beginning of the twentieth century two of the best known women making public appearances on theatre stages operated on different sides of the world, but each owed her fame to having mastered the Japanese combat system known as ju-jitsu, a form of martial art in which an opponent's strength and aggression is employed against him.

In Great Britain, Mrs Edith Margaret Garrud, who was born in 1872, became the first leading instructor in the sport and gave many demonstrations of it all over London, although she was only just 5ft tall. Together with her husband, the gymnasium owner and teacher of physical culture, William Garrud, Edith attended courses of lessons in ju-jitsu given by Sadekazu Uyenishi, one of the first Japanese experts in the art to visit Great Britain. William Garrud soon became an assistant to Uyenishi and, when the latter returned to Japan, Garrud took over the gymnasium and continued to give lessons. His wife Edith became responsible for teaching it to women and children.

Edith Garrud became very interested in the Suffragette movement, campaigning for the right of women to vote. Members of the organisation were often arrested and manhandled by the police when they protested in the streets. Matters grew worse when the Suffragettes adopted a policy of protest and public disorder to draw attention to their cause.

In an effort to protect Emmeline Pankhurst, the founder of the group, and other leading Suffragettes, a group of about twenty-five women known as 'the Bodyguard' was selected to maintain order at meetings. They even wore Indian Clubs in their belts. To aid their cause, Edith Garrud volunteered to use her skills to teach this inner circle the arts of ju-jitsu. Her lessons were so effective and well received that Edith then toured public halls in London, giving demonstrations of this form of self-defence to women and urging them to learn how to look after themselves. She appeared at theatres, public halls, clubs and even skating rinks.

Edith's reputation spread. She became particularly well known after *Punch* magazine printed a cartoon showing a triumphant Edith Garrud advancing upon a group of apprehensive London policemen. She told the London *Evening Standard*:

> I have already had the pleasure of ejecting one youth from a woman's franchise meeting and after we have had our new society in full swing for some months we hope to have a regular band of ju-jitsu officers who will be able to deal with all the male rowdies who bother us.

Edith Garrud divorced her husband but continued giving exhibitions of ju-jitsu and running a gymnasium for women, which became something of a safe haven for militant Suffragettes. On one occasion, half a dozen of her pupils had been demonstrating outside shops in Oxford Street and had fled to avoid arrest by the police. Edith Garrud's ju-jitsu *dojo* (or gymnasium) was handily situated in Argyll Place, so they made their way there and explained breathlessly to their tutor that the forces of the law were close behind them.

Quite unperturbed, the ever-resourceful Mrs Garrud made them take off their top clothes and don their ju-jitsu training attire. She concealed their clothing and a few missiles left over from their shopping expedition under the floorboards of the gym. When the police arrived, Edith met them at the door. After the officers of the law had explained the reason for their visit, Edith replied with a frosty, 'I have a group of lady students in training. We don't expect the police to come in here!'

She would admit only one of the constables, who under the forbidding glares of the instructress and her six pupils, made the most cursory examination of the premises and left, apologising for the unwarranted intrusion.

In 1907, Mrs Garrud played a leading role in a ju-jitsu instructional film entitled *Ju-jitsu Downs the Footpads*. Four years later, she choreographed the fight scene for a self-defence instructional play called *What Every Woman Should Know*.

Upon the outbreak of the First World War, Emmeline Pankhurst ordered the cessation of militant actions among Suffragettes and the Suffragette Bodyguard was disbanded.

On the other side of the world, another female ju-jitsu exponent was achieving success. Florence LeMarr, known to her friends and fans as Flossie, was born in New Zealand in 1885, where she became an expert in the recondite sport of barefoot skating. She became interested in physical culture when Eugen Sandow made a successful tour of Australia and New Zealand in 1902 and 1903.

Florence married an English wrestler, Joe Gardner, who taught her ju-jitsu. Showing a natural flair for the art, together they toured Australasian music halls for eight years, with a sketch involving demonstrations of ju-jitsu. Florence was also an early feminist and she made much of the fact that any woman should be able to defend herself in a male-orientated world. She advertised her act with the slogan 'No lady in New Zealand should miss this show'.

Although she was only in her twenties, she called herself the world's champion female ju-jitsu performer. Her advertising matter announced that Gardner and LeMarr would be appearing in a dramatic production entitled *The Hooligan and the Lad*, 'in which it is shown how it is possible for a lady with a knowledge of ju-jitsu to protect herself from ruffianly attacks'. Her act began with the sketch of a demure, inoffensive respectable lady (played by herself) who was attacked by a thug, using a series of increasingly threatening and potent weapons. Her husband Joe portrayed her assailant. Florence used her knowledge of ju-jitsu to overpower Joe Gardner as he menaced her successively with a stick, a bludgeon, a knife, a chain, a bottle, an iron bar and finally a revolver.

The sketch was usually well received. It would be followed with Flossie and Joe engaged in an exhibition contest. Finally Florence gave a series of lessons on the finer points of the Japanese art.

The era of professional strongwomen did not last long, nor, with the possible exceptions of Lulu Hurst and her successor as the Georgia Magnet, Annie Abbott, did they usually top the bills, but they were fascinating women and by making their way as strength athletes in what was regarded generally as being a man's world, they displayed character and resolve.

In their male-dominated society they were among the few women who physically and mentally regularly stood up to the male sex in public. Kate Sandwina and a number of her peers wrestled against men and took part in weightlifting competitions with them – often successfully. Lulu Hurst, Annie Abbott and all the other Magnetic Girls delighted in challenging men, singly and in groups, to resist their physical challenges and defied their attempts to overcome them in their stage performances.

The strongwomen also encouraged other members of their sex to be independent and to think for themselves. Edith Garrud and Florence LeMarr showed in their ju-jitsu exhibitions that women could learn to look after themselves. Lulu Hurst made no attempt to hide her pleasure in matching herself against members of the male sex. Again and again she is recorded as giggling with delight as she impelled men challenging her from the audience to make helpless exhibitions of themselves onstage. Kate Sandwina was always her own woman, whether encouraging women to do away with their corsets or admonishing them, perhaps tongue-in-cheek, to drink a daily glass of beer. Annie Abbott made it clear that she might on the surface appear to be a demure, feminine 97lbs, but her abilities – and those of her colleagues – were such that she and they could justly be described, as she was in the Minneapolis *Star Tribune* of 15 October 1890, as 'a wonderful woman'.

Above all, the strongwomen added to the gaiety of nations, both in their public performances and in their lectures and writings. They encouraged other women to be free and lead independent lives, just as these doughty performers so obviously did.

10

THE RUSSIAN LION

E very time it looked as if the strongman craze might falter beneath the weight of charlatans and gimmicks, another theatrical headliner seemed to appear from nowhere to revive the cult. There was no shortage of applicants. After all, posing on the stage of a music hall was infinitely preferable to working in a factory or on a farm or being beaten up on a regular basis as a professional boxer or wrestler.

Unfortunately, the shrewd Sandow apart, most strongman acts still tended towards monotony. Managers and agents started to cast their nets wider in order to meet the demands of the audiences for new strongmen with fresher and livelier routines.

A young, brash and ambitious would-be entrepreneur named C. B. Cochran made the necessary breakthrough when he discovered the so-called Russian Lion and kick-started professional wrestling in Great Britain. So far Cochran had dabbled without success in a number of theatrical ventures. After a sojourn in the USA as a secretary to an actor, he returned to Great Britain determined to become a theatrical agent. Cochran had no money and few contacts but possessed enormous energy, a thick skin and a resolve never to take no for an answer. By chance, within a few days of his return he encountered the unsuccessful Estonian wrestler Georg Hackenschmidt.

Wrestling had existed in the British provinces for centuries. Cornish grapplers wore jackets and gripped one another's shoulders. Devonshire wrestlers wore straw shin guards and clogs and kicked each other in the shins. Lancashire wrestlers stood well apart, with knees bent and arms outstretched. The Greco-Roman and catch-as-catch-can formats made famous by William Muldoon in the USA had not yet caught on in Great Britain. Its practitioners had to cross the Atlantic to earn a steady living.

One wrestler, however, had broken on to the music hall circuit, albeit towards the bottom of the bill and usually in provincial and outer London circuits. His name was Jack Carkeek, a smooth-talking American. He was an experienced wrestler with a convincing line of patter and a witty way with hecklers. He was certainly not setting the Thames on fire, but he was making a steady living at the turn of the century with his act. A skilled self-publicist he would keep his name in the public's eye by sending occasional self-laudatory communiqués back to the USA, exaggerating the state of his success.

One *Police Gazette* paragraph supplied by the wrestler provided a slightly optimistic account towards the end of his British tour: 'He saved his salary, which amounted to nearly £1,000 a week, as he played on average in three or four music halls nightly.' Even in the dubious event of Carkeek obtaining so many regular engagements, he would have been unlikely to have earned much more than a tenth of the sum claimed as a 'dumb act' appearing towards the bottom of the bill.

One night in 1902, all this was to change. In a rare appearance in the West End at the Alhambra in London's Leicester Square, the

40-year-old American was throwing out his customary challenge to the audience for any man to wrestle with him for ten or fifteen minutes without being pinioned to the stage, when an enormous young man stood up in one of the boxes. It was Hackenschmidt, resplendent in white tie and tails. In front of the amazed audience he stripped off his clothes to reveal that beneath them he was wearing wrestling trunks. Jumping down on to the stage he accepted Carkeek's challenge.

Hackenschmidt had been in London for some days but had been unable to secure any wrestling engagements. Later he wrote, 'I was on the point of leaving England when it came to my knowledge that Carkeek, believing me to have already gone, had challenged any professional wrestler then in London to wrestle with him.'

George Jowett, later to become a professional strongman, was in the audience that night. In his 1930 book, *Strong Man Stunts Made Easy*, he described the crowd's reaction to the challenger's imposing physique:

> The first murmurs of surprise from the audience became an uproar, with everybody talking at once, thrilled by the marvellous specimen of humanity that confronted them. No wonder! If Hercules had been resurrected before them they could not have visioned a more spectacularly muscled body.

If the Estonian had hoped for a repeat of the Sandow–Sampson scenario of over a decade ago he was to be disappointed. He was rebuffed firmly by the wily American. Carkeek recognised his would-be challenger at once as the winner of a recent wrestling tournament at the Folies Bergère. Although he was only twenty-three, Georg Hackenschmidt was already a successful wrestler in

Europe, although completely unknown in Great Britain. Carkeek was going to have nothing to do with the enormous Russian. As Hackenschmidt described in his autobiography, the American turned to appeal to the audience.

'You are Englishmen!' he cried self-righteously. 'This man is a famous foreign professional. He comes here tonight for cheap advertisement. I will gladly meet him in a properly arranged match. My challenge is to British wrestlers only!'

Billed as 'the King of Wrestlers', Carkeek had always been a quick-witted man with an eye on the main chance. For some years he had been wrestling in the West Country, the home of his parents, using the jacketed Cornish style in which grips could only be held on the coats and the object was to throw an opponent flat on his back.

Carkeek would take on all comers, defying any of them to last fifteen minutes against him. He would then end his act with the usual hackneyed displays of manual strength. The *Cornishman* described the climax of Carkeek's performance at a hall in Penzance in 1888: 'Carkeek threw two volunteers from the crowd. He then allowed them to stand on his chest while he rested on his hands and feet.'

After a lucrative sojourn, the American finally had to flee the area after complaints that the results of a number of bouts in which he had been engaged had been fixed in advance in order to facilitate betting scams. The *West Briton* newspaper of 15 December 1887 censoriously had exposed details of such a prearranged match between Carkeek and a wrestler called Sam Rundle and a subsequent court case, emphasising the fact that Carkeek was involved in a match with a pre-arranged verdict: 'Carkeek, Rundle and a man named Pascoe had arranged the match. Rundle knew that the match was a bogus one.'

At the Alhambra Theatre, in the space of a few minutes the resourceful Carkeek had managed to make the tongue-tied Russian appear a double-dyed villain intent only on perpetrating a fraud on the innocent English public. The audience began to hiss the now bewildered Hackenschmidt and shout at him to go home. Disconsolately the Russian wrestler walked off the stage.

It had been a long journey from his Dorpat birthplace in 1878 to the inhospitable stage of the Alhambra. By the time he was sixteen, Hackenschmidt already had a local reputation as a muscular prodigy and all-round athlete. His speciality was declared to be having a horse lowered by a pulley on to his shoulders and then walking a few paces carrying the animal. He attracted the interest of Dr Wladislav von Krajewski, a physical culture guru who ran a gymnasium in St Petersburg. The physician started training the young Hackenschmidt, promising the youngster, as Hackenschmidt said in his autobiography, 'I will make you the strongest man in the world.' What the Estonian did not know was that von Krajewski believed that sex was a great weakener for young athletes. As Hackenschmidt morosely complained for the duration of his stay in St Petersburg, he was chaperoned as carefully as a young girl.

With such stories, true or false, circulating, it was not long before the young Hackenschmidt had attracted the attention of one of the many touring wrestlers roaming from tournament to tournament on the Continent. The grappler was George Lurich, a well-known strongman. Lurich took the young Hackenschmidt under his wing, coaching the youth in the rudiments of wrestling and helping him to develop his muscular strength even further.

By 1898, Hackenschmidt's burgeoning reputation was such that he was invited to display his strength in St Petersburg by Count Ribeaupierre, who held the ceremonial title of Master of Horse to the Tsar. Hackenschmidt impressed an invited audience with his new party piece. He stood between two horses, each facing in a different direction. Hackenschmidt grasped their harnesses, tensed his mighty muscles and resisted all efforts by the straining animals to tear him in half. Experienced strongmen muttered that the feat was not quite as impressive as it looked, because by pulling in opposite directions the two horses had each nullified the effect of the other. However, this was a display for seasoned strongmen. Few young men could have pulled off such a stunt and Hackenschmidt now certainly looked the part of a strongman.

He also continued with his wrestling. In the same year the Russian won several amateur tournaments and was feted when he pressed a weight of 279lbs above his head. In 1899, he was recruited into service in the Life Guards but was released after five months to sally into the wide world and win glory for the Tsar and his adopted motherland as a professional wrestler. Wrestling in the static Greco-Roman style, which did not permit holds below the waist, he toured Europe, winning tournaments in Moscow, Paris, Budapest, Vienna and Constantinople. The Moscow championships were a real test of stamina, extending over a forty-day period.

After the Viennese tournament, Hackenschmidt had claimed the Greco-Roman heavyweight championship of the world, but then as now there was no authoritative international sanctioning body and the Russian was only one of many wrestlers laying claim to the title.

Nevertheless, the word was beginning to spread among the strength fraternity that in Georg Hackenschmidt a new star, both in wrestling and weightlifting, was beginning to emerge. Almost inevitably, it would seem, Hackenschmidt cemented that reputation against the perennial fall guy, Charles A. Sampson.

Their meeting occurred, or rather did not occur, in St Petersburg. Sampson, on tour as usual, was going through his customary routine at a theatre in the city when he heard that the young Georg Hackenschmidt was in the audience. Sensing a chance for additional publicity and always happy to embarrass younger strength athletes, Sampson challenged Hackenschmidt to come up on to the stage and lift the long, heavy steel pole that the older man had just finished hoisting above his head. Unfortunately Sampson's reputation for deviousness had preceded him even as far as Russia. Hackenschmidt and his companions had noticed that the challenge pole had been discarded, as if by chance, behind a curtain. Hackenschmidt surmised correctly that while it was out of sight in this fashion the Frenchman's assistants had been busily filling the hollow steel cylinder with lead shot, increasing its tonnage considerably.

Nevertheless, Hackenschmidt strolled nonchalantly on to the stage and agreed to attempt to lift the weight – as long as Sampson would elevate it above his head one more time first! As was his wont, Sampson argued and blustered, but adamantly refused to attempt the lift again, knowing it to be impossible. Triumphantly Hachenschmidt turned to the audience and in stentorian tones explained what had happened, exposing the other man as a fraud. In an attempt to alleviate matters, Sampson insisted that he only needed more time in order to prepare for this unexpected challenge contest. He defied Hackenschmidt to come prepared for a trial of strength with him on the following Friday night. The Estonian agreed willingly. At this the crowd's catcalls turned to cheers. However, when Hackenscmidt and the spectators arrived at the hall a few days later it was to discover that Charles Sampson had broken his theatrical engagement and had fled from the city.

The day after his abortive attempt to challenge Jack Carkeek in London, the disconsolate and almost penniless Hackenschmidt was on the point of returning to the Continent when he met C. B. Cochran. The introduction was effected by Harry Taft, an American comedian outside the Tivoli theatre. He had seen Hackenschmidt wrestle on the Continent and described the Russian's prowess in glowing terms. The opportunistic Cochran immediately offered to become Hackenschmidt's manager. The Englishmen knew nothing about wrestling but he was not about to let a little thing like that stand between him and a potential meal ticket. Initially Hackenschmidt was dubious about the proposed business relation-ship with a stranger, but Cochran was persuasive and the wrestler had nothing to lose. With some reluctance he agreed to allow the would-be entrepreneur the opportunity to steer him to the prom-ised gold and glory.

Cochran was aware that he would have to capitalise on Georg Hackenschmidt's ability as a wrestler. He was also aware that the real money was to be earned as a strongman on the music hall stages. The Russian was a very well-built man, possessed great natural strength and could easily be taught a few strongman tricks. Accordingly the fledgling manager bombarded newspapers with florid handouts describing the shy and retiring Hackenschmidt as 'the wonder of the age'. It was not all bombast. C. B. Cochran's privately expressed opinion of the Russian Lion was just as laudatory as his public utterances: 'The most perfect specimen of physical manhood I have ever seen. He had not the bulging muscles of Sandow or Sampson, the strongmen, but the smooth rippling muscles of a greyhound, and a slender waist.'

The breakthrough came surprisingly quickly when the *Daily Mail* published a glowing puff in the shape of an article with the heading 'Is Strength Genius?' Hackenschmidt was a thoughtful, philosophical and surprisingly temperamental man. He did not conform to the public image of a strength athlete, and the article made great play with his theories of the cosmos.

More to the point, as far as Cochran was concerned, the publicity bore fruit in the shape of a week's booking at a music hall for his new client, at a rate of £70. Dutifully Hackenschmidt went through the usual hackneyed stage routines of lifting weights, giving posing exhibitions and challenging any member of the audience to wrestle with him.

By now other newspapers were writing about the Russian, leading to an appearance in the boxing ring at the National Sporting Club, where he stripped to his posing trunks and gave a display of muscle flexing.

Cochran was doing his job well, but trouble lay over the horizon. Flushed with triumph, Hackenschmidt next accepted a fee of £150 a week to appear for five weeks at the London Tivoli. He flopped. The Russian's steadily decreasing audiences could not help noticing that the stolid Hackenschmidt was no showman. His physique was impressive but his weightlifting displays were dull and his onstage wrestling bouts were over almost as soon as they had begun. Hackenschmidt simply could not grasp the concept of 'carrying' a challenger from the audience for a few minutes in order to entertain the audience. Nor could the agitated Cochran at first persuade his protégé of the necessity of spicing up his act.

By the end of the Tivoli booking, word of the Russian's boring stage routines had spread among the other music hall proprietors and Hackenschmidt and Cochran were both unemployed again. In desperation Cochran turned to the city of Liverpool. Wrestling was quite popular in Lancashire. Tom Cannon was a local veteran, a former champion of England who still laid claim to the European title bestowed upon him by someone who happened to be passing after an obscure provincial match as long ago as 1894. No one in the sporting world paid much attention to such claims, which were the stock-in-trade of most professional wrestlers of the era.

A more genuine claim on the part of the Liverpool man was that he had probably been the first English wrestler to earn a living in the emerging grappling market in the USA. Little is known of the contests he engaged in there, but he is on record for having been annoyed by the Solid Man, William Muldoon, and even to have challenged him. An edition of the *New York Times* on 21 December 1882 described how the Englishman issued his defiance at a sports meeting organised by the Metropolitan Rowing Club before a crowd of five hundred:

> Mr Tom Cannon caused a sensation by preceding a wrestling exhibition by saying that Mr William Muldoon, who was present, had been stating through newspaper columns that Tom Cannon was no good. 'I am good enough for him!' continued Mr Cannon, 'and I now challenge him to step upon this platform to wrestle me either Graeco-Roman or catch as catch can.' Loud and prolonged cries for Muldoon followed Mr Cannon's challenge but Mr Muldoon remained in his seat.

Cannon was an interesting and courageous man. If he had come along a little later when the wrestling boom was at its height, and if he had been able to secure the services of a manager as lively as C. B. Cochran, he might have become a major figure in the early grappling world. As it was the best that he could do was use his strength and skills to meet the needs of a wanderlust practically amounting to restlessness. Tom Cannon was a muscular fidget.

Like many brawny Lancashire men of his age and class, Cannon started by working in the pits. He then served for a time as a policeman, where he honed his wrestling skills to such an extent that he was encouraged to turn professional. He never secured enough backing to make a great deal of money and he was never the 'house' fighter, aided by a sympathetic promoter to build up an impressive winning record. This meant that throughout his career Cannon sometimes had to wrestle to order, losing to much inferior wrestlers when the wagers were laid. Still, in the vernacular, when his chains were off and he could fight freely, in his prime he could be a fearsome opponent, especially when he abandoned the staid Lancashire and Greco-Roman styles and concentrated on the more spectacular catch-as-catch-can form of grappling.

In 1881, he is recorded as losing to 'Little' Joe Acton in a match billed for the catch-as-catch-can championship of the world. By 1887 he was wrestling in New Zealand. At the end of the same year he had moved across to Australia and was lodging at a hostelry owned by a man called Tom Taylor near Randwick Racecourse in Sydney. He was challenging all comers to matches under the rules of all or any of the five major currently recognised wrestling styles. His weight was recorded as 200lbs and his height as 5ft 8in.

By 1888, Cannon had visited the USA, where he defeated such highly rated performers as the Japanese Sorakichi and the original Ed 'Strangler' Lewis. A typical itinerary on this tour was impressive. On Monday he wrestled in Rochester. Tuesday saw him grappling in Buffalo. On Wednesday he appeared in Cleveland against the formidable Tom Jenkins. By Friday he was back in Cleveland. He ended the week with a bout in Cincinnati.

It was on this tour that Tom Cannon reached the nadir of his professional career when he was forced to tour briefly in a tent show with the notorious psychopath Clarence Whistler, who had the habit of turning a pistol on co-stars with whom he had fallen out. At the end of that year Cannon returned to London to grapple the Frenchman Eugen Bazin at the Royal Aquarium. In 1889, he was in Paris, where he made the acquaintance of Louis Uni, the mighty Apollon, and for a time became his manager and trainer, looking after the big man when he took on challengers at a wrestling and strongman show in the Avenue de Neuilly.

Cannon also had a few bouts in the French capital but obviously was not putting his all into his contests. In 1890, the Paris correspondent of the *Sportsman* wrote,

The grand wrestling match at the Folies Bergère between Tom Cannon and Felix Bernard which has been advertised all over Paris as a genuine contest for ten thousand francs, was, after all, nothing but a hoax.

The contest at the Winter Garden was so tame, with both contestants rolling aimlessly all over the stage, and so incensed the crowd, convinced that it was being cheated, that there were cries of '*A bas les voleurs!*' ('Down with the robbers!'). Spectators stormed the box office to get their money back. The gas was turned off, a customary precaution in such riots, and the police summoned. The crowd was driven into the street by a number of forced charges, but not before almost all the tables and chairs in the hall had been smashed.

Nothing daunted, Tom Cannon then went on to wrestle Carl Abbs at the American Theatre in Berlin, losing after eighty minutes. He next popped up in India, where he was matched against Karim Bux in Calcutta. Bux was the favourite wrestler of the wealthy Maharajah of Cooch Behar, who played a prominent part in proceedings from the ringside. Cannon was adjudged the loser. He left the theatre furiously, saying that the Maharah had influenced the judges to give Bux the decision. Cannon declared that he would no longer remain in a place where such high personages could be guilty of mean, unsportsmanlike and unjust behaviour. He (Cannon) intended sailing to Ceylon and Egypt, where he hoped to pick up some matches and be treated better than he had been in India.

Cannon stopped off briefly in Paris in 1896, where a wrestling manager of dubious reputation called Antonio Pierri hired him to referee a bout at the Cirque d'Hiver in Paris, between Yousouff, 'the Terrible Turk' and Ibrahim Mahmout. Preparatory to a tour of the USA, Pierri was trying to gain Yousouff a reputation as a wrestler who would stop at nothing to win. At one point in the bout Yousouff pretended to go berserk and attacked his opponent wildly. Adhering to the script, Cannon picked up a stick and beat the wrestler with it, before sending for the police.

He then spent some years giving wrestling exhibitions in circuses, notably Hengler's in London and Liverpool, but soon was on the move again. In April 1897 the London *Mirror of Life* wrote that Tom Cannon 'has elected once more to seek fresh woods and pastures new, where, by his indomitable courage and determination he will endeavour to subdue all aspirants who may oppose him for the proud title of champion'. The newspaper went on to say that a large crowd had seen Cannon off on the midnight train from Liverpool to Southampton, where he was due to catch a boat for South Africa.

A year later Cannon was embarking upon another two-year tour of the USA, wrestling all over the country. In 1900, he secured a top-billed spot with a circus, claiming to be the world Greco-Roman champion. He lost credibility – and the job – when reporters pointed out that over the past twelve months Cannon had lost to Antonio Pierri, Joe Acton, Dan McLeod and a number of others.

Time was running out for the ageing Lancashire man. He tried one more tour of Great Britain, taking on all comers at a Liverpool music hall, offering £10 to any wrestler, amateur or professional who could last fifteen minutes against him. By now he was in straitened circumstances and allowed himself to be matched against Madrali, the Terrible Turk, the latest overseas sensation to appear on the wrestling scene. A shadow of his former self, Tom Cannon was defeated easily in what was described as a grievous mismatch. It was 1906 and Tom Cannon was fifty-nine years old. Hopefully, he announced, 'I was forty years old before I began to appreciate the finer points of wrestling.'

He was merely whistling in the dark. He was home again, exhausted and impoverished after his recent unsuccessful tour. Originally a Greco-Roman wrestler, his style had been regarded as boring in the USA and he had adopted the more freestyle and fluid catch-as-catch-can form of the sport. Now his luck had turned for the worse to such an extent that he even started working again in the pits he had left with such relief all those years ago.

Cochran heard of Cannon's plight and for his own ends deliberately set out to resurrect the Lancashire man's grappling career. He issued a public challenge to Cannon on behalf of the much younger Hackenschmidt. The had-been local wrestler could hardly believe his good luck in being offered an unexpected payday when he thought that his ring career was over. He accepted the challenge at once and went into training. Using all his publicity skills,

C. B. Cochran set out to persuade the inhabitants of Liverpool that the forthcoming contest would turn out to be the most exciting ever witnessed in the northwest.

For once the promoter did not have to go out of his way to garner publicity. Events conspired to provide the delighted manager with as much precious newspaper space as even he could desire. Wrestling was seldom witnessed on the stage – apart from the exhibitions provided by Jack Carkeek and a handful of others – and Cochran could not persuade any of the city's music hall proprietors to stage the proposed bout. Theatre owners even doubted if the sport really constituted a variety act.

As a last resort Cochran decided to promote the contest himself. He secured a three-month lease on the derelict Prince of Wales Theatre in Clayton Square and announced that after the inaugural Hackenschmidt–Cannon match there would be more bouts on succeeding evenings, many of them featuring the Russian Lion. Suddenly Cochran was confronted by the horrified owner of the theatre, fearful of losing his licence should such a degrading spectacle as professional wrestling be featured in his establishment. He insisted that the contest, now being billed as the European championship, be cancelled.

Cochran ignored the proprietor. He sent out hundreds of men bearing display boards advertising the match. The distraught theatre owner retaliated by dispatching his own sandwich-board men, announcing that the bout most certainly would not take place. Feelings between the rival factions reached such a pitch that whenever the opposing board carriers met in the street, fights would sometimes break out between them.

The resultant publicity was tremendous. On the opening night the hall was besieged by would-be patrons demanding admittance.

But the enterprising theatre owner was not yet beaten. Before the spectators could start surging into the theatre, all the lights in the building went out. The gas pipes had been cut, almost a reflex action in such situations. Cochran rose to the occasion. While he sent his minions out to scour the city for gas fitters he addressed the mob. Hoarsely he assured the crowd that if only everyone was patient the fight would assuredly go on.

In a short time the required technicians were rounded up. As an added inducement Cochran promised the leading fitter that if the lighting could be restored, the man could act as timekeeper for the main event. The incentive worked. Eventually the lights fluttered into life and the show began.

The opening night turned out to be highly successful. The Russian Lion had little trouble in disposing of the ageing Tom Cannon but Hackenschmidt's impressive strength and physique awed the audience. Later Hackenschmidt described the contest:

> The English champion now something of a veteran, had had a very wide and exceptional experience, and was able to bring into play some very skilful, if somewhat painful moves, which he had picked up from Turkish wrestlers.

Hackenschmidt won the bout by a single submission after thirty-three minutes, having placed Tom Cannon in a hammerlock. But the dogged owner of the Prince of Wales struck again. He had discovered in the fine print of the contract a clause stating that the lessee had to vacate the theatre by midnight after every performance. On the night of the second performance at his theatre he saw to it that the police escorted Cochran and Hackenschmidt from the hall. As soon as the lessees had been ejected, the proprietor led a gang of hired thugs into the building and locked and barricaded the doors from the inside.

The following morning, a determined Cochran stirred his wrestling troupe with an impassioned address and led them into Clayton Square to storm the theatre. After a frantic struggle the wrestlers wrenched one of the outer doors off its hinges and rushed up a narrow flight of stairs. At the head of the stairs the proprietor and his men were waiting. They turned a fire hose on Cochran and his followers, driving them back. In *A Showman Looks On*, Cochran told how three times he'd led a charge up the stairs and on each occasion the concentrated jet drove the gasping attackers back. At the fourth attempt the bedraggled grapplers reached the head of the steps. The men manipulating the hosepipe lost their nerve at the sight of the approaching horde of soaked and vengeful mammoths. They turned and fled.

Throughout the hectic battle for possession of the stairs, Charles Cochran had been urging on his men with great vehemence but somehow, in the excitement of the final successful surge, he had lost contact with the main body of wrestlers. He found himself hurtling round a corner on his own. He stopped when he saw half a dozen of the owner's hired hands waiting for him in pleased anticipation. The men leapt on the promoter, hustled him to the head of another flight of steps and hurled him down them with such velocity that he skidded on his back out into the street.

Bruised and winded, the young showman dragged himself to his feet and staggered back into the Prince of Wales. By this time the main conflict was over. Only a few minor skirmishes were still being conducted. The local hard men had been no match for the professional wrestlers. Once again C. B. Cochran was in charge of the theatre.

It turned out to have been a pyrrhic victory. The proprietor had not been idle overnight during his tenure of the theatre. During the uproar not only had the gas pipes been severed again but most of the seats in the auditorium had been removed as well. There would be no more wrestling in Liverpool that month.

Nevertheless, the publicity engendered by what the newspapers termed the Battle of Clayton Square had been invaluable, for both Cochran and Hackenschmidt. Other cities began to clamour to see the Russian Lion in action, although in a more peaceful context.

Acting quickly, Cochran signed a contract for Hackenschmidt to appear in Manchester, at £150 a week. At last the manager persuaded his charge to polish up his act and introduce more razzle-dazzle and showmanship into his music hall appearances. Former opponent Tom Cannon was recruited for the tour to train the Estonian in the art of presentation. With an eye to the future, the Lancashire wrestler introduced Georg Hackenschmidt to the intricacies of catch-as-catch-can wrestling, which was soon to eclipse the staid old Greco-Roman form in the public's favour.

Cochran also took on a German wrestler called Schackmann to play the part of the group's resident 'heavy'. Schackmann soon became an indispensable part of Hackenschmidt's music hall routine. Night after night, the shapeless German would loom up out of the audience loudly challenging Hackenschmidt to a bout. The Russian Lion would feign amazement and then fury at such effrontery and the contest would be on. From the outset Schackmann would break every rule in the book. He would elbow Hackenschmidt, head-butt him, stamp on the Russian's toes and even throw the referee out of the ring, before finally being subdued by his squeaky-clean opponent, to great public approbation, night after night.

Cochran, who, like Hackenschmidt, was still learning on the job as far as screwing every last penny out of the music hall patrons was concerned, finally settled on an acceptable range of tariffs for his wrestler, which would sound agreeable when announced from the stage. His rates were to be taken up by many other music hall grapplers. The Russian Lion offered to pay £25 to any challenger who could last for fifteen minutes against him in a challenge bout. A generous £100 would be handed over to anyone from the audience who could gain a fall over the brawny professional. As a sign that no one was banned, Hackenschmidt and Cochran also promised to pay £50 to any challenger who could show that Georg Hackenschmidt had failed to meet him in the ring within twenty-four hours of being challenged.

If challenges from the audience were slow in coming, there was always the reliable old Tom Cannon on hand to step into the breach by pretending to go the distance with Hackenschmidt, thus securing a return match later in the week for a 'sidestake'. With the heading of 'Evergreen Cannon', the *Montreal Gazette* reported on 22 November 1900:

> Tom Cannon, who for sixteen years held the championship of the world, lasted the time with Hackenschmidt, won £25 and the right to challenge him for £60 later in the week.

As he further burnished Hackenschmidt's act, which now by public demand included the obligatory exhibitions of weightlifting and muscle flexing, as well as wrestling, Cochran saw to it that the now conciliatory Hackenschmidt allowed a few hopeful challengers from the body of the theatre to last the full fifteen minutes with the champion and thus secure the cash prize. A heavily publicised return match would then be arranged at the hall for another night. This time Hackenschmidt would win without exerting himself, while C. B. Cochran pocketed any sidestake which had been arranged, or else bet a substantial sum on Hackenschmidt to win with enthusiastic but misguided fans of the local hopeful.

Within twelve months, Georg Hackenschmidt was famous all over England with his music hall act. Like many of his contemporaries he started writing books and articles on physical culture. Where he differed from most of the others eager to sell their postal courses, was in his frank acceptance that regular training with heavy weights was essential in order to build substantial strength and muscle. In Hackenschmidt's *The Way to Live*, he also advocated the beneficial effects of running:

> Run as much as you can and as often as you can, and whenever you come across a hill run up it. This will force you to inhale deep breaths and will also accustom you to breathing through your nose. Beside the chest and lung development resulting there from, you will soon appreciate the benefits which your leg muscles will develop.

Hackenschmidt became so well known that the popular song 'In the Shade of the Old Apple Tree' was rewritten in his honour:

> When Hackenschmidt grappled with me
> He pulled like the roots of a tree.
> He gave me a punch where I just had my lunch
> And he mixed up my dinner and tea.

Georg Hackenschmidt's music hall strongman and wrestling act had become so popular that he attracted grapplers from all over the world to Great Britain hoping to emulate the Estonian's success, just as weightlifters had flooded into the country in the wake of Eugen Sandow. They came in all shapes and sizes, but their intention was not to wrestle one another, although they would do so as a last resort. The grapplers realised that the big, steady money lay in securing lucrative music hall or vaudeville tours. First they had to attract the attention of the bookers, next they had to work up interesting stage acts, involving a combination of strongman stunts, wrestling, drama and humour. Once they had accomplished this they could stay on the twice-nightly entertainment circuit for years, even decades, without ever again having to risk life and limb in genuinely ferocious wrestling matches.

Managers and agents started importing wrestlers they hoped to be able to turn into professional strongmen. 'The whole country went wrestling mad,' gloated C. B. Cochran, who held a trump card in Georg Hackenschmidt.

For most of the first decade of the twentieth century there was a craze for ethnic grapplers who could offer the public glamorous backgrounds and suitably embellished exotic biographies. The first group to arrive came from India, a country with a long tradition of wrestling. Most princes of the different states had their own palace wrestlers, who were treated very well as long as they continued winning.

The Indian wrestlers were assembled and imported to Europe by a promoter called R. B. Benjamin, who toured with a wrestling circus, offering to take on all comers. A Bengali millionaire called Shavat Kumar Mishra met the expenses of the tour. He was eager to see how the best Indian wrestlers would fare against European professionals.

The impetus for the visit was the emergence of a wrestler many considered to be the best ever to come from the Indian continent. Gulam Mohammed was born in 1888, the son of a wrestler, and began grappling at the age of five, embarking upon a gruelling training regime designed to improve his strength and stamina. Eventually he reached a weight of 230lbs at a height of about 5ft 8in. Raised by his grandfather and an uncle, he began wrestling competitively at the age of fifteen. In 1906, he had won so many contests and displayed such skill that he was appointed a court wrestler. Three years later, he claimed the championship of India.

R. B. Benjamin's wrestling circus had a mixed time of it in Great Britain. The promoter made a great fanfare of the titles possessed by his troupe – Gama, the Indian champion, undefeated in two hundred matches; Imam Bux (Gama's younger brother), the champion of Lahore; Ahmed Bux, the champion of Armritsar; and Gamu, the champion of Jullundhur. As a codicil, Benjamin added to the posters the reassuring information that the visitors from such a far-flung part of the Empire were all loyal British subjects.

At first all went reasonably well. Benjamin, the promoter, secured a bout for Gama against Dr Benjamin Roller, 'the Pride of Seattle', a leading American wrestler. Roller was a genuine practising medical doctor and an interesting man: a former college athlete who had played American football for the Philadelphia Phillies, claimed a hotly disputed world record for throwing the discus, lectured at Washington University and had written a chapter on anaesthesia for a textbook on gynaecology. He had taken up wrestling to pay his way through college, but after a bout with wily old Jack Carkeek, allied to a minor betting coup, earned him enough to purchase his first house outright, he began to contemplate a long-term career in the sport.

In an effort to make the big bucks, Roller once wrestled twenty-one times in a month, claiming to have lost only five of the contests. As befitted his medical background, his wrestling speciality lay in claiming in most of his bouts to have sustained spectacular injuries to parts of his body that laymen could not identify on an anatomical chart if they tried, but then battled on through transparent agony to conquer.

The Great Gama defeated Roller by two falls secured in very quick time, impressing the wrestling public. Those inside the sport were less easily won over; lurking in the background was the form of the Machiavellian and unscrupulous US promoter Jack Curley, who had accompanied Roller across the Atlantic. It was rumoured that Curley was considering importing Gama to the USA and that the Pride of Seattle, who was known to be amenable to surreptitious deals when the price was right, might have gone into the tank in order to gather publicity for Gama on the far side of the Atlantic.

True to form, Benjamin Roller claimed to have broken two of his ribs in the contest, but no one was really bothered. A more immediate result of Gama's first victory was that R. B. Benjamin's Indian Wrestling Circus secured an engagement at the Alhambra Theatre. The experienced manager worked out a convincing routine for his grapplers, including exhibition bouts between the Indians, challenges to anyone in the audience and displays of strength, including lifting heavy rocks. The highlight of the performance consisted of the Great Gama going through a modified training routine, lifting members of the audience above his head with one hand and bursting asunder a potato held between his fingers while Benjamin gave the audience an account of his regular physical regime. As a Muslim, Gama eschewed meat and ate a specially prepared vegetable broth six times a day, supplemented by copious draughts of milk. He spent most of his time preparing his body for his wrestling career. He would perform endless stretching and bending exercises. He also performed thousands of deep knee squats, often holding a heavy stone above his head, as well as push-ups and self-resistance exercises, in the course of a day. To strengthen his grip he would manipulate handfuls of thick clay between his fingers for thirty minutes at a time.

Hackenschmidt was doing well with his music hall tours, where he was now clearing £200 a week after covering the wages of his supporting acts and paying all expenses, but he ignored Gama's challenges. This led to Benjamin overplaying his hand. He matched Gama against Stanislaus Zbyszko, a top Polish wrestler, a squat, dour character with a reputation for erudition, who had been winning many matches on the Continent. His real name was Stanislaw Cyganiewicz but he had changed it to Zbyszko after a fictional Polish knight. Zbyszko was 5ft 6in. tall, bald and later was to attain a weight of almost 300lbs. He had started his career as a professional strongman and weightlifter. One opponent said that he resembled 'a cross between a gorilla and the egg of some gigantic prehistoric bird'.

The match, sponsored by the magazine *John Bull*, turned out to be a disaster. It took place at the Shepherd's Bush Stadium in September 1910 for a sidestake, it was claimed, of £250 a side. Zbyszko trained in a gymnasium at Rottingdean, while Gama fitted in his preparations between London music hall appearances. Twelve thousand people attended, to be greeted by demure Japanese women in kimonos, handing out flowers. The spectators seemed lost in an arena capable of holding almost seventy thousand.

From the start, Gama revealed his inexperience of modern western wrestling techniques. Almost at once he allowed Zbyszko to take him down to the mat. The Russian then squirmed over on to his stomach, with Gama lying ineffectually on top of him, and there the pair of them remained for over two hours.

It was a bizarre encounter, officially timed at two hours and thirty-five minutes. Long before the end of that time, spectators were heading for the exits. For almost the entire duration of the bout, Stanislaus Zbyszko lay obdurately on his stomach beneath the Indian wrestler, like a supine tortoise, refusing to depart from this cautious, ultra-defensive strategy. Sometimes he rose on to his hands and knees but always he returned to the safety of his prone position on the mat, as Gama tried in vain to prise the Russian loose. In the end, while the handful of remaining spectators cheered ironically, the referee Jack Smith declared the so-called contest to be a draw.

Health and Strength condemned the Polish wrestler for being 'woefully lacking in enterprise', but almost incredibly a return bout was arranged for the following Saturday. This time Zbyszko did not turn up. His manager claimed that the grappler's mother was ill, but others scoffed that the Pole was busily wrestling easier opponents in France. The matter was abandoned with relief.

The Great Gama's European foray was almost over. He had engaged in two farcical matches, the jig-time encounter with Benjamin Roller and the protracted bore against Zbyszko. Georg Hackenschmidt was not interested in a contest and music hall bookings had dropped off alarmingly. In an effort to recoup his losses, R. B. Benjamin took his circus to Paris, but there was little interest there either. The troupe was disbanded and the Indian champions returned sadly to their own country, where they remained pre-eminent for many years. Gama retired in 1919, but returned to the ring a decade later for one final strange encounter in India against Zbyszko, whom he defeated in a matter of seconds on this occasion.

As if in an attempt to show Benjamin and other would-be promoters how the career of a champion should be handled, C. B. Cochran withdrew Hackenschmidt from the halls temporarily to present him to the public in several well-mounted major matches in London. In direct contrast to Gama's matches against Roller and Zbyszko, the Russian Lion's bouts were spectacular and lucrative.

It was generally acknowledged that Hackenschmidt was flourishing because he had the promotional genius of Cocharan behind him. The promoter was particularly shrewd in finding the right opponent for the Russian Lion, and one had just appeared. The newcomer was called Madrali and was backed by Antonio Pierri, a manager and former wrestler who called himself the Terrible Greek. Towards the end of his career he had fought Hackenschmidt and lost quickly. He was cross-eyed and had a bald head. His favourite catchphrase was 'Pierri is a very straight man'. Cochran considered him about as straight as a corkscrew.

Believing that the old ways were the best ways, Pierri took the traditional route to challenging Hackenschmidt. He and Madrali appeared in the stalls of a hall at which the Russian Lion was appearing. The two men stood up, wearing long coats, and challenged Hackenschmidt to a bout. Cochran knew that the appearance of the huge and ugly Madrali would fit in with the current desire for strongmen with exotic and enhanced backgrounds.

As soon as the match was made it caught the fancy of sporting London. Cochran took one of his punts and courageously hired the mammoth Olympia stadium for the night. Pierri did his part, publicising Madrali as hard as he could. There were rumours that this latest Terrible Turk was in fact a Marseilles stevedore of Bulgarian extraction. Pierri would have none of it. Ahmed Madrali, he declared, was the Sultan of Turkey's favourite court wrestler and had recently been appointed chief bodyguard to his master's personal harem of four hundred women. What was more, he ate twenty meat cutlets for breakfast every morning.

London went mad over the forthcoming contest. It was billed as 'The Greatest Feat of Athleticism Ever Witnessed'. Every ticket was sold weeks in advance, some ringside seats changing hands at twenty-five guineas each.

Behind the scenes there was considerable mutual antagonism between Pierri and his wrestler, but Madrali was bound to his manager by a cast-iron contract. Pierri doled out £5 a week to his athlete, although he was taking in £100 for his music hall act. To make the meagre stipend look larger, Pierri paid it out in three-penny pieces and coppers. He claimed to feed Madrali on a leg of mutton a day. In reality the leg had to last a week and was supplemented with low-quality rice, purchased by the sackful.

Madrali was very strong. He weighed 220lbs but hated most forms of training, especially roadwork, almost as much as he detested his manager. On several occasions, a pursuing Pierri found the wrestler playing cards in a pub along the route of his training run.

Strangely enough, the rather naive Georg Hackenschmidt approached the contest with some apprehension. He started to believe his opponent's pre-match publicity and genuinely felt that Madrali, who was a favourite in the betting, might beat him. This spurred him into some vigorous training sessions. He did his daily preparation at a public house in Shepherd's Bush. A feature of his workout was carrying a sack of cement weighing over 500lbs on his shoulders, with a heavyweight sparring partner balanced on top of the sack. He drank eleven pints of milk a day and ate vast quantities of raw fruit and vegetables.

Throughout their training period, aware of the real source of their incomes, both competitors persisted with their music hall appearances. Hackenschmidt performed twice nightly at the Paragon Theatre in Canterbury, while Madrali headed the bill at the Pavilion Theatre.

Hackenschmidt's entourage was not quite as varied but his name alone was enough to draw in the crowds all over the country. As back-up he employed the usual comic singers, soubrettes, illusionists, mimics and tenors, while to make him look good in his wrestling exhibitions were the docile Gunner Moir, former boxing champion of England and heavyweight wrestling champion of the army; Bert Wood, wrestling champion of the navy; and Herr Charles Axa, the champion of Germany. It was announced that in addition to grappling exhibitions and accepting challenges from the audience, Hackenschmidt would lift weights and also appear in 'instructive and interesting scenes of "Poses Plastiques"'. In the run-up to the much-hyped Olympia match, each strongman would end his stage performance by boasting to an enthusiastic audience of what he would do to the other man when they clashed in the ring in January.

The day of the match was overcast. It rained most of the morning and afternoon. Hackenschmidt spent the afternoon in bed while Madrali relaxed at a sporting club. That evening, traffic jams extended from Olympia to Piccadilly, one of the capital's greatest traffic pile-ups so far. The hall was filled hours before the fight. To while away the time, Lieutenant Forrest's celebrated Light Infantry Band played selected airs, including the acclaimed *Entry of the Gladiators*.

Madrali was the first to enter the ring, wearing a brown dressing gown with fur trimmings. Hackenschmidt followed, looking pale and nervous. He was greeted with a great roar of approbation. The introductions of the wrestlers were shouted through a megaphone. There was a puzzling variation to the Terrible Turk's presentation. Almost as an aside the announcer bellowed 'No one in the world would ever buy him for a fixed fight!' Those in the know at the ringside took this to be a sideswipe from Cochran at some of his rival promoters, who were putting on more and more patently rehearsed matches. The two wrestlers shook hands, returned to their corners and shed their gowns. The referee blew a whistle to start the bout.

It was all over inside two minutes. Hackenschmidt rushed straight across the ring at Madrali. He missed with his first attempts to secure a hold but then clamped a grip around the Terrible Turk's body. As he felt the breath being squeezed out of his lungs, Madrali stuck his fingers up his opponent's nostrils, drawing blood. Hackenschmidt jerked himself free and swung Madrali to the ground, falling across him and pinning him to the canvas. The referee blew his whistle to signify that Hackenschmidt had won the first fall. When both men stood up it was apparent the Terrible Turk's arm was hanging at an awkward angle. It was dislocated. Madrali immediately conceded the match to his opponent.

At once C. B. Cochran sent the Russian Lion on a tour of the country at an enhanced salary to cash in on the publicity engendered by the bout at Olympia, though not before allowing the Estonian wrestler to return to London for one more match. In June, Hackenschmidt met an American, Tom Jenkins, a one-eyed, illiterate former steel worker. His trade in the dreadful mills had been that of a 'rougher' seizing red-hot iron bars in a pair of gigantic tongs and feeding them through rollers. Hackenschmidt won the bout easily and claimed the world title. Then, almost as a last hurrah in Great Britain, he added more kudos to his reputation by throwing a redoubtable Scottish wrestler called Alec Munro.

Munro, a former blacksmith, was feared not so much for his wrestling ability as for the fact that he was a police inspector in the Govan force, whose proud superiors threatened to close down the theatre should any touring wrestler defeat their man. To keep Munro on his toes, the local equivalent of the Watch Committee also threatened to dismiss their inspector if any of his performances should not come up to scratch. In the event, Hackenschmidt managed to circumvent the threats being issued by competing against an almost tearfully distraught Munro in the open air at Glasgow Rangers' Ibrox football stadium in the pouring rain, in a best of two falls competition. He threw the policeman in twenty-two and eleven minutes respectively. Sixteen thousand people watched the match.

Then the Russian Lion made the mistake that was to ruin his career and inadvertently begin the end of the professional strongman era. He parted company with C. B. Cochran.

Shortly before he gave up trying to establish himself in England, The Indian wrestler the Great Gama issued one final desperate appeal for work. It read:

A Sensational Challenge India v Japan

Gama is prepared to throw every one of the thirty Japanese wrestlers now showing at the Exhibition in one hour – actual wrestling time. Gama will guarantee to carry out the contract, the only stipulation being that the men stand five yards apart, and as soon as the signal is given to start they approach one another and begin wrestling. Ten minutes' rest to be allowed after Gama throws the first fifteen. £100 a side. Gama is also prepared to throw the champion of the Japanese ten times in thirty minutes for £100 a side

The fact that there were as many as thirty ju-jitsu performers in London in 1910 was a sign of the popularity of the sport on the halls – and it attracted the interest of women like Edith Garrud and Florence LeMarr who took up the martial art and encouraged other women to do so. In fact, exponents of the Japanese wrestling art probably represented the last large-scale influx of professional strongmen to the British music halls. At the end of the nineteenth century, there were few Japanese citizens living in Britain. One of the few was Takashima Shidachi, a representative of the Bank of Japan in London. He practised ju-jitsu and taught it to small groups.

It was, however, an Englishman who planted the roots of the art in Great Britain. His name was Edward Barton-Wright. He was born in India in 1860 and was one of the great eccentrics of the British Empire, of whom there were a fair few scattered about at a time when much of the globe was coloured red to indicate British possession.

Barton-Wright worked as an engineer, specialising in the smelting process, in a number of tough mining camps in different parts of the world, and developed an interest in the martial arts of different countries. In 1899, he returned home from Japan and opened a martial arts academy in London. He soon sent for one of his previous instructors, Yukio Tani, to teach ju-jitsu at his institution.

Barton-Wright's 'School of Arms' in Shaftesbury Avenue concentrated on teaching a form of self-defence called bartitsu. The name was a combination of Barton and ju-jitsu. It was a mixture of a number of different fighting sports of all nations, including boxing, fencing, wrestling, stick fighting, ju-jitsu and the French type of kick boxing known as savate. They were combined by the sport's originator to be used in conjunction with everyday objects like walking sticks and umbrellas.

Barton-Wright was not often on the mark with his timing of events but he had chosen the right moment to launch his self-defence school. The public in general was growing increasingly apprehensive about the growing wave of crime in the rapidly expanding cities. Bartitsu was given an extra fillip when Sir Arthur Conan Doyle chose to make his master detective Sherlock Holmes an expert in the combat art – even if he did spell it 'baritsu' in error, possibly because he miscopied the word from a report in *The Times* newspaper.

Where Edward Barton-Wright was less successful was in his quixotic ambition of trying to make ju-jitsu a commercial success on the music halls. The initial effort failed on all levels. When he first broached launching it commercially to his Japanese instructors, many of them recoiled in horror. Most of them were staidly middle class in origin and revered their art. Most of them refused to profane ju-jitsu by performing it on the stage, and some even resigned and went home in protest.

Yukio Tani, however, was more pragmatic and commercially minded. With a partner, he agreed to give the scheme a try. After much desperate wrangling, Edward Barton-Wright managed to secure the two Japanese a booking at the Tivoli music hall. Their display was a success, but not in the way that Barton-Wright and the two exponents had intended. Members of the audience thought that they were watching a knockabout comedy act and roared with laughter throughout. Tani was furious and refused to go through such a humiliating process again.

Edward Barton-Wright was seriously worried. His school of arms and his brain-child bartitsu were both in need of some favourable publicity. He arranged to give a display before the Prince of Wales at the Gallery Club, but fell off his bicycle while cycling along a country lane before the show and was too badly bruised to perform on the night. Another display at the Alhambra had to be cancelled because his two principal Japanese instructors had both been hurt while teaching their art to over-enthusiastic pupils.

Barton-Wright decided to risk everything on a public performance. At his own expense he put on a great bartitsu tournament at St James's Hall. It was well attended, with representatives from newspapers and magazines present, but the evening proved to be yet another embarrassing fiasco.

Due to scenes of confusion behind the scenes, the show was late in starting. Finally a flustered Barton-Wright emerged from behind the curtains to announce that the first item would in fact be the one billed as the third; an exhibition of unusual ways in which to use a walking stick to defend against attack followed. Next came an exhibition of ju-jitsu between Sadakazu Uyenishi and Yukio Tani, beginning with a display of falls, causing the reviewer from *Sandow's Magazine* to yawn: 'This display was ingenious, certainly, but in the absence of any real contest failed to carry conviction.'

A proposed wrestling bout between Uyenishi and the Cornish and Devonshire heavyweight champion did not materialise. No reason was given for this. Instead the evening continued with a catch-as-catch-can wrestling match for a side bet of £5 a-side between A. Cherpillo, the Swiss champion, and Joe Carol, champion of England. A reporter noted disapprovingly, 'It was in connection with this event that there occurred the unseemly bickering and wrangling which marred the otherwise sportsmanlike conduct of the tournament.'

This may have been due to the fact that most of the great names in the music hall strongman cult had been attracted to the occasion, each with strong opinions of his own. The editor of the *Sporting Life* had agreed to hold the stakes and appoint the referee. At the last minute he sent a telegram to the organisers, announcing that the arbiter should be Ferdinand Gruhn, a sparring partner of Georg Hackenschmidt. Uncertain of the provenance of the telegram, Barton-Wright refused to accept him. This led to loud and prolonged wrangling in front of the audience. Barton-Wright took offence at something shouted from Joe Carol's corner and insisted indignantly that he was a straight man and everyone knew it. Finally, after many names had been proposed and discarded, it was reluctantly agreed that Tom Burrows, the club swinger, would officiate. The ever-present Tom Cannon came forward with a meaningful scowl directed at Burrows and grimly remarked that if he was not satisfied with the judging, he personally would lodge an objection with the stakeholder.

For some time Carol's clique, described as 'particularly obstreperous' continued to heckle, object and utter threats. All this took so long that two other items on the programme were cancelled to make room for the wrestling bout, which was won by Cherpillo with a fall, after one hour and twenty minutes, in what was described as a steady and occasionally monotonous display by both men.

Edward Barton-Wright continued to run his academy, although both instructors and students were draining away. He was also beginning to fall out with his star Yukio Tani, finding the Japanese to be dilatory and argumentative. For his part, Tani was still smarting from the failed music hall ju-jitsu act so ineffectually masterminded by Barton-Wright.

The situation changed with the reappearance of William Bankier, the Scottish Hercules. By this time Bankier was running down his theatrical appearances and beginning to concentrate on various entrepreneurial ventures. He still had ambitions to rival Sandow as a physical culture emperor and believed that suitably adapted ju-jitsu exhibitions could be successful as a part of the strongman oeuvre. Bankier persuaded Tani and a number of other ju-jitsu practitioners to leave Barton-Wright and sign up with him as their manager. He was everything that the founder of bartitsu was not: tough-minded, streetwise, practical, efficient and vastly experienced in all aspects of show business. He took over his new recruited coterie of ju-jitsu experts and polished and transformed their acts. Instead of rambling displays of the different throws, Bankier taught his charges how to include the usual popular strongman routines in their performances – breaking chains and lifting weights. He beefed up Tani's physique with a specifically designed bodybuilding routine and sent him out on to the halls as 'the Pocket Hercules' on what was to become an uninterrupted six-month tour of the country.

For several years the ju-jitsu invasion of the British music halls was very successful. It coincided with the unexpected success of Japan in the 1904–5 Russo-Japanese war, leading to a wave of sentiment for the 'plucky little Japs' and the increased popularity of their martial arts displays, in which small men symbolically humiliated larger ones.

The best exponents topped the bills and filled the theatres. Chief among them was Yukio Tani, who adapted well to Bankier's tutelage. He freely admitted to being only a third-rate practitioner of the art in his own country, but in his matches in Britain he seemed able to paralyse giants. He claimed that only once did he lose a contest onstage, when fellow Japanese expert Taro Myaki defeated him in 1905, although tough Joe Carol was reputed to have overpowered him once in a rough-house match that got out of hand at a theatrical performance. Even the veteran Jack Carkeek took lessons from Tani and included elements of ju-jitsu in his perennial act.

A typical ju-jitsu performance would start with the practitioner giving a quick-fire strength display, breaking chains, splitting planks with the edge of the hand and lifting weights. Then he would start demonstrating the more spectacular throws and falls with a partner. This would be followed by the leading practitioner in the partnership challenging any man in the audience. At first Tani offered £1 for every minute, up to a maximum of five minutes, that any challenger could survive, or £5 to anyone actually defeating him. He became famous for the cheerful smile that never left his face during even the toughest of bouts.

One week at an Oxford theatre, Tani beat thirty-three opponents, several of them professional wrestlers. On average he fought and defeated about twenty opponents from the audience every week. These adversaries were all required to wear orthodox ju-jitsu jackets, which gave the professional additional handholds for his throws.

William Bankier called in a number of favours from his strongman peers in order to boost the publicity of his ju-jitsu team. Thomas Inch, weighing 210lbs, wrestled Uyenishi, 70lbs lighter, and described the experience years later in an article in *Health and Strength* magazine:

The more I exerted myself the more I fell down, first one way and then the other. I found my strength not the slightest use, and it was evident that Uyenishi knew just how to use it against me.

As long as Hackenschmidt and Sandow and their imitators, and spin-offs like the ju-jitsu practitioners prospered, so did the music hall strongman acts generally. The cult was even depicted frequently between 1908 and 1910 in a sketch put on by Fred Karno's famous 'Mumming Birds' troupe, one of the most popular comedy acts on the halls. The sketch ended with a drunken swell falling out of a box on to the stage and being forced to fight a professional wrestler, introduced as Marconi Ali, the Terrible Turk. After a hilarious slapstick contest, the fop defeated the wrestler by tickling him and pinning his opponent while he was helpless with laughter. The swell was played by an unknown comedian called Charlie Chaplin, who later was to try his luck in Hollywood.

11

FINAL CURTAINS

When Eugen Sandow tumbled breathlessly on to the stage of the Imperial Theatre in time to defeat Charles A. Sampson in 1889, the music hall and vaudeville strongman cult kicked off. By the beginning of the second decade of the twentieth century, its star was certainly fading. With a lifespan of about twenty-five years, it was a very fair run in the entertainment world for what had started as a series of clunky curtain raisers, back in the days when Houdini had been one of the first dumb acts to achieve the status of a vaudeville headliner.

Before the decline set in there were several brief fluttering revivals of strength acts, especially in vaudeville in the USA. With Hackenschmidt on tour, the hub of professional wrestling was transferring from Great Britain to the USA. When Antonio Pierri discovered in France yet another Terrible Turk and, almost inevitably, claimant to the title of the Sultan's favourite wrestler in the form of Yousouff Ishamaelo, he paused only briefly with him in London before crossing the Atlantic with his latest protégé. Pierri made no attempt to glamorise the shambling wrestler, freely admitting that Yousouff ate like a pig and never washed. The ruthless Pierri treated Yousouff as badly as he had Madrali, paying him only $25 a week and virtually imprisoning the wrestler in a tenement room in the Bowery area of New York.

In return, Yousouff made matters as difficult as he could for his manager. For all his size and strength he hated fighting. Pierri responded by dressing a hired thug in a policeman's uniform, ordering him to force the reluctant wrestler into the ring for his bouts at gunpoint. Once, driven almost crazy with hunger and frustration, Yousouff threw an opponent in the first three minutes and then lay sprawled across his prostrate opponent for several hours, snarling menacingly at anyone who approached to try to separate the two men.

Temporarily things took a turn for the better for the Turk when his contract was purchased by the American showman William A. Brady. Brady changed the wrestler's image, removing his rags and dressing him in a red turban, baggy green pants and a gold-laced jacket. For publicity purposes Brady encouraged Yousouff to consume gargantuan meals in the windows of restaurants, before sending him on a very successful vaudeville strongman tour.

Brady also paid Yousouff in gold pieces, which the delighted wrestler kept in a money belt around his waist. This proved the Turk's final undoing. He was sailing back to Europe on the vessel *La Bourgogne*, off Sable Island close to the coast of Nova Scotia, an area dubbed by seamen as 'the graveyard of the Atlantic', when the vessel sank, with 546 drowned. Yousouff, the Terrible Turk, was one of the casualties. It was said that he was carried to the bottom of the ocean by the weight of the gold in his belt, although this could have been just one final posthumous knee-jerk publicity stunt on the part of the master showman William A. Brady.

The strongest men on earth lingered on for a while in the USA, but in a much-altered state. Vaudeville and burlesque still drew the crowds in rural areas but in a much less sophisticated form for the audiences. Typical of the new breed of touring strongmen was 'Mexican' Billy Wells, who probably came from Italy or the Netherlands. When he had been eight years old, Wells had fallen 15ft from an upstairs window to the sidewalk below, while he had been watching a parade go by. Examining physicians informed the unharmed boy that he had an exceptionally thick skull. Later the youth used this attribute as his entrée into show business.

Wells developed an act in which men from the audience were encouraged to use sledgehammers to break stones placed on top of his head. For his performances he wore evening dress, with a blanket draped over his skull. He always used stones which were 6–10in. thick and 2ft square. The strongman always claimed that these stones were of the hardest possible quality. He had a long and successful show business career, but could not have claimed to have been underemployed. While travelling with the Barnum and Bailey circus he gave up to twenty-three shows a day. This marathon was exceeded only at Stuart's Waxworks in Edinburgh, where Wells declared that on a public holiday he had once performed on fifty-three separate occasions.

Famous athletes had been performing on vaudeville and burlesque stages for decades, but by the beginning of the twentieth century there was a sudden demand for celebrities of all types to make well-paid stage appearances. The heroic William F. Cody, better known as Indian scout Buffalo Bill, had been particularly inept in his early show business career. He was reputed once to have seen his wife in the audience, stop his monologue and shout despairingly, 'Hello, Mamma, I'm such a bad actor!' A singer billing himself as Lord Kenneth Douglas Home MacLaine, declared that he was singing in vaudeville in order to pay off a mortgage of £190,000 on his ancestral home in Scotland. A comic appearing on the same bill commented that the peer's voice was not good enough to pay for a birdbath.

Boxers had been touring vaudeville since the days of John L. Sullivan, because their stage appearances allowed them to take part in exhibition contests, even in areas where genuine bouts were banned. John L. Sullivan was in the William Cody class when it came to acting. Once the great heavyweight rushed on to the stage roaring 'I'll save you, mudder!' only to be stopped in his tracks when a voice from the upper regions of the hall drawled, 'Save her? You can't even pronounce her!'

Another world heavyweight champion, the British-born Bob Fitzsimmons, a former blacksmith, toured with an act in which he lifted weights, and boxed and wrestled with sparring partners. He ended his performance by shoeing a horse onstage. He had a habit of playing jokes on members of his audience by handing out souvenir horseshoes which were still red-hot. There were few regrets among the patrons of one of his performances when Fitzsimmons was kicked in the groin by the horse he was attempting to shoe.

Even lesser known fighters like Andy Bowen could earn $200 a week by appearing in a sketch called 'Fun in a Gym'. Bowen, a gritty New Orleans fighter renowned for his stamina, had become famous when he and Jack Burke had set a world record for the longest gloved fight in history: 110 three-minute rounds lasting seven hours and twenty minutes, which ended when both contestants were too exhausted to leave their corners. As soon as he had recovered, Bowen was thrust into the hastily written sketch and sent round the variety circuits. His theatrical career did not last long. Occasionally leaving his tour to participate in genuine bouts, he took on Kid Lavigne at the Auditorium Club on 14 December

1894. During the eighteenth round he was knocked down by his opponent and struck his head on the floor of the ring with enormous impact. Bowen never recovered consciousness and died the following morning, shortly before his thirtieth birthday.

Not all the ex-boxers treading the boards proved to be outright successes. One of them, Leach Cross, known as the Fighting Dentist and unpopular for his persistent bending of the rules within the roped square, admitted, 'In the theatres it's the same as when I fight. I pack the house with people who come to see me lose!'

Another boxer who was subsumed by vaudeville was the notorious Joe 'Iron Man' Grim, born Savario Gianonne in Italy, in 1881. Grim was a squat middleweight who often fought heavyweights, and was known for his durability. Over a career of several hundred fights he probably won only about ten, but although he was sent crashing to the canvas on many occasions, he almost always got up and lasted the distance. After he had absorbed his latest thrashing, he would totter to the ropes in his bright pink and blue trunks, wave defiantly to the crowd and through bloodied lips shout 'I am Joe Grim and fear no man on earth!'

Bob Fitzsimmons knocked him down nine times but could not put Grim away. In another fearsomely one-sided fight, another former heavyweight champion in Jack Johnson sent Grim tumbling to the canvas on at least eighteen occasions, until ringside reporters stopped counting, but still the Iron Man went the distance.

Crowds flocked to see Grim's vaudeville act, in which he gave sparring and training exhibitions, performed feats of strength and allowed spectators to whack him in the stomach with a broom handle. With no more worlds to conquer, or even lose in, Grim embarked upon an extended sea tour of the Pacific with a variety troupe, going through his stage act wherever the vessel docked and picking up the odd bout in the ring whenever he could. In 1909, he fought Malley Jackson unsuccessfully for the heavyweight championship of Tasmania at the Gaiety Theatre in Zehan on the west coast of Tasmania, after suffering twenty rounds of heavy punishment.

In November of the same year, Grim lost a bout in Brisbane for a sidestake of £30 against Spider Kelly. The referee disqualified the American visitor for throwing his opponent to the floor. In retaliation the Iron Man struck the referee several times. The seconds of both men joined in the mêlée and eventually police were called in to break up the brawl.

Doggedly, Grim continued fighting until 1913, when he went in against a young unknown called Joe Borrell. True to form, the Iron Man was knocked down in every round, six times in round six. But here he departed from his usual script by actually suffering a knockout defeat. Grim retired from the ring and his vaudeville career also came to an end. There were few bookings to be had for an Iron Man who had revealed that he was no longer made of iron.

As the numbers of performing strongmen and challenge-issuing wrestlers dwindled in vaudeville and burlesque, so their places were taken by celebrities or eccentrics with weird backgrounds who could offer at least a minimal element of the strength athlete's routine in their performances. Impresario Willie Hammerstein, father of the Broadway lyricist Oscar, was the first major showman to specialise in celebrity bookings and actively seek out oddities for his shows.

In 1912, the great Olympic athlete Jim Thorpe was deprived of the pentathlon and decathlon gold medals he had won in Stockholm, because as a youth he had played professional baseball, albeit briefly. A vaudeville syndicate offered him $1,000 a week to tour their theatres with a hastily cobbled together strongman act. Thorpe refused, preferring to become a full-time baseball player.

Other athletes, however, seized their opportunities. The *New York Times* of 13 December 1909, reviewed one of them in the following terms:

Sam Mahoney, the man who likes ice water externally, made his first appearance on the vaudeville stage in New York at Keith and Proctor's Fifth Avenue Theatre yesterday afternoon. His stage act consists in giving exhibitions of plain and fancy swimming in a tank containing water and large pieces of ice. A light effect to represent the Aurora Borealis adds to the apparent frigidity.

Most Americans of the period preferred ice as an adjunct to their drinks, but Samuel Mahoney claimed to have swum in it often. He was a swimmer and skilled self-publicist who parlayed a minor talent into a fairly successful show business career. He had moved to the USA from Ireland to work as an engineer, where he supplemented his income by working as head lifeguard at Revere Beach, Massachusetts.

He made his breakthrough into a series of vaudeville bookings by claiming to have been the second man after Captain Webb to have swum the English Channel, although there was absolutely no record of his having done so. This did not stop his giving detailed accounts of his alleged swim from France in 1908 to reporters when he returned to the USA:

...at 4.30 a.m. I was a quarter of a mile from the shore, and could hear the shouting of the party on the tugboat encouraging me on. I felt then that I had won, and swam with one long, final spurt with my arms until finally I felt the sloping beach under my numbed feet, and a moment later I crawled ashore, amid the cheers of my friends. (*Taranaki Herald*, 15 March 1909)

Mahoney, a natural showman, said that he had remained in the water for twenty hours, during which he covered forty-one miles before he waded ashore near the South Goodwin lighthouse. Novelty-seeking theatrical managers booked him for a substantial tour in which he swam in a glass-fronted tank containing floating pieces of ice, pausing every so often to give a lecture of the benefits of swimming every day in the sea for the development of health.

He claimed to have developed his own magnificent physique in this way and displayed a testimonial from Dr Dudley Sergeant of Harvard University, declaring that Mahoney was the only perfectly developed man he had ever examined. Sergeant, who tended to be over-generous in his commendations, had said much the same thing a few years earlier when he had run the rule over the touring Eugen Sandow.

Another entertaining charlatan who talked his way on to the vaudeville circuit for a while was Leopold McLaglen, who claimed to be the world ju-jitsu champion. He was a gigantic 6ft 6in. height and bore a strong resemblance to his brother Victor, who went on to become an Oscar-winning Hollywood film star.

Victor had also been a circus and vaudeville strongman for a time, as well as a silver miner, railroad policeman, pearl diver, boxer, soldier, circus performer and all-round soldier of fortune as he made his way round the world. His stage act had consisted of being the bearer in an acrobatic act called the Great Romanos, giving posing displays and demonstrating the favourite punches of well-known boxers.

Leopold was a much more devious character. One of eight enormous sons of a clergyman, he claimed to have studied ju-jitsu at the age of twelve with a Japanese student brought back to England by an uncle who had worked in an overseas legation. In 1901, Leopold served in the Boer War in an undisclosed capacity, although he claimed to have fought in the mounted infantry. He then went off to see more of the world. Somewhere on his travels he claimed to have won the title of ju-jitsu champion of the world, before a crowd of fifteen thousand, a claim scorned by those who knew anything about the art. Undeterred, McLaglen used the title and offered to teach ju-jitsu to anyone who would pay him for lessons. When he ran out of pupils, which seemed to have been soon, he put together a music hall strongman act and started touring South Africa with it.

His performance consisted of the usual strength stunts, culminating with an exhibition of ju-jitsu and a challenge to any man in the audience. His tour came to an ignominious end when one night a much smaller opponent refused to be cowed by the giant's bluster and chased McLaglen screaming for help from the stage.

In December 1907, the *San Francisco Call* revealed that the wanderer had surfaced in the USA:

Leopold McLaglen, who claims the ju-jitsu championship of the world, is training at the San Francisco Athletic Clubrooms for a match with two Japanese experts, which will be held a week from tonight at Dreamland Pavilion... McLaglen does not have to risk his life in this dangerous sport, as he could live at ease should he desire. His father is Right Rev. Lord B. McLaglen, Bishop of Scotland.

In fact, McLaglen senior, who had been a Nonconformist bishop in South Africa, not Scotland, and never achieved a peerage, appears to have been as feisty and eccentric as most of his sons. A few years later, upon the outbreak of the First World War, the former bishop offered to box six fast rounds with any other clergyman, all proceeds to go to a War Relief fund.

In the USA, Leopold McLaglen secured a few small-time vaudeville bookings on the west coast but was reduced for a time to working as a cinema doorman in Milwaukee. He then took the first names of two of his boxing brothers, Victor and Fred, and, announcing himself as Victor Fred McLaglen, persuaded a gullible promoter that he was an experienced heavyweight boxer. He was matched against a seriously good title contender called Fireman Jim Flynn, who knocked Leo out in three rounds. This infuriated his brother Victor, who fired off letters to a number of newspapers, accusing Leopold of being a charlatan and besmirching the family name.

Next McLaglen promoted a ju-jitsu match between himself and a Japanese man called Kukamuachi. This time he actually made a profit on the enterprise by the simple expedient of running off with all the gate money in two suitcases.

It was almost the end of Leo McLaglen's vaudeville career though there was to be one last hurrah. Soon after the outbreak of World War One, he turned up in Wellington in New Zealand, via India, Shanghai and Singapore. By this time he had written a book on self-defence: *Jiu Jitsu: a Manual of the Science*. He wasted no time in announcing his presence. Within days posters were declaring:

Railwayman's Belgian Effort
Town Hall Friday 26th March
Realistic Assault-St-Arms by the khaki boys from Trentham
UNIQUE JU-JITSU BY CAPT. LEOPOLD MCLAGLEN

THE WORLD'S CHAMPION
BAYONET FIGHTING UNDER CAPTAIN MCLAGLEN'S
JU-JITSU SYSTEM BY SQUADS FROM TRENTHAM CAMP
GRAND PATRIOTIC CONCERT

See Captain McLaglen, the Irish giant, withstand the combined pulling power equal to that of two draught horses. Captain McLaglen
is at present in Wellington under engagement to the Government.
The McLaglen System of Bayonet Fighting. Captain McLaglen has
instructed some 30,000 Australian and New Zealand troops.

It was too good to last. Within months, suspicious local newspapers
were making pointed remarks about the so-called gallant captain's
apparent civilian status in a world racked by war. Never one to
outstay his welcome and with a firm belief that it was always harder
to hit a moving target, Leopold McLaglen moved on again. There
are no more records of any theatrical bookings for him. In 1920,
he appeared fleetingly in a silent movie called *Bars of Iron*. Ten
years later, uncharacteristically vague about where he had spent the
previous decade, he returned to California. His brother Victor, by
now an established part of Hollywood's English colony, tried to get
his brother moved on, on the grounds that there was only room for
one McLaglen in the USA. In return, Leopold sued Victor unsuccessfully for attempting to ruin his reputation and prevent him
from securing employment. In 1938, Leopold was back in court,
charged with trying to extort money with menaces from a millionaire. Described as 'a former Hollywood physical culture instructor',
he was barred from the USA for five years.

In Europe, as long as the famous Sandow reigned supreme, so the
strongman cult could put up a good fight to retain its shaky status

on the halls. When Sandow suddenly faltered, however, the muscle-man cult also reeled and never really recovered. Slowly the strength athletes' routines were relegated once more to the status of 'dumb acts', starting and closing the bills. Before long, the manipulation of heavy weights was no longer considered interesting enough for the sophisticated and constantly changing tastes of modern audiences. They were replaced to a certain extent by acrobatic, posing and hand-balancing acts, but by 1914 the heyday of the physique acts in general was over.

Sandow continued to struggle to maintain his supremacy but he was now in his forties and had lost his taste for touring and appearing on the halls. In addition, he had a vast physical culture empire to run and this took up most of his time. His magazine, gymnasiums and business enterprises were still bringing in the money. Between 1905 and 1906, he went on well-received lecturing tours to India and the Dominions, giving demonstrations of his system. In 1909, when Lord Esher appealed for 11,000 recruits to bring the county of London territorial regiments up to full strength, Sandow offered at his own expense to provide physical education lessons for sub-standard recruits. He also provided free physical training to the Church Lads Brigade. His reputation received a momentary boost when, in 1911, the strongman was appointed Professor of Physical Culture to King George V. Keeping busy, he gave evidence and made recommendations to the royal commission on physical education in Scottish elementary schools.

Almost inevitably he over-extended himself, branching out into the manufacture of embrocation, cocoa, chocolate, cigars and even corsets. The cocoa business went under first. The major manufacturing companies like Cadbury deliberately undercut the strongman's prices until he had to go out of business. Before that there had been a long-running court hearing at which the shocked strongman was told that he could not legitimately use the world 'Health' to describe his drink. There was further annoying litigation with an actress over his patented Health and Perfect Fitness corset.

Worst of all, with the approach of World War I and the growth of increasing anti-German sentiment in Britain, the Prussian-born Sandow became the object of mistrust. When the war broke out there were vicious rumours that Sandow was a spy, planted in the community to work for the Kaiser, even though he had been a naturalised English citizen for some years. There were even stories that Sandow had been arrested and incarcerated in the Tower of London for treason. With most of the young men away at the war, purchasers of his bodybuilding courses dwindled. By 1915, his business empire was experiencing difficulties on all sides. A year later Sandow Ltd went into liquidation.

Having lost its acknowledged leader, the strongman cult was danced off the stage by the emergence of the terpsichorean art. Almost everyone suddenly wanted to perform and witness exhibitions of the tango, the cakewalk, the grizzly bear and the two-step. In Europe and the USA, hundreds of dance halls and academies were opened. Performers who could display a flair for dance were hastily promoted to the tops of the bills. Vernon and Irene Castle, Joe Frisco, Gaby Deslys and from the classical stage even Pavlova and Nijinsky all had their followers.

With the decline of Sandow and the commensurate lack of interest in weightlifting and posing acts onstage, professional wrestlers continued to top the bills in Great Britain and the USA, but interest in their stage performances was also dying off. It was becoming increasingly obvious that too many professional wrestling bouts were being choreographed. In August 1909, the magazine *Health and Strength* wrote:

> Professional wrestling is simply a part of a series of music hall turns, 'a show' – to be treated as such. Mind you, a man must be above the average as regards skill and strength; then, with a smart manager, and a working agreement with others in the business there is money in the game.

Most of this money was still to be found on the halls. Hackenschmidt had shown the way by wrestling exhibitions and giving posing and strength displays six nights a week all over the world, with the occasional major bout to keep his name in front of the public, and others were following enthusiastically in his wake. C. B. Cochran, disillusioned and embittered by the way in which the Russian Lion had abandoned him, started to look for a replacement for the Estonian, but with little success. For a time the impresario toyed with the idea of backing Stanislaus Zbyszko, and the Polish wrestler did well for a time on a tour of provincial music halls.

The promoter even arranged several big-time matches for the Pole in London, with one against the latest sensation, a Turk called Kara Suliman, 'the Champion of the Bosphorous'. Zbyszko and Suliman put up an exciting music hall scrap and there was talk of matching them again in one of the capital's major arenas. Then Cochran suffered a major embarrassment when *Sporting Life* disclosed that Suliman was in reality a Bulgarian called Ivan Offthoroff. What was worse, Offthoroff was a paid employee of both Cochran and Stanislaus Zbyszko, and had even shared the same London address as the latter. Their spectacular music hall bout had been a fake designed to build up interest in a return contest.

This disaster for C. B. Cochran coincided with another dangerous promotion when he matched Zbyszko against Ivan Padoubney, the Russian Cossack, at the London Pavilion. After what turned out to be a very dirty contest, with much butting, punching and back-handing, the Russian was disqualified after twenty minutes. A disqualification result should really have meant that the purse and any sidestakes were returned to the wrestlers and their backers, but Cochran outwitted Antonio Pierri, the Cossack's manager, by catching a cab to the office of the editor of the *Sportsman*, who was holding the stakes, assuring him that Padoubney had been declared a genuine victor and absconding with the money.

It was a shrewd stroke of business, but with Pierri known to be an extremely dangerous customer who was backed up by Padoubney's seconds, the enormous Louis Uni and the spiteful Charlie Mitchell, and that, to the horror of its owners, the London Pavilion had subsequently been wrecked by disgruntled patrons after the disqualification, Cochran decided in future to detach himself from the wrestling game and concentrate on his theatrical productions.

It was bad enough that the general public discovered some of the major wrestling contests in London and New York were being fixed, but when it became public knowledge that the music hall and vaudeville wrestling challenges, the main source of income for professional grapplers at the time, were equally pre-arranged, it sounded the death-knell for the sport as an entertainment. In March 1906, a court case involving Ahmed Madrali, the Terrible Turk, and his manager Antonio Pierri was widely reported in the newspapers.

On behalf of Madrali and his troupe of wrestlers, Pierri sued a music hall manager called Barney Williams, who refused to pay the wrestlers the sum of £120 which he had agreed to give to Pierri for his wrestling group to top the bill at his theatre for a week. Williams claimed in his defence that the displays of the wrestlers had been dull and sub-standard, while the challenges from the audience had emanated from wrestlers paid by and planted there by Pierri, to fight to order and make the stage performers look better than they were. These wrestlers, claimed Williams 'were scattered about the hall … [and] … would rise dramatically in response to the challenge issued by Madrali'. The audiences had seen through the subterfuge and attendances had dwindled greatly during the week.

In addition, Pierri had promised that some time during the week, Madrali would engage in a contest onstage with the celebrated Scottish wrestler Alec Monroe. Monroe had not turned up. Pierri had guaranteed that the bout would be fixed and Monroe, a local favourite, would be allowed to last the full ten minutes. As an excuse, Antonio Pierri explained that Monroe had withdrawn at the last moment because the Scottish grappler wanted to secure a much more lucrative bout against Madrali in London later in the year.

The magistrates agreed that Madrali's act had not been the genuine exhibition of wrestling that had been advertised and that the music hall manager did not have to pay the withheld reimbursement.

He was not aware of it, but Georg Hackenschmidt had selected a course that was to culminate in the ruin of professional wrestling and at the same time put an end to the music hall strongman genre which had nurtured him so well and for so long. At first, after he had parted company with Cochran to manage his own affairs, matters went well enough for the Estonian. He undertook a profitable music hall tour of Australia where, in feature matches, he defeated the touring Indians Buttan Singh and Gunga Brown and also pinned Weber, the Australian champion, in ten minutes. An article in the New South Wales *Singleton Argus* of 5 November 1904, announced his imminent arrival:

> Hackenschmidt … claims to be the strongest man in the world, and has competed in forty championship matches, and won them all. He is also a champion weightlifter, for which he holds fourteen world records.

He then criss-crossed the USA with his troupe, with time out to defeat Tom Jenkins again in a major match, and went on with his vaudeville displays to Canada, gaining headlines with the manner in which he threw Maupas, a highly regarded French Canadian, in twenty minutes.

The Russian Lion then returned to Great Britain to fulfil a number of outstanding variety engagements and personal appearances. By public demand he was called back to the USA for another cross-country tour with his strongman act. Then he made his mistake. He allowed himself to be matched to defend his world title against Frank Gotch, the leading American wrestler of the time.

Gotch's local Iowan newspaper the *Humboldt Independent* gave some idea of the local wrestler's popularity as he prepared for the bout with Hackenschmidt:

> From the remotest corners of Iowa – and from the vastness of the Dakotas, stalwart sons of the open prairie make their pilgrimages

to witness the work of their idol – for in no small measure, Frank Gotch is a deity.

Gotch was also a ruthless and merciless competitor who was quick to work out deals with competitors who might give him trouble in the ring and equally ready to break the arms and legs of any novices he should come across in the way of duty. Much was made of his 'good ole boy' image but he was backed by one of the shrewdest and most influential wrestling cartels in the USA, busily plotting their man's path to the world championship with clinical efficiency. The group included former champion Farmer Burns, who had both fought the farm boy and then trained him earlier in his career. In 1901, his employers had tested their prospect's ability to cope under pressure by sending Gotch on a tour of the rougher prospecting areas of the Klondyke Gold Rush, where he worked on a claim belonging to a man called James Brown. Gotch went north as a ringer, the term given to an already experienced wrestler pretending to be a novice. For this purpose he was given the name of Frank Kennedy. In the Klondyke, he teamed up with a conniving manager and former grappler called Joe Carroll, who had adopted the name of Ole Marsh for a separate scam he had already been pursuing in Alaska. With the aid of several crooked associates, the party set about introducing a confidence trick to the goldfields. Carroll would arrive in one of the wealthy mining communities, claiming to be the champion of some remote region. He would make himself feared and unpopular in the area with his swaggering bullying antics around the camp and in its saloons. A few days later Gotch, under the pseudonym of Frank Kennedy, would turn up at the same camp in the guise of a guileless greenhorn young prospector only recently arrived in the goldfields.

In front of as many spectators as possible, Carroll would pick a fight with the new arrival. One of the accomplices would suggest that 'Ole Marsh' should meet 'Frank Kennedy' for a sidestake in a wrestling bout. The contest would be arranged, with hundreds of miners paying to watch. Practically the whole camp would bet on the experienced Marsh to win the bout. Secretly Joe Carroll and his co-conspirators would bet all their money on Gotch to win, at very long odds. When the bout started Carroll would put up a reasonably convincing show, but would lose in an upset decision to his callow opponent. The members of the badger game would collect their winnings and move on hastily to the next remote mining area, where the whole performance would be gone through again.

Only once did Gotch put a foot wrong. After a number of spectacular victories against novice miners, he began to believe in his own publicity. He allowed himself to be matched in a boxing match with a veteran Australian called Frank Slavin who was trying his luck in Alaska as a prospector and part-time barfly. Slavin was not a young man but he was still far too good with his fists for Gotch, and won on a disqualification when his opponent tried to resort to wrestling.

This blip apart, over the span of one summer Carroll and Gotch made a great deal of money for themselves and their sponsors from their nefarious tricks, and even managed to get out of the territory alive to spend it. In Iowa, the *Daily Leader* of 19 March 1902, printed an ingenuous account of the scam:

He (Gotch) left the Klondike two months ago with the sincere respect of the sporting public. In spite of their heavy losses the people bade farewell to the young man who had defeated their every veteran, and wished him well. Gotch is back in Humboldt, leading a quiet life again. But his advice to the wrestler who seeks financial assistance is, 'go to the Klondike and stay six months'.

Gotch's backers were delighted with the way that the young grappler had conducted himself during the lucrative scam. As a reward they saw to it that he won the American wrestling championship from the veteran, and probably at the same time bought-and-paid-for, Tom Jenkins. Then they matched their wrestler with Hackenschmidt for the world title.

The two men met at Dexter Park Pavilion in Chicago on 3 April 1908. Hackenschmidt had been too busy raking in the money on one of his many vaudeville tours and too complacent to bother to train properly. Gotch, on the other hand, had prepared for the fight of his life. From the opening bell he bullied a bewildered Russian Lion around the ring. Hitherto, Hackenschmidt had been accustomed to intimidated opponents treating him with a respect amounting to awe as he advanced upon them with outspread arms. Instead, the ferocious Frank Gotch was on the attack from the start. He tore into his startled European opponent, head-butted him, slapped the Estonian's face and kept up a constant stream of abuse directed at his adversary. Hackenschmidt had never been treated in such a cavalier fashion and did not know how to cope with the American. To make things worse, Gotch had coated his body liberally with oil and Hackenschmidt found it difficult to get a secure grip on his opponent. In vain the champion complained to the referee. After two hours and three minutes of mounting pain, indignities and slights he submitted to his opponent, saying with commendable self-control considering the circumstances, 'I surrender the championship of the world to Mr Gotch.'

It was not long before Hackenschmidt had abandoned this role of the good-losing nice guy and was accusing Gotch of winning the title by underhand means. Cutting his losses and realising that as an ex-champion his drawing power would soon be considerably reduced, Hackenschmidt went on the road for another three years with his music hall act. At the end of this time, with bookings drying up and the music hall strongman cult in Europe petering out, somewhat reluctantly he decided to go for one last big payday and signed up to meet Gotch in the ring again.

Gotch too had almost abandoned competitive wrestling in favour of touring the sticks with a vaudeville act, which he later also took to England. He played the lead in a short sketch entitled *All About a Bout*. He portrayed a college wrestler forced by circumstances to challenge a professional European champion called Atlas. The sketch ended with a well-choreographed wrestling match. While he was reasonably successful with this venture in the USA, the dour, sullen and suspicious Gotch in show business parlance could not draw flies when he ventured too far from home. It became apparent that he was not going to replace the Russian Lion as an international drawing card on the halls.

He and Georg Hackenschmidt met in the open air on 3 May 1911, at the recently opened Comiskey Baseball Field in Chicago. Hackenschmidt was paid $10,000 while his opponent received more than twice that amount. In addition, each man was scheduled to receive a percentage of the motion picture rights. The size of the attending crowd was estimated as being somewhere between twenty thousand and thirty-five thousand people. Even at the lower end of the estimate it would have been the largest crowd ever to attend a wrestling match in the western world.

This time Hackenschmidt trained hard for the bout, but towards the end of his period of preparation the Estonian's knee was badly damaged in a sparring match. For years there were rumours that the 'accident' had been carefully arranged by Frank Gotch's backers, who had inserted one of their own grapplers on to Hackenschmidt's training staff, with orders to partially disable the challenger. Some asserted that the veteran Dr Benjamin Roller had been the bribed culprit, while others placed the blame on a grappler called Abe Santel.

Hackenschmidt tried to pull out of his championship challenge but the tough and underworld-connected promoter Jack Curley would have none of it. It was made plain to the Estonian that wrestling with a damaged leg would be immeasurably less painful than the alternative. Hardly able to keep a straight face, Frank Gotch piously promised that he would not touch Hackenschmidt's knee or apply one of his dreaded toeholds.

Curley swung into action, even employing a Hackenschmidt lookalike to go on long training runs down dimly lit lanes at night for the benefit of reporters. But it would take more than that to fool the gentlemen of the press. Rumours started to spread that something was amiss with the forthcoming match. Fearful for the safety of his beloved park, owner Comiskey called the promoter, referee, wrestlers and their managers to him an hour before the match. He told them plainly that they could not use his field to stage the robbery of the public. He and some others had taken the matter up with the chief of police, who ordered the referee Smith to call off all bets.

Frank Gotch's only contribution to the meeting was that it didn't matter to him whether the bout was being faked or not; his only intention was to inflict as much damage upon his opponent as possible. Georg Hackenschmidt appeared to be sulking. The *New York Times* remarked 'This was a trying day for Hackenschmidt's trainers. The great wrestler was as petulant as a spoilt child.'

Just before the contest started, the city chief of police, called McWheens, entered the ring and announced tersely that all bets on the championship were off. This was tantamount to an accusation that the contest was not going to be on the square. An angry roar went up from the crowd as rumours of possible double-dealing spread. Gotch and Hackenschmidt were hustled into the ring. Frank Gotch wore long purple tights while Hackenschmidt's tights were dark green in colour. Both men were bare-chested. With painful memories of their first bout neither man had been allowed to use oil on his body, allowing each man to secure a grip on his adversary.

The contest was dull and one-sided. Hackenschmidt hobbled pathetically about the ring, perpetually on the retreat, while Gotch pursued him menacingly. The champion secured the first submission in a little over half an hour and the second in a derisory five minutes. Both men left the ring to boos and catcalls. Hackenschmidt was in tears.

To his dying day Georg Hackenschmidt swore that he had tried his hardest at Comiskey Field. Most fans of the game and many newspapers disagreed. The *Chicago Tribune* summed up the general feeling about the Russian Lion:

> The public had no intimation that he would lie down at the first plausible opportunity but that, as since discovered, was exactly what he intended to do – and did.

It was a significant turning point in many ways. The reputation of professional wrestling was besmirched beyond measure and stopped being considered a sport as it transformed into the meaningless slapstick imbroglio of posturing over-developed clowns that was to persist for a century and continues to exist in its current embarrassing form. Whereas before the second decade of the twentieth century some bouts had been on the level, soon after this watershed all of them were fixed. After Comiskey Field, Jack Curley became the Czar of wrestling, appointing and demoting champions and contenders at will and sending his lesser hired hands out to wrestle all over the country (in those areas in which wrestling had not been banned by the local authorities), sometimes as often as four or five times a week.

Before long it became increasingly difficult for wrestlers to earn a living on the halls. The strongman cult was almost over. Its practitioners dispersed all over the world.

Sandow died in 1925. The official medical diagnosis was an aortic aneurism. There were stories that he had been involved in a car crash and had strained his heart attempting to pull the vehicle out of a ditch. It is possible, however, that the notoriously philandering strongman died as the result of complications brought upon by a dose of syphilis. His wife had him buried in an unmarked grave.

Others among the pioneering strongmen also drifted away from the stage. Chang Woo Gow, the Chinese Giant, one of the most popular of the big men, left Barnum and Bailey, married an English girl and settled in Bournemouth, where he opened a popular teashop. His wife died in 1893. A few months later the Chinese Giant had also passed on; it was said of a broken heart. He was fifty-two. John Holtom, the Swedish original Cannonball Man who took up his dangerous career after a spell as a more orthodox strongman, also retired to England, dying there in 1919.

For a time the mighty John Marx kept a London public house before returning to Luxembourg where he died of cancer. To keep up his spirits, on his deathbed doctors and nurses pretended that he still retained his once awesome power, and would feign pain when he seized their hands playfully and tried to squeeze them. He was in his forty-fourth year. The Great French Canadian strongman Louis Cyr also died young, at the age of forty-nine. He had spent his last few years bedridden at his daughter's home, suffering from Bright's disease, an inflammation of the kidneys, which paralysed his legs and brought with it associated heart problems and asthma attacks.

Cyr's great rival Louis Uni, Apollon, kept working for most of his life, and even appeared in a silent movie, but he fell upon hard times. He invested most of his savings in Russian imperial stock which became worthless after the 1917 Revolution. He was reduced to advertising for a post as a guard or caretaker. A heavy smoker for most of his life, he died after suffering from a throat abscess in 1928, at the age of sixty-seven.

William Bankier continued to resent the fact that Eugen Sandow had beaten him to the title of King of the Bodybuilders, but remained in the strength business. He teamed up with another strongman, Monte Saldo, to open a popular gymnasium, the Apollo-Saldo academy in London's West End. He was twice elected King Rat, the highest office in the variety artistes' charitable organisation, the Grand Order of Water Rats. At the age of forty, he won the heavyweight boxing championship of the music halls on a second-round knockout. Later he became a leading wrestling promoter. He died at the age of seventy-nine.

William Muldoon, the Solid Man, also lived to a good old age. In 1921, he made good use of his political connections to obtain the post of Chairman of the New York Athletic Association, controlling boxing and wrestling in the state. He died at the age of eighty-one. He had claimed to be a lifelong bachelor but after his death it was discovered, in addition to his false claims to have served in the Civil War, he had been married twice.

Bernarr Macfadden, who had been inspired to become a physical culture guru when he saw Eugen Sandow at the Chicago Exposition, developed a huge magazine publishing consortium with a total circulation of over seven million. One magazine alone, *Physical Culture*, achieved a readership of half a million. He became eccentric in his old age but lost none of his initiative and courage. He exercised and swam in the sea until the end of his life. He married four times, was imprisoned for non-payment of alimony and was making parachute descents when he was over eighty. He died in 1955, at the age of eighty-seven.

A number of strongmen were affected in different ways by the First World War. Edward Aston, the strongest man in the world, lost several fingers in the conflict. He still returned to the stage in an adagio act with a series of nubile young women. Tom Burrows, the club swinger, treated wounded Australian soldiers as a physiotherapist. Alexander Zass, who performed under the titles of the Amazing Samson and Iron Samson, built up his enormous grip strength by bending green branches as a young man. He served with the Russian army against the Austrians and was badly wounded and taken prisoner. Grimly he rebuilt his strength by bending the bars of his cell and while detailed with other prisoners of war to perform heavy labour on a road gang. After several unsuccessful attempts, he escaped to freedom with a small travelling circus and took up his career again.

Launceston Elliot, the Olympian, continued with his music hall appearances until he was fifty, spent a few years farming and then went to live in Melbourne. He died of cancer of the spine at the age of fifty-six, in 1930. Towards the end of his strongman career a match had been mooted between Elliot and the new up-and-coming strength star Thomas Inch, but Elliot decided that he could not compete successfully with the next generation. Many years after his death, writer David Walker used Elliot's story as the inspiration for his novel *Geordie*, later made into a movie, about a lonely Scottish boy who develops enormous strength via a correspondence course and represents Britain as a hammer thrower in the Olympics.

Thomas Inch had a gambling habit and lost much of the money he had made with his successful postal bodybuilding courses at the racetrack. Until close to the end of his life in 1963, he could still lift his challenge dumbbell. He never disclosed its secret, if there was one.

Some of the strength athletes continued performing until ripe old ages, not always by choice. The Scottish all-rounder Donald Dinnie lost most of his savings in ill-advised business deals. He was still doing a strongman act around the London halls when he was in his seventies. He lifted weights and then supported a table while two dancers performed a Highland fling on it. In 1912, as he approached seventy-six, the London County Council withdrew his licence to perform, on the grounds of his advancing years. Friends arranged a public benefit for the Scot, raising about £80, which was used to purchase a small annuity. He then ran a fish and chip shop and accompanying tearoom. He died in London in 1916.

Rosa Richter who, as Zazel, the Human Cannonball, had become one of the first strongwomen to transfer from the circus to the stage, gave up her cannonball act because it was too dangerous. She became a high-wire walker with Barnum's Circus. Ironically she fell and injured her back. She retired, married a circus publicist and settled in Great Britain.

Of the two original Georgia Magnets, Lula Hurst lived a life of contented domesticity with her husband William in Madison until his death in 1931. Lula died in 1950, at the age of eighty-one. Annie Abbott had a much more tormented life, with domestic strife, separations from some of her children, and long departures from the stage. In 1911, she became housebound, dying four years later in Macon, Georgia, aged fifty-four. Some of her neighbours regarded her as a witch and spread rumours that on her deathbed Annie had placed a curse on anyone who ever stood between her grave and the sun.

Edith Garrud lived to be ninety-nine, dying in 1971. She lost a son in the First World War and later divorced her husband. Almost to the end of her life she was still giving the occasional interview to newspapers about her time as a ju-jitsu expert and tutor to the Suffragette Bodyguards. Florence LeMarr also divorced her husband and gave up her music hall ju-jitsu career. For a time, she coached police in the martial arts and then retired to sell confectionary from a cinema stall.

Kate Williams, the Welsh strongwoman and heroine, continued to live with her on- and off-stage partner William Roberts for fifty years, but never married him. Towards the end of her life she was for the first time slowed down a little when she was injured in a street accident. Kate Sandwina, the strongest and most beautiful woman in the world, accompanied by her faithful husband Max in a marriage that lasted for fifty-two years, was as successful in vaudeville as she had been in the circuses. Eventually the pair retired to open a restaurant in Queens, New York. She spent her spare time plotting the career and supervising the training of her son Ted, a leading professional heavyweight boxer.

Several prominent strongmen seemed to disappear. Charles A. Sampson, who was defeated by Sandow in 1889, continued as a headliner for almost another fifteen years, and then vanished from the annals of music hall history. He is recorded as appearing in London in 1904, but after that there is no further record of him.

Leo McLaglen, the great charlatan, was spotted on a number of occasions after he had been banned from the USA for extortion. In 1938 he was in Australia, selling a strange weapon he had designed, consisting of a combined dagger and cosh, after a postal ju-jitsu course he had attempted to market had failed. In 1948, he turned up for one last time in South Africa. Tromp von Diggelin, a strongman who had once shared a music hall stage with McLaglen, reported that he had encountered the former giant in a dreadful state. He was in very poor health and part of his tongue seemed to have been removed. McLaglen said that he had been captured and tortured by the Japanese in the Far East during the Second World War. Von Diggelin reported that he later heard that the self-anointed ju-jitsu champion had died in Nairobi soon afterwards.

The fiasco of the second Gotch–Hackenschmidt bout and the anointing of Jack Curley as the new virtual controller of wrestling put an end to the sport as a major attraction. Gotch and Hackenschmidt soon both retired from the ring after their Chicago encounter. Gotch retired to his farm, tried to make a brief comeback and then died from a kidney ailment at the age of thirty-nine. Hackenschmidt, derided as either a quitter or a faker after the Comiskey Field debacle, lived to be ninety-three. He spent the remainder of his life as a philosopher and writer. On 30 December 1950, he was the subject of a short paragraph in the *Sydney Morning Herald*:

Georg Hackenschmidt, the greatest wrestler of the classical school in modern times, has become a philosopher. At the age of 74, 'Hack' spends his time in a small London flat meditating not on his past triumphs, but on his own ideas for composing the problems of mankind.

Tom Jenkins, the one-eyed former steel worker who wrestled everyone, everywhere, did as well as any of his contemporaries in later life. He was appointed wrestling instructor at West Point Military Academy, where he remained for thirty-seven years, revered by generations of students, including future President Dwight D. Eisenhower.

Stanislaus Zbyszko, who attracted the interest of C. B. Cochran and almost inherited the mantle of Georg Hackenschmidt, settled in the USA and spent many years there, ending up as a manager of wrestlers. In 1929, he showed an unexpectedly sensitive side to his nature when he sued the *New York American* for libel. The newspaper had published a picture of the wrestler, next to one of a gorilla. The caption read 'Stanislaus Zbyszko, the Wrestler, Not Fundamentally Different from the Gorilla in Physique'. A court agreed that the Pole had been traduced, and ordered that he be paid a few dollars in damages and costs.

Zbyszko then retired to run a chicken farm in New Jersey. He was rescued from this bucolic life by the film director Jules Dassin, who cast him at the age of seventy as an ageing wrestler opposite Richard Widmark in the 1950 movie *Night and the City*. The old grappler died in 1968, aged eighty-eight.

A few less fortunate of the original wrestlers-cum-strongmen continued to roam the world living by their wits. Jack Carkeek, a contemporary of Hackenschmidt and Gotch, who had refused to wrestle the young Russian Lion at the Alhambra, continued to tour the remaining halls and arenas for years, settling back in the USA. In spite of his advancing age he returned to wrestling, but with little success. In 1910, the *Steven Points Journal* reported that Hali Adali, a gigantic Turk, had failed to throw Carkeek in a Milwaukee bout: 'The match put the game in bad odour in Milwaukee, it being claimed that the Oriental [sic] deliberately allowed his opponent to stick out the time.'

Next, after an inglorious spell as a detective, the wrestler became involved in a notorious series of confidence tricks perpetuated by the notorious Millionaires' Club, led by J. C. Maybray. A wealthy, gullible victim would be enticed to an alleged wrestling match, prizefight or race meeting, carrying a large sum of money, usually between $10,000 and $50,000, to bet upon what he was assured was a sure-thing, fixed event. The venue would either be out in the sticks or in a small town like Galesburg, Illinois, with a population of about 29,000, whose law-enforcement officers had a relaxed attitude towards tourists being fleeced.

Carkeek's role usually was as one of the wrestlers involved. The mark would be persuaded to hand over his bankroll to one of the gang to bet for him. Soon after the bout had started, other members of the gang dressed as policemen would break up the match. The crowd would scatter. As the *Washington Post* put it in 1910, 'The club members would rush around in fear for a minute or two and then stealthily decamp.' The mark would never see his friends or his money again.

As a variation on a theme, the Millionaires' Club would sometimes organise a faked race meeting. Soon after the race had started, the jockey on the syndicate's horse would fake a heart attack and fall dramatically from the saddle, just as the stage police force swung into action and broke up the event. Specialists in playing the part of the lawmen included one John Fletcher, a pseudonym used by Carkeek when his wrestling skills were not needed in the ring. When the criminal group was broken up and most of the participants brought to trial, the fraudsters pleaded in mitigation that they would sometimes slip their dupe enough money for the cheapest railroad ticket home. They were all sentenced to terms of imprisonment. When Jack Carkeek was released he went to live in Cuba, then a wide-open island as far as crime and morality were concerned. Even a hardened globetrotter like Carkeek discovered that this time he had travelled too far from his normal habitat. One night in 1924, he was mugged, robbed, stripped and left dead in an alley in Havana.

While he was pursuing his itinerant life, Carkeek paused long enough to write an obituary in the *Mirror of Life* for Matsada Sorakichi, the former sumo wrestler who had tried to break into the catch-as-catch-can scene. The Japanese died penniless at the age of thirty-two, discarded by his manager and associates. Little attention was paid to weight divisions in the early days of wrestling, which favoured the bigger contestants. Carkeek wrote in the *New York Times* of his efforts: 'The plucky little Jap suffered numerous defeats because he tackled all the best men of the day, no matter what their size or weight might be.'

There was one brief resurgence at the end of the golden age of the strength athletes. It concerned a performer who, with the benefit of hindsight, could almost be called the last of the strongmen. His name was Zisha Breitbart and he was a Polish Jew, born in Lodz in 1883. His entry into show business mirrored that of many other ambitious youths. He was apprenticed to a blacksmith but at the age of thirteen ran away to join a passing circus. He grew to be large and strong, and embarked upon a career as a professional strongman. During the First World War, he entertained German troops with his act and continued as a circus star in the postwar era.

Soon he was starring in Vienna, with the usual, if well-presented, strongman tricks of weightlifting, chain breaking and boulder smashing. Often he appeared onstage in the costume of a Roman gladiator. He was billed modestly as the Superman of the Ages.

What marked Breitbart out from his contemporaries was his immense pride in his Jewish heritage and his fascination with Zionism. Whether he was wearing a Roman tunic or a blacksmith's apron for his public appearances his costumes were always embellished with the Star of David. Whenever possible he included references to the Biblical Samson in his act.

In 1923, billed as 'the Jewish Superman', Breitbart took part in a highly successful tour of the USA. He became an American citizen and sponsored a postal bodybuilding course. At the peak of his fame he returned to appear in Poland again. In the city of Radom he was performing one of his lesser tricks of pounding a nail with his fist into a plank. The nail, which was rusty, went through the wooden board and penetrated Breitbart's knee. Blood poisoning set in and both of the strongman's legs had to be amputated. He died in a Berlin hospital after ten operations in 1925.

Zisha was the last strongman to top a music hall or vaudeville bill but it wasn't quite the end. After Breitbart's death there were few out-and-out strongman acts left to parade on the vaudeville and music hall stages, but the legacy of Eugen Sandow was still apparent in the proliferation of postal bodybuilding courses available in the 1920s to the 1940s. Chief among those offering such courses was the ubiquitous Charles Atlas. He received his imprimatur from Bernarr Macfadden who, in turn, had been inspired by the public performances of Eugen Sandow on his tour of the USA in the 1890s.

Born in Italy in 1892, Angelo Siciliano emigrated to Brooklyn with his parents. He started developing his body from a young age, with a picture of Eugen Sandow pasted to his bedroom mirror to inspire him. By 1921, he was so well developed that he won the title of the world's most perfectly developed man, sponsored by Bernarr Macfadden's *Physical Culture* magazine. He changed his name to Charles Atlas, linked up with a British physician and health writer called Frederick Tilney and started his enormously successful postal bodybuilding course, which costed $29.95, avowedly aimed at '97lb weaklings' accustomed to getting sand kicked into their faces by beach bullies. He employed slogans which spread around the world – 'You Too Can Have a Body Like Mine'. Tens of thousands of young men signed up for the course and by the time of his death in 1972 at the age of eighty, Atlas had a massive business empire.

A few other bodybuilders, usually former weightlifters, achieved fame, this time on the big screen. At the peak of his fame the highest-paid actor in Europe, Steve Reeves became the star of a few sword and sandal epics, while Austrian Arnold Schwarzenegger parlayed a number of bodybuilding titles into a successful Hollywood career and even took office as Governor of California.

Despite these later successes, the great age of the stage strongman was over. From Eugen Sandow's leap on to the stage of the Imperial Theatre to challenge Charles Sampson in 1889 until the advent of world war in 1914, the strongman heyday lasted less than twenty-five years. But those years were fascinating ones. Some of their number were rogues and others charlatans, but most of the strongmen were both brave and resourceful. Their attitude to danger is best summed up in the words of the Polish-born strongman-juggler Paul Cinquevalli, who worked the halls in the 1890s. For the climax of his act he spun a huge cartwheel on a pole, knocked the support away with a flourish, stooped and caught it – still revolving – on the spike of a helmet he was wearing. A reporter once asked him if this hurt. Cinquevalli's response entered the lexicon of show business one-liners.

'Hurt?' he asked. Pausing, he shook his head. 'No, I just lose consciousness for a few seconds!'

BIBLIOGRAPHY

Books and booklets

Adam, G. Mercer, *Sandow on Physical Training* (London: Gale & Polden, 1894)

Alltree, George W., *Footlight Memories: Recollections of Music Hall and Stage Life* (London: Sampson Low & Co., 1932)

Aston, Edward, *Modern Weight-Lifting & How to Gain Strength* (London: C. T. Trevor, 1935)

Atilla, Louis, *Professor Atilla's 5 Pound Dumbbell Course* (New York City: Richard Fox, 1913)

Belzoni, Giovanni, *Narrative of the Operations and Recent Discoveries within the Pyramids, Temples, Tombs, and Excavations, in Egypt and Nubia* (Brussels: H. Remy, 1835)

Booth, J. B., *A 'Pink 'Un' Remembers* (London: Werner Laurie, 1937)

Booth, J. B., *The Days We Knew* (London: Werner Laurie, 1943)

Brady, William A., *Showman* (New York: E. P. Dutton, 1937)

Busby, Roy, *British Music Hall: An Illustrated Who's Who From 1850 to the Present Day* (London: Elek 1976)

Calthrop, Dion Clayton, *Music Hall Nights* (London: John Lane, 1925)

Cashin, Fergus, *Mae West: A Biography* (London: W. H. Allen, 1981)

Chapman, David L., *Sandow the Magnificent: Eugen Sandow and the Beginnings of Bodybuilding* (Illinois: University of Illinois Press, 1994)

Chapman, Mike, *Frank Gotch* (Buffalo: William S. Hein & Co., 1991)

Chidsey, Donald, *John the Great. The Times and Life of John L. Sullivan* (London: Chapman & Hall, 1974)

Cochran, C. B., *Secrets of a Showman* (London: William Heinemann, 1925)

Cochran, C. B., *I Had Almost Forgotten* (London: William Heinemann, 1932)

Cochran, C. B., *Showman Looks On* (London: Dent, 1945)

Daley, Caroline, *Leisure and Pleasure: Reshaping and Revealing the New Zealand Body, 1900–1960* (Auckland: Auckland University Press, 2003)

Dibble, R. F., *John L. Sullivan: An Intimate Memoir* (Boston: Little, Brown, 1925)

Dreiser, Theodore, *Twelve Men* (New York: Boni & Liveright, 1919)

Ernst, Robert, *Weakness is a Crime: The Life of Bernarr Macfadden* (New York: Syracuse University, 1991)

Fair, John D., *Muscletown USA: Bob Hoffman and the Manly Culture of York Barbell* (Pennsylvania: Pennsylvania State University Press, 2008)

Felstead, Theodore, *Stars Who Made the Halls: A Hundred Years of English Humour, Harmony and Hilarity* (London: Werner Laurie, 1946)

Fields, Armond and Fields, L. Marc, *From the Bowery to Broadway: Lew Fields and the Roots of American Popular Theatre* (Oxford: Oxford University Press, 1993)

Fields, Armond, *James J. Corbett* (London: McFarland, 2001)

Fleischer, Nathaniel Stanley, *From Milo to Londos: The Story of Wrestling Through the Ages* (New York: C. J. O'Brien, 1936)

Freedland, Michael, *Al Jolson* (London: W. H. Allen, 1972)

Gaines, Charles, *Pumping Iron: The Art and Sport of Bodybuilding* (New York: Simon & Schuster, 1974)

Gaudreau, Leo, *Anvils, Horseshoes and Cannons* (Alliance: *Iron Man*, 1978)

Gibson, Walter B., *Houdini's Escapes* (Harcourt, Brace & Company, 1930)

Gilbert, Douglas, *American Vaudeville: Its Life and Times* (New York: McGraw-Hill, 1940)

Gillis, James D., *The Cape Breton Giant: A Truthful Memoir* (Nova Scotia: Cape Breton Books, 1988)

Griffin, Marcus, *Fall Guy: The Barnums of Bounce* (Chicago: Reilly & Lee, 1937)

Hackenschmidt, George, *The Way to Live: Health & Physical Fitness* (London: *Health & Strength*, 1908)

Hackenschmidt, George, *The Complete Science of Wrestling* (London: *Health & Strength*, 1910)

Haley, Bruce, *The Healthy Body and Victorian Culture* (London: Harvard University, 1978)

Harding, James, *Cochran* (London: Methuen, 1988)

Harding, James, *George Robey and the Music Hall* (London: Hodder and Stoughton, 1990)

Hewitt, Mark, *Catch Wrestling: A Wild and Wooly Look at the Early Days of Pro Wrestling in America* (Colorado: Paladin, 2005)

Higham, Charles, *Ziegfeld* (London: W. H. Allen, 1973)

Holland, Charlie (comp.), *Strange Feats and Clever Turns* (London: Holland & Palmer, 1998)

Jones, Colin Spong, *Percy Hunt: The Great Marvello* (One-Off Publishing, 1999)

Jowett, G., *The Strongest Man that Ever Lived* (*Your Physique*, 1940)

Isenberg, Michael, *John L. Sullivan and His Times* (London: Robson, 1988)

Kilgarriff, Michael, *Grace, Beauty and Banjos: Peculiar Lives and Strange Times of Music Hall and Variety Artistes* (London: Oberon Books, 1998)

Lamb, Geoffrey, *Victorian Magic* (London: Routledge and Kegan Paul, 1976)

Larsen, Erik, *The Devil in the White City* (New York City: Doubleday, 2003)

Levy, E. Lawrence, *The Autobiography of an Athlete* (J. G. Hammond & Co., 1913)

Liederman, Earle E., *Secrets of Strength* (Manchester: Universal Institute of Physical Culture, 1938)

Livingstone, Belle, *Belle Out of Order* (London: Heinemann, 1960)

McCabe, James D., *Lights and Shadows of New York* (Deutsch, 1971)

Macfadden, Bernarr, *Encyclopedia of Physical Culture*, vol. 1 (PC Publishing, 1911–1912)

Machray, Robert, *The Night Side of London* (Macqueen, 1902)

MacMahon, Charles, *Feats of Strength and Dexterity* (1927)

McNeal, Violet, *Four White Horses and a Brass Band* (New York: Doubleday, 1947)

Macqueen-Pope, W., *Twenty Shillings in the Pound* (London: Hutchinson & Co., 1948)

Macqueen-Pope, W., *Ghosts and Greasepaint* (London: Robert Hale, 1951)

Macqueen-Pope, W. *Back Numbers* (London: Hutchinson, 1954)

Marcuse, Maxwell, *This Was New York!* (New York: LIM Press, 1969)

Marx, Groucho and Anoible, Richard J., *The Marx Brothers Scrapbook* (London: W. H. Allen, 1974)

Maxick, *Muscle Control* (London: Ewart, Seymour & Co., 1910)

Muller, J. P., *My System* (*Link House*, 1904)

Muzumdar, S., *Strong Men Over the Years* (Lucknow: 1942)

Neil, C., *Modern Physical Culture* (London: C. Arthur Pearson, 1904)

Newton, H. Chance, *Idols of the Halls* (London: Heath Cranton, 1928)

Pierce, Dale, *Wild West Characters* (Golden West Publishers, 2000)

Radley, Allan Stuart, *The Illustrated History of Physical Culture, Vol. I: The Muscular Ideal* (Blackpool: Radley, 2001)

Ransome, Arthur, *Information About the ABC of Physical Culture* (London: Drane, 1904)

Roach, Randy, *Muscle, Smoke and Mirrors*, vol. I (USA: Authorhouse, 2008)

Roach, Randy, *Muscle, Smoke and Mirrors*, vol. II (USA: Authorhouse, 2011)

S. D., Trav, *No Applause – Just Throw Money: The Book That Made Vaudeville Famous* (New York: Faber & Faber, 2005)

Sampson C. A. *Strength: A Treatise on the Development and Use of Muscle* (Chicago: Rand, McNally & Co., 1895)

Sandow, Eugen, *Strength and How to Obtain It* (Aldershot: Gale & Polden, 1897)

Sandow, Eugen, *Bodybuilding* (London: Gale & Polden, 1904)

Saxon, Arthur, *The Development of Physical Power* (New York: Healthex Publishing Co., 1905)

Scott, Harold, *The Early Doors: Origins of the Music Halls* (London: Nicholson & Watson, 1946)

Shaw, Desmond, *London Nights in the Gay Nineties* (New York: R. M. McBride & Co., 1928)

Stein, Charles W., *American Vaudeville As Seen By Its Contemporaries* (New York: De Capo Press, 1984)

Steinmeyer, Jim, *Hiding the Elephant – How Magicians Invented the Impossible* (London: Arrow, 2004)

Taylor, Robert Lewis, *W. C. Fields: His Follies and Fortunes* (New York: Doubleday, 1949)

Trevor, Charles T., *Training for Great Strength* (Mitre Press, n.d.)

Van Diggelen, Tromp, *Worthwhile Journey* (London: William Heinemann, 1955)

Van Every, Edward, *Sins of New York* (New York: Stokes, 1930)

Webster, David, *Barbells and Beefcake* (D. P. Webster, 1979)

Webster, David, *Bodybuilding: An Illustrated History* (New York: Arco, 1983)

Webster, David, *The Iron Game* (D. P. Webster, 1976)

Webster, David and Dinnie, Gordon, *Donald Dinnie, the First Sporting Superstar* (Ardo Publishing, 1999)

Weider, Ben, *The Strongest Man in History, Louis Cyr, 'Amazing Canadian'* (Vancouver: Michell Press, 1976)

Wiley, Barry H., *The Georgia Wonder: Lulu Hurst and the Secret that Shook America* (Seattle: Hermetic Press, 2004)

Wilson, Charles M., *The Magnificent Scufflers Revealing the Great Days When America Wrestled the World* (Stephen Greene Press, 1959)

Zass, Alexander, *The Amazing Samson* (London: Samson Institute, 1926)

Periodicals

Apollo's Magazine
Baltimore Sun
Bodybuilder
Boston Globe
Brain and Brawn
Californian Daily Alta
C. B. Fry's Magazine
Chicago Tribune
Cleveland News
Daily News
The Era
Health and Strength
Iron Game History
Iron Man
Journal of Sports History
Klein's Bell
Manx Advertiser
Milo
Montreal Gazette
Montreal Star
Mr America
Muscle Builder
Muscle Power
National Police Gazette
New York Dramatic Mirror
New York Sun
Physical Culture
Sandow's Magazine

Sporting Life
The Strand Magazine
Strength
Strength and Health
The Strongman
Sydney Morning Herald
Taranaki Herald
The Times
Western Mail
Your Physique

Academic Theses

The Operational Aesthetic in the Performance of Professional Wrestling
William P. Lipscomb III
Ph.D. thesis, Louisiana State University, 2004

An Exploration of Weightlifting as a Reflection of the Major Socio-Political Events and Trends of the 20th Century
Mark Kodya
MA thesis, State University of New York Empire State College, 2003

Building Strength: Alan Calvert, the Milo Barbell Company and the Modernization of American Weight Training
Kimberley Ayn Beckwith
Ph.D. thesis, University of Texas at Austin, 2006

Archives

Evanion Catalogue (British Library)
National Fairground Archives (Sheffield University)

INDEX